This Business of Writing

D0806852

Published in 2006 by
Institute of Chartered Accountants in Ireland

CA House, Pembroke Road
Ballsbridge, DUBLIN 4

Designed and typeset in Minion and Gill Sans by Marsha Swan
Printed by MPG Books, Cornwall, United Kingdom

ISBN Hardback   0 903854 24 4
    ISBN-13   978 0 903854 24 5

ISBN Paperback   0 903854 17 1
    ISBN-13   978 0 903854 17 7

The opinions expressed in this publication are those of the authors and do not necessarily represent the views of the ICAI. The text is designed to provide accurate and authoritative information in regard to the subject matter covered. It is sold on the understanding that the ICAI is not engaged in rendering professional services. If professional advice or other expert assistance is required, the services of a competent professional should be sought.

This Business of Writing

Terry Prone and Kieran Lyons

Institute of Chartered Accountants in Ireland
Dublin

CONTENTS

ACKNOWLEDGEMENTS

Generous contribution to the first edition was made by friends and colleagues. We owe an enormous debt of gratitude to our editor and designer, Marsha Swan. Ever forthright and challenging, she engaged with our text and constantly questioned our assumptions and conjectures. This book could not have happened without her. Amy Hayes took time out of her life as managing editor of Tottel Ireland to proof the final draft. Tom Savage read the manuscript and made observations, particularly about Latin tags. Pádhraic Ó Ciardha offered help on use of the Irish language, and Jo O'Donoghue provided guidance on Irish expressions now fully adopted into the English language family. Aviva Cohen checked out and revised the memorandum section, and Michael Brown and Barry McCormack cast eagle eyes over our checklists. The detailed index was compiled by Gráinne Farren.

A great joy, for the reader of a book like *This Business of Writing*, is to spot an error or a deficit in it. The authors welcome input to later editions, and can be reached at the Institute of Chartered Accountants in Ireland. We feel properly guilty for any failures, for which we take complete responsibility.

INTRODUCTION

Some people write because they want to. Some people write because they have to. Some people write because they feel fully alive only when they have managed to hammer out a certain number of words in a given day.

Writing is about stating one's existence, even if that statement is no more than a scribbled signature or a couple of identifying initials. Hence the graffiti found in Pompeii, the messages ground into mortar and then sealed into old bridges, and the carved initials of writers like George Bernard Shaw and William Butler Yeats preserved to this day on the tree in Coole, Lady Gregory's home in the West of Ireland.

One step up – but an important step up – from the graffitist is the storyteller. Every culture in the world is founded on stories, and in every literate culture, those stories are written down.

Before the invention of the printing press, scribes committed stories to vellum, in the process creating beautiful illuminated manuscripts like the Book of Kells. Alone in his candle-lit cell, one eighth-century scribe wrote a little bit of doggerel about his pet cat in the margin of an illustrated manuscript of the Epistles of Saint Paul.

He seems to have been working in a monastery founded by Irish monks, miles from where he'd been born. We know nothing about him, other than his craftsmanship, that he sought to understand his narrow world by writing about it, and that he had an acute sense of the importance of the written word.

Today, some writers still 'sit with book and pen'. Booker Prize-winner John Banville handwrites all of his novels, finding that the pace

'Me and Pangur Bán my cat,
'Tis a like task we two are at.
Hunting mice is his delight.
Hunting words I sit all night.

Better far than praise of men,
'Tis to sit with book and pen…'

Anon

When Oscar Wilde, imprisoned in the last years of the nineteenth century, set out to write *The Ballad of Reading Gaol*, prison regulations allowed him so little paper that he was forced to draft the poem in his head before committing a final version to paper. Nor was he permitted to keep in his cell the earlier sections of the poem. They had to be entrusted to the post, leaving the writer to depend on his recollection of what he had written while he crafted the latter portions of the work.

'Writing and teaching have always been, for me, so richly rewarding that I don't think of them as work in the usual sense of the word.'

Joyce Carol Oates

dictated by the passage of pen over paper better suits his thinking process than inputting to a computer.

Most fiction and non-fiction writers today use PCs. Not only do those computers allow the writer to conduct instant research via the Internet, but their word-processing programs will alert the writer to grammar, syntax and spelling flaws. In addition, most programs offer cut-and-paste options.

All of which gives today's writers immeasurable advantages over wordsmiths of the past. The fact is that publishing is easier these days – a lot easier. For little or no cost, aspiring writers can set up a web log, or blog, disgorge the data of their daily doings, and perhaps parlay the blog into a published book, as has happened in the last couple of years to several writers on both sides of the Atlantic.

A business writer facing the deadline for a report, not one word of which has yet been written, might find it difficult to imagine that any writer might be delighted to sit down at a keyboard and gleefully input a few thousand words each day. Yet Joyce Carol Oates, one of the most critically acclaimed and prolific living writers, maintains that she has no sense of working especially hard, or, indeed, of 'working' at all. She is unusual in that regard. Thousands of people desperately want to write, but are fearful of breaking rules they neither know about nor understand. Just as many individuals have studies or careers that demand that they write and find the task extraordinarily daunting.

This book is about demystifying the business of writing. It sets out to offer guidance to simplifying the task, helping writers make better use of their time. Whether you're a creative writer embarking on a novel, a student preparing a thesis, a manager preparing a PowerPoint presentation, a politician writing a speech, or a business executive crafting a report, you will find answers to your questions and solutions to your problems in this volume.

Good writing is never easy, but it can and should be simple. It can and should be enjoyable. All that is required is to kick the obstacles out of your path.

We hope this book will help you do that.

I. APPROACHING LANGUAGE

LET'S START AT THE VERY BEGINNING...

Journalists all over the world employ, every day, a formula of approach immortalised in doggerel by one of the most prolific and successful writers of the past, Rudyard Kipling. Good professional writing always starts with Kipling's 'six serving-men': What, Why, When, How, Where and Who, in no particular order. Here's how you can apply them to any writing task:

- Why am I writing this book/report/speech/feature?
- Who is the target audience?
- What should they learn or remember from it?
- When is it due?
- Where will the data come from?
- How will I get started?

Why am I writing this? Many reports and theses get written because the writer has no choice. That's as good a reason as any, but can be used as justification for postponement when writers convince themselves that if they didn't *have* to produce these words in this particular form, they would find the task easier. The fact is that most reports and theses are based on data (which does not have to be created) and the central task is to order the presentation of that data so the reader can understand and gain from it, in most cases utilising a standard format. None of which removes the desire to do something, anything, other than write what must be written. That desire tends to emerge from a fear that the task is a huge shapeless threat – a fear best managed by application of the old

'I keep six honest serving-men
(They taught me all I know);
Their names are What and Why
    and When
And How and Where and Who.
I send them over land and sea,
I send them east and west;
But after they have worked for me,
I give them all a rest.'

Rudyard Kipling

advice on how to eat an elephant: slice it thinly and allow several days for consumption.

If the answer to the question 'Why am I writing this?' is, 'Because I want to write a bestselling novel,' think again. Surprise bestsellers do happen, but the vast majority of creative writers do not make a living from it. Many writers have analysed the formula of bestselling novels and set out to produce one, only to see it remaindered at a humiliating discount. Dr Johnson said that only a blockhead wrote for anything other than money. But writing in the hope of a runaway bestseller is almost a guarantee of grievous disappointment – and may do serious damage to the quality of what might otherwise be produced.

Be clear in your objective before you start writing. If you know your destination, you stand a better chance of getting to it.

Who is the target audience? The honest answer, especially if you're writing a novel or a memoir, may be 'Me.'

However, the writer is not the target audience for most books, reports, speeches or features – and too many writers begin the writing task without giving enough consideration to the person or people they want to reach, influence, inform or change. A good approach is to *profile* your target audience in advance by filling in a short questionnaire along the following lines:

- Who is my target audience?
- What do they know about the topic/issue at this point?
- What is their attitude to it?
- What age are they?
- How sophisticated are they?
- How much time do they have?
- What kind of writing will best meet their needs?

Thinking about the audience in advance can usefully inform the structure, length, style and language of your writing.

What should the audience learn or remember from this writing? Business reports frequently open with an Executive Summary. An Executive Summary, if it's good enough, ensures that readers who lack the time or motivation to read the entire document nevertheless get the gist of what is being reported or recommended. But it serves another central purpose. It forces the writer to identify the essential issues that *must* be communicated. (See Writing an Executive Summary, Section 2.)

'Say you're writing a brochure for an investment firm, giving financial advice to the newly widowed. You'll want to sound serious but not gloomy, honest and direct but not intrusive. A wisecrack about the River Styx would not be appropriate. If you were advising college students, on the other hand, humor might be in order. Your tone and choice of words would be very different.

'For better or worse, audience is everything, no matter what you write. Unfortunately, some audiences seem to *require* bad writing: dullness (the phone book), pretentious language (an academic paper), hype (advertising copy). Take the academic paper, for example. Ask yourself who will be reading, then aim at that target. It may be that you hate pompous words like *syncretism* and *etiology*, and would rather use plain words like *joining* and *cause*. But since the professor or dissertation committee or scholarly journal expects gobbledygook and would reject anything else, you hold your nose and write "syncretism" and "etiology." If they want stuffy, give them stuffy.'

Patricia T. O'Connor, former *New York Times Book Review* editor

Even if your document does not contain an Executive Summary, it's a good idea, for your own clarity of thought, to produce one before you embark on the overall task. Knowing what the audience *must* learn or remember, having read the full text, will help you order and emphasise the points you need to make interesting, understandable and memorable.

When is it due? This is the piece of information that freezes the writer's heart. The deadline. Waiting until the last minute and flogging yourself with repeated doses of Red Bull throughout a night or two nights of frantic typing, punctuated with self-comforting peeks at the wordcount, is acceptable when you're a student. When you're an executive with a demanding day-job, it makes no sense at all.

A deadline should be the stimulus for project-management. Try this sequence of steps:

Step 1   **Add contingency.** Because illness and accidents do happen but cannot be predicted, it's always a good idea to set yourself a false deadline two or three days in advance of the real thing.

Step 2   **Sub-divide the task.** What elements add up to the overall? Does a research phase need to be included? Will you need time to read and collate materials? Will it be necessary to formally seek permission to use quotations from other books or publications, and how long will that take? Have you worked out how many chapters or sections are involved? How many words have to be written and how many words – typically – do you write in any one day? Should the draft material be submitted to a lawyer?

Step 3   **Allocate time to each segment.** Once you have put the segments of the task in order and allocated a reasonable time-slice to each, you have reduced the great black cloud of the final deadline into a series of much smaller clouds. More to the point, you have created your own calendar of achievements, allowing you to pat yourself on the back as each chunk of work is complete.

Step 4   **Tell everybody.** By 'everybody' we mean friends, family and workmates. We know no writer who delivers clean manuscripts on time who does not severely limit their social life while they write. On the other hand, we know an awful lot of writers who take time off from work to write at home, only to get sucked into every family exigency, ranging from the baby's chicken-pox to the cat's fleas.

Deadlines are met by writers who fiercely guard their writing time and who make it clear to everybody around them that they're engaged in an important task and that real life must be postponed until it's finished. Don't tell anyone the details of the content – that's another way to avoid writing them down. Just tell everybody that, short of a world-class emergency, you are not to be disturbed.

Where will the data come from? Instant research on the Internet has greatly speeded up the process of data-gathering for writers. It has also multiplied the pot-holes. (See Using the Internet for Research, Section 3.) But, while search engines can be enormously useful to business writers, the reality is that executives producing an in-company report have to get their information from within their own organisation, and that can be much more difficult. The best way to get information is to ask for it, face-to-face, or – if the source is in another branch or country – by phone. Indicate precisely what you need and for what purpose, and give a realistic deadline that fits well within your own timeline. Once the person has agreed to be helpful, confirm that agreement and your requirement by e-mail. Check in a positive way at a couple of interim dates to ensure progress. It may, for instance, be helpful to hint that you'd prefer to get the material as it becomes available, rather than receiving the whole lot right up against the deadline. It's also helpful to acknowledge the help you receive within the document itself and in any presentations you may make using it.

How will I get started? Just do it. One of the best pieces of advice given to any writer is the old axiom: *Don't get it right. Get it written.*

Sticking that slogan on your desk can be a useful reminder to avoid taking refuge in counter-productive perfectionism. Of course you want the perfect opening line – and we'll get to that later in this book. But the first task is to get started. Writing is a no-excuses business. Set yourself a number of words to be inputted every day. If necessary, set your alarm clock an hour earlier than the time it usually goes off, get up and start writing then. *Irish Independent* political correspondent Bruce Arnold wrote four splendid novels without taking time off, just by getting up

Long before it was possible to take career-breaks from the civil or public service, a Royal Mail employee managed to complete several novels just by getting up earlier in the morning. Anthony Trollope, to whom Britain owes its red post-boxes, wrote for two-and-a-half hours before heading for the day job. When the time came for him to set off for work, he stopped wherever he was, even if it was the middle of a sentence, knowing that he would pick up the following morning in the same place. If he happened to reach the end of a novel one-and-a-half hours into his allotted writing time, he would write the words 'The End', tidy the manuscript to one side of his desk, and embark upon the next.

earlier in the morning. Nobody interrupts you at that time.

Don't kid yourself that talking about what you're writing is the same as writing. It isn't. Building up a document, sentence by sentence, section by section, is rewarding. The only thing more rewarding is holding the final printed version in your hand.

And the sooner you get started, the nearer you are to those magic words: The End.

Reference
Patricia T. O'Connor, *Words Fail Me* (Harcourt Brace, 1999).

PLAGIARISM

2006 may go down in literary history as The Year of the Plagiarist. The main event was the massively publicised trial of Dan Brown, whose *The Da Vinci Code* had become one of the all-time bestselling novels, helped not a little by the fact that the Vatican condemned it, thus delivering free publicity worldwide.

The Da Vinci Code may have its merits, although they're not obvious. Its plot, suggesting that Jesus Christ did not die on the cross but lived on, married Mary Magdalen and fathered a family, fascinated millions of readers in a plethora of languages. The problem was that the writers of an earlier novel on the same theme decided Mr. Brown had nicked their work. They sued him for plagiarism. They lost. The sales of their own book revived, but are unlikely to produce the £2 million of legal costs they now have to pay. *The Da Vinci Code* court case not only educated many readers about what is copyright and what is *not* copyright, but also revealed a wealth of information about how this particular novelist goes about his business.

Earlier in the year, another bestselling author fell foul of the copyright law, although in this instance the case did not end up in court. Raj Persaud is a household-name psychiatrist with eight degrees, a columnist with *Cosmopolitan*, and a regular radio and TV presenter. He has produced bestsellers like *Staying Sane*, which manage to straddle the popular and the scholarly.

And he's a plagiarist.

The 'inadvertence' excuse clearly does not stand up in some famous instances of plagiarism. Take, for example, the lifting by Senator Joe Biden of bits from a Neil Kinnock party political broadcast to beef up a Biden speech about the poverty and deprivation of his background. It was marvelous, stirring stuff, delivered with passion and apparent spontaneity by Biden in a broadcast from the Iowa State Fair.

'I started thinkin', as I was comin' over here,' he confided, 'why is it that Joe Biden is the first in his family ever to go to a university?'

This rang a bell in the minds of some journalists watching, motivating them to go back to the Labour Party political broadcast, where they found Kinnock being emotional on the same topic.

'Why am I the first Kinnock in a thousand generations to be able to get to a university?' the then Labour Party leader asked.

Downhill it went from that point on. Or rather, down mine. Biden talked admiringly about his ancestors going down into the coalmines of north-east Pennsylvania and coming up twelve hours later to play football. Cut to Kinnock, whose ancestors spent a more modest eight hours down the mines before dashing onto the football pitch. Cut back to Biden opining that what held his grandfather and great-grandfather back was absence of a platform to stand on. Which matched, almost word for word, Kinnock's claim about his forebears and damaged the Democratic senator's hopes of future preferment.

In 2006, Raj Persaud published an article in a scientific journal. Thomas Blass, a professor in the University of Maryland, read the article with interest, because it dealt with an area in which he himself worked. His interest increased as he noted the similarity between Persaud's text and some of his own published research. The similarity was eerie. He went back to his own material and found whole paragraphs which, but for a couple of phrases, matched Persaud's paper word for word.

Professor Blass protested to the publishers, who investigated and published a formal retraction and expression of regret. Persaud's explanation? It was a cut-and-paste error.

Meaning that when he cut a sizeable chunk of text from Professor Blass's work and pasted it into his own manuscript, 'the references at the end were inadvertently omitted'.

Catch the passive voice in that explanation. It wasn't that Persaud didn't give credit where credit was due. It was that somehow, the computer just chopped off the credits.

That's a classic defence of the academic plagiarist: 'Wasn't me, Guv, the computer did it.'

Inadvertence tends to be the first claim of any plagiarist. In many cases where fiction has been cogged from earlier novels, the perpetrators have claimed that – for example – their mothers read the earlier work to them while dandling them on a maternal knee, so that the material lodged in their subconscious, ready for retrieval years later and accidental presentation as their own work.

Accusations of plagiarism tend to be less damaging when the accused is demonstrably more eminent, successful or creative than the victim whose work gets stolen. Recent suggestions that Nabokov's *Lolita* owed much to a story published in his youth have been regarded as an interesting curiosity, rather than a threat to his reputation. The assumption is made that Nabokov might have come across the story, with its paedophile theme and its heroine with the same name as the eponymous nymphet he later created, but forgot the encounter, which seeped through his subconscious decades later. That benign assumption is greatly helped by the demonstrable fact that Nabokov was a world-class writer, whereas the unfortunate who produced the Lolita germ-story during Nabokov's youth was a minor writer.

Whether they do it consciously or unconsciously, for reputation or money, plagiarists who get found out tend to behave in remarkably similar ways. They apologise for error, but never take responsibility.

They claim inadvertence. And if they can, they pay off the person whose work was misappropriated and stitch a confidentiality clause into the agreement. Most of them suffer grievously, despite payoffs and confidentiality clauses. Damage to reputation is permanent, not least because search engines will always kick up references to controversies in a writer's career. Financial damage can also happen: Raj Persaud was dropped by the BBC as presenter of a planned TV series in the aftermath of his plagiarism problem.

New writers, strangely, tend to be much more worried about having their work stolen by other people than by the possibility that they might steal someone else's words or ideas. Many newcomers constantly worry about submitting even a feature to a newspaper, lest some editor read it, like it, and assign a staff writer to produce a marginally different version of it. Sometimes, those newcomers believe this has actually happened to them. They recount how they e-mailed a thousand words on the dangers of the new kiwi-fruit diet, or the perils of using year-old mascara, or the diminishing population of Jews in Ireland, only to see a feature on the same topic, written by another writer, in the paper to which they sent their work.

To the new writer, the crime is obvious. Case closed. To more experienced writers, it seems more likely that a particular issue simply happened to be topical at the time, and so attracted the attention of more than one writer at the same time. Most newspapers, offered a coherent feature by a freelance writer, are more likely to sub-edit and use it than steal the idea, partly because of moral reasons, but also because the newer the freelancer, the smaller the fee, so it makes more economic sense to use the submitted item.

No writer should hold back from submitting a feature out of fear that it might be stolen. Nor should the writer caveat their work up to the gills by sticking COPYRIGHT all over it or predicting dire consequences for any potential plagiarist. Assume the best of editors and that's what you're likely to experience. Typing in the copyright icon or the word does not add to the protection of the work. Once a piece of writing has been created, it is automatically copyright. All the author needs to do is save it on a computer. The computer will retain the details indicating when it was created. (A literary work stays copyright for 70 years after the writer's death.)

In non-fiction work, as indicated earlier in this chapter, the real and present danger is that, in trawling through source books and other

The novice writer who gets paranoid about the possibility of having their work stolen is wasting their own time and possibly other people's time too. The real danger is that the new writer may plagiarise someone else's work. In fiction, this is dangerously easy. You must not appropriate anything, even a phrase from a song that's been rattling around in your head since your teens, without putting quotation marks around it and paying for it. Yes, paying for it. If one of your characters sings a song to another of your characters, it's going to cost you, unless he sings a song that's so old, it's out of copyright.

You can, for example, have a character sing all of the words of 'Greensleeves' without paying any royalties. King Henry VIII is reputedly the writer of that song, but even that litigious old monarch has no rights to it after this length of time. It's in the public domain and you can make whatever use you want of it.

If, on the other hand, you would like your hero to leave a voicemail on his beloved's phone that quotes Blake Shelton's voicemail song 'Austin', every quoted word will require you to seek permission and pay a royalty. This can be quite restrictive. Using words of songs can be evocative of a particular period of time, but the cost can add up, for writer and publisher alike. The costs of such quotations are often borne by the writer rather than the publishing house.

documentation, you may confuse yourself to a point where you incorporate someone else's thoughts into your own prose.

Preventing inadvertent plagiarism

Use Post-it flags on every page of any book holding a fact or a quotation that interests you. Use a highlighter pen on key text within a flagged page. Yes, we know, it pleats your moral core to so mark a book. Trust us, it's necessary. Buy yourself a virgin copy of the book out of the royalties when your own is published.

When you do research on the Web, print out any source material you select, flag and highlight it. Simply cutting and pasting electronically from Web document to your own text carries a huge danger that you'll forget where it came from and eventually assume it to be your own.

If you have a publishing contract, you should send your editor a package containing all the flagged books and documentation when you submit your manuscript. A prestigious publishing house may have a couple of subject-matter experts to whom they will submit the manuscript, and those experts are likely to be familiar with the texts and to spot accidental theft. But a good line-editor will punctiliously read your work and your source material side-by-side to assess possible breaches of the boundary lines. It's an extra insurance policy.

Facts are not copyright. Opinion and phraseology are copyright. Which sounds simpler than it is. Let's say you write a book about Joe Bloggs, in which you out a little-known fact that he tortured budgies in his youth, according to his third wife, who discovered court records of an arrest for caged-bird-abuse. That's a fact. But if the sequence 'little-known, discovered by third wife in court documents' follows precisely the sequence in someone else's book and uses a few of the same terms, then the other writer may feel you've stolen something from them. Acknowledging the other book as a source does not obviate this danger: the two writers who sued Dan Brown had been generously acknowledged in *The Da Vinci Code.*

Having said that facts are not copyright, some facts can be circumscribed by circumstance. Let's say a writer visits a nudist colony, signing an agreement not to subsequently reveal all (or, indeed, anything) in print. Many years later, said writer produces a novel set in a nudist colony. She makes sure to give the leader of the colony a beard, since he was clean-shaven when she met him in reality. Problem: he grew a beard in the meantime, sued and forced her to pay damages. It happened. In this

Plagiarism or placement? Some thoughts ...

'God, I wish I'd said that.'
'You will, Oscar, you will!'

Oscar Wilde in conversation
with James McNeill Whistler

Eighty percent of what you'll write has been written before. Any feature, essay or presentation starts from a series of sources: press cuttings, commentary, company reports, published articles, journals, textbooks, the Internet. Three questions:

- What do you bring to the table?
- How do you approach source material?
- Do you want to call yourself a writer or a stenographer?

As much depends on intent as on content. Journalists, for example, know that public-relations people want their news releases printed as written. (The cunning ones compose in the classic pyramid format, tailored to the tone of the publication they're targeting, counting on laziness, copy deadlines or pressure to fill space.) They're being driven by a PR agenda, urge to place product and compulsion to deliver free advertising for clients. Which may be fine, just as long as the journalist knows it. But the same applies to everyone writing in business today. There's often a background agenda to background data.

The margarine checklist

This exercise is often used in US journalism courses to illustrate the need to verify source material.

The headline:

'Low-Cal Technology: All the Taste, Without the Terror'

The questions before pressing 'Print':

- What's the vehicle? (A newspaper feature? A high-traffic health website? The *Journal of the American Medical Association*?)

- Is the information correct? (What makes this spread so innovative? How does it compare with others in the supermarket fridge?)
- How do you know? (Did you take a trip to Costco's? Study an FDA trial report?)
- Have you checked the veracity of the claim? (What if it's not low-fat? What does low-fat mean?)
- What are the consequences of not checking? (If it's an artery-clogger, will you encourage someone to eat something that will kill him?)
- Can you live with yourself if you don't bother with the above?

Living with the lies, showbiz style

The constant cry of the Jennifer Anistons and Brad Pitts of this world is that once something has been reported about them, although it may be found to be inaccurate, defamatory and even retracted, the material has already found its way into archives and press libraries, to be repeatedly rehashed. It will surface endlessly, hurting the parties, their loved ones and maybe an indemnity insurer. In July 2006, *The National Enquirer* paid substantial damages to Britney Spears and Kate Hudson, and had to print apologies. The agencies that carried the stories in Europe were seen heading for the hills. Moral of the tale: check the source.

Celebrity gossip can affect the everyday reader. However well-intentioned the story, Sir Cliff Richard does not wear a colostomy bag. He has quietly denied the rumour several times, even on his website, but to no avail. Mistake becomes mythology. Does it matter in the greater scheme of things? Not to you or me perhaps, but maybe to those patients who discover that the story was not true and they can never have the quality of life that he enjoys.

Some writers lift bits of other people's lives and get away with it, by sheer force of genius. Budd Schulberg, the man who wrote *What Makes Sammy Run* and several other bestsellers that were made into films, fascinated Scott Fitzgerald with his stories about Schulberg père and his life in Hollywood. Schulberg was later startled to read about his father, under another name, in one of Fitzgerald's novels. He didn't do anything about it, because he admired Fitzgerald so much as a writer, but it rankled, nonetheless, because Fitzgerald had lifted more than facts: he had lifted the personification of an era and a glamorous context.

instance, the issue seems to have been two-fold: breach of a confidentiality agreement *and* possibly bringing an individual into disrepute.

Because the information superhighway is knee-high in abandoned litter it's always tempting, when you come across an unattributed clever phrase or observation, to regard it as an orphan and give it a good home in your thesis or report. Err on the side of caution, remembering that what made it attractive to you will make it attractive to others of the same profession, and sooner or later, someone will quote it to a third party, who will know day, date and detail of the original and take enormous delight in drawing them to your attention or, more damagingly, to the attention of the public.

Give credit where it's due. Append a bibliography of source material to all business documentation, even if the main target audience has no interest in it. And if you cannot find the source of a particular quotation, indicate somewhere in your book that you will be happy to attribute it correctly in the next edition if the writer contacts you.

FACT-CHECKING – SAYS WHO?

Evidence is valid only when it's defensible and provable. Nothing is more dangerous to the writer than conviction without evidence. Newspaper editors dread the reporter who, when asked about a statement in their published material, says, 'Well, I just *knew*.'

Let's say, for example, that the reporter has done a story on child development, in the course of which she has claimed that children whose parents read to them every day are much more likely to succeed in school. Of course she just *knew* that was true. Except that no objective data exists to prove it. It *is* provable that children coming from homes where there are a lot of books tend to do better in school. But nobody is sure if that's because homes with a lot of books are usually owned by reasonably wealthy, literate, middle-class people, or because of some other factor in those homes. Pushing the 'lots of books' fact into a statement about the reading habits of parents vis-à-vis their own children is turning a correlation into a cause.

That example would not get the writer into much trouble, although some child-development expert may write a letter to the editor criticising the original report. But extrapolating from data in that kind of way in a story related to a crime could get the writer into serious trouble. One of the writers of this book did precisely that. In a book about Irish murders, she stated that an individual who played a minor, innocent-bystander role in a pre-war murder had been fired on the day of the murder for a specified offence. The individual was still alive, and sued, because the statement about the firing was contained in the evidence given by the murderer and was unproven and – the libelled individual claimed – unjustified.

Freelance writers, who survive on the number of words they can sell to a newspaper or magazine, are always under pressure, direct or perceived, to come up with scoops and sexy stories, and so the temptation to over-egg the pudding is enormous. Editors employing large numbers of freelancers need to be extra rigorous in their assessment of the incoming material. But the responsibility for fact-checking falls squarely on the writer. It is time-consuming, but an essential investment in your long-term credibility.

Names and numbers

Fact-checking starts with names. Never assume that because you've *heard* a name, you know how to spell it. Karyn sounds the same as Karen. Carol sounds the same as Caryl. Featherstonehaugh sounds like Fanshaw. Ask your source how they spell their name and double-check that you have it right. Apply the same rigour to place names and technical terms. Your source will be impressed, not irritated, by your eagerness to get them right.

Numbers are the second bane of the fact-checker's life. Billions and millions and kilometres have to be made understandable to the reader in the text itself, not just in the graphics that may accompany the text.

It is acceptable – even desirable, depending on your audience – to simplify figures to their most understandable level. Take, for example, a point about mobility.

'2.3 people on average are to be found in commuter cars each morning.'

That may be statistically accurate, but it fails to deliver understanding. It also creates a weird image. Which bit of the third person is present? Is a severed torso to be found in the back seat of most cars as they head to the city each morning? It's safer to say that the average is two people,

Traditionally, fact-checking was a shared function of the editor and the writer. However, because of the speed of newspaper and book production today, editors have less time to fact-check. A number of high-profile cases of fact fabrication by young writers underlines this change. In one case, a colour-writer on an American newspaper was nominated for a major prize because of her heart-rending story about an eleven-year-old drug addict. The nomination started the process of unravelling the story, as the newspaper that had published it sought more information about the child and encountered odd contradictions in the writer's responses. Eventually, it emerged that she had made the whole thing up and passed off fiction as fact. The prize was withdrawn, as was her job, and the editors who had allowed her creative writing to make it into print under the guise of fearless reporting were mortally embarrassed.

occasionally three. But, if you make such a change, it can be useful to go back to your source in order to ascertain if the change in some way falsifies the data.

Quotations

Quotations are enormously valuable in any form of writing.

> The fact that quotations tend to be indented means that the reader's eye is pulled to the quotation. The quotation, therefore, has an advantage over solid blocks of text. It indicates to the reader that someone's talking at this point, and the reader always reacts to a quotation.

Getting quotations right is crucial. That applies to historic quotations just as much as it applies to present-day quotations. Writers should never assume that because a quotation is familiar to them, they have remembered it accurately. Or that it was written by the person they believe wrote it. For example, nowhere in the four novels and more than fifty short stories Arthur Conan Doyle wrote about Sherlock Holmes does the latter say, 'Elementary, My Dear Watson.' It was a much later screenwriter who put the words into the mouth of the character, played by Basil Rathbone.

Conan Doyle won't sue if you attribute something to him that he didn't say. However, living subjects can and do sue, or at least get vexed, when misquoted.

A useful preventative measure is a tape-recorder on a desk between you and your source or attached to your telephone, to support your memory and your notes. If you put a tape-recorder on a surface during a meeting, defuse any anxiety it may create by a casual explanation: 'I'm going to make notes of what you say, of course, but this is my back-up.'

When interviewing someone on the telephone, the same kind of explanation should be offered. In some situations, it is illegal to tape-record someone for later publication without their knowledge: it is also discourteous and duplicitous.

A tape recorder shouldn't stop you taking notes, but it frees you to make more notes of surrounding circumstances and observations, in addition to simply getting quotations correct. In the absence of a tape-recorder, it's still possible to document quotations with absolute accuracy. All you have to do is stop the interviewee: 'Whoa,' you say. 'Hang on. You just said something very interesting, and I don't want to get it wrong.'

When Europe changed from a myriad of national currencies to the euro, Ireland was widely regarded as having managed the transition much better than many larger EU states. A pivotal decision (which, in retrospect looks tiny) was made by the campaign's communication advisors.

The original plan was to tell people that:

€1 = IR£0.787564

The experts in communication pointed out that this starts with the unfamiliar and then delivers the incomprehensible.

Instead, Ireland went with this formula:

IR£1 = €1.27

Much later, when consumers had the new coins in their hand, it was possible to move on to an explanation starting with the euro coin.

Then you write down what the person said – or ask them to say it again. Few experiences are more flattering than having one's words faithfully transcribed. Interviewees never mind repeating themselves or waiting for the note to be fully taken.

None of which obviates the possibility that your interviewee makes the first half of an interesting point in the third minute of the interview, and the second half of the same point in the second-last minute. You may not join up those quotations without going back to him or her. However, going back to an interviewee is fraught with dangers. Your first duty is to your reader. Journalists are warned against submitting their draft features to individuals being profiled, because the individuals invariably want to tinker. They may have said precisely what they've been quoted as saying, but when they see their words in cold print, they lose confidence and begin to amend them. Interviewees invariably amend towards blandness.

First time around, they said something like:

'I have nothing to offer you but blood, toil, tears and sweat.'

When their red pen has reworked it, the quotation reads like this:

'It is undeniable that the mid-term future will generate particular challenges, the specific nature of which is somewhat opaque at this point in time.'

It is unwise to promise or agree to show a source the totality of your feature or report. It is, however, quite acceptable and helpful to indicate that you'll ring them to check facts with them or to run past them any edits you might want to make in their quotations. The edits about which you might want their input do not include necessary tidying-up. If a source wanders all over the shop and interlards their every sentence with 'em' and 'sort of' and 'you know' or 'right?' or 'you with me?', you will do them a favour by removing this padding from around the essence of what they have said. Indeed, if you include all the garbage, you can make someone who sounded reasonably coherent in person appear to be completely incoherent in print, which does neither them nor the reader any service.

Before you telephone a stranger to do fact-checking, rehearse what you plan to say, so they understand quickly what it is you're asking them to validate. Make it clear you're asking a favour if they don't stand to gain out of it. Tell them Joe Bloggs told you they were the greatest expert on

Tips on finding your source

Never underestimate the telephone book. Since mobile phones were invented, an assumption has grown up that the telephone book is irrelevant. Most people still leave their landline numbers in it, and it's no fun to detail for a contact the lengths to which you went to reach them, only to learn that if you'd lifted the big tome from the telephone company, you'd have found them there, first go.

Let's say you need to reach someone in a multinational with plants all over the world and you have no clue where the individual is located. Telephone the nearest branch of that multinational early in the morning, before the receptionists get drowned with incoming calls, and throw yourself at their mercy.

Reaching CEOs and chairpeople is also best done early. Many of them have got to their current eminence by workaholism. So they pitch up at their desks at 7.30 or 8.00, and if you telephone at that time, you may get through to them without having to breast the wave of opposition represented by a good personal assistant. In the corporate world, a piece of advice from Irish communications expert Tom Savage is relevant: 'It's much more important to know the doorman than the President.' When it comes to checking data, knowing the first name of the doorman, or the secretary, or the researcher, is often more useful than being on first-name terms with the top people.

the topic and so you've taken your courage in your hands and you want to run precisely five statements or chunks of detail past them to make sure you're not making serious errors.

If you're writing a book, promise you'll send them a copy, and make sure to deliver on the promise. Inscribe the book with a message indicating your gratitude and if appropriate, include them in your acknowledgements section. Ask them first, though. Some civil servants and people in a couple of professions (like law or medicine) are endlessly helpful to writers, but prefer *not* to be acknowledged in publications.

It has been suggested that any human being is six degrees separated from any other human being. We are more connected than we think. If you need to check a fact with someone eminent or famous, do a little brain-storming among your friends and colleagues. Sooner or later, one of them will say 'Oh, hey, I had a friend in Singapore and his sister-in-law was a cousin of that guy.' Contact the friend in Singapore and ask for help. Don't be self-conscious about it. People love to be asked to exercise their expertise – and they *love* to be helpful, particularly to writers.

Never rely on secondary sources. Newspapers are secondary sources. Just because a story appears in several newspapers does not mean that any one of them has the facts. Another problem with newspapers is that, when they get it wrong, the correction a) tends to be much smaller than the original story, and b) depending on the amount of litigation involved, may appear months or years after the offending report.

If, therefore, you trawl through the archives of a newspaper and find a story making lethal allegations about a public figure, you would be ill-advised to lift the allegations and incorporate them into your own work. For all you know, the paper was forced into a retraction a year-and-a-half later and you are laying yourself open to be sued, just as they were. Find the reporter, if they're still alive, or, better still, go back to the people named in the story.

'Don't get it right, get it written,' is good advice at the start of a report or feature. It's after you have the first draft complete that you go through the process of getting it stand-up-in-court right.

AUTHENTICITY

Writers are born – and made. They are made by the books they read. Children's essays reflect what they've most recently seen on TV or read at bedtime. Undergraduates veer from reproducing the elaborate intricacies of James Joyce one week to the achieved simplicity of Hemingway the next as they progress through their reading lists.

The prolific and engaging Stephen King happily confirms that, in his early days, he wrote in the style of whatever writer he was reading at the time. He went through a Ray Bradbury phase and a James M. Cain phase. His writing went from eerie to hard-boiled to embroidered. He was unconsciously trying out various styles prior to the point where his own 'voice' emerged.

Most good writers are readers. But it's important to move away from the writers you admire, lest their style overwhelm your own. A good analogy to what can happen was provided in Stendhal's advice 'not to purchase engravings of fine views and prospects seen on one's travels, since before very long they will displace our memories completely, indeed one might say they destroy them'.

Don't try to imitate another writer. If you're doing creative writing, then it's a good idea not to read novelists or short-story writers you particularly like at the time you're crafting your own work. The danger of cross-contamination is too great. If you're doing either creative or business writing, select your reading matter carefully during the drafting stage. No, that doesn't mean immersing yourself in some highbrow text, adjudged by the critics to contain sentences of limpid lucidity. It means reading something exciting, which takes you away from the topic about which you're writing, written by a master of the simple sentence and accurate observation.

What's most interesting about an authentic individual style is that we all develop it without trouble in the spoken word. Most people, by their teens, have a distinctive way of talking. The problem is that when they sit down to write, they iron it flat. They reach for a formal version of the written word that removes all personality from their work. The French novelist Gustave Flaubert was so aware of this problem that he used to go out on his balcony and speak his thoughts to the wind, to test out his phraseology before he committed it to paper. It's a good habit, for a number of reasons, starting with content mastery.

Hearing yourself articulate your points out loud can startle you, the

'If you want to be a writer, you must do two things above all others: read a lot and write a lot. There's no way around these two things that I'm aware of, no shortcut. I'm a slow reader, but I usually get through seventy to eighty books a year, mostly fiction. I don't read in order to study the craft; I read because I like to read.'
Stephen King

lone listener. You may find you don't quite believe what you're saying. Or that there's something more important than the point you planned to start with. Matt Cooper, when he edited the *Sunday Tribune*, used to ask younger journalists to tell him the essence of their story before they wrote it. 'If you don't clearly understand your own point,' he would say, if they dithered, 'how do you expect your reader to understand it?'

Developing a distinctive 'writer's voice' starts with speaking aloud. That's the positive approach. It's the first step towards avoidance of posturing. Posturing is when you seek to be more authoritative, more literary, and more impressive than you believe yourself to be. Posturing shows up in posh language when a writer chooses multi-syllabic verbiage instead of mono-syllabic minimalism. (And that means big grey words where small colourful words will do.)

As Mark Twain put it: Eschew surplusage. When a client reads a consultant's report, for example, they should have the sense that the consultant is on their side of the issue, talking to them, rather than talking *at* them, or posturing at them.

That doesn't mean that you shouldn't use an unusual word if only that word will fully express what you want to convey. But – especially for the business writer – it means reminding yourself at all times that you're trying to create *understanding*, not setting out to impress another mind. The Americans have an acronym: KISS. Meaning: Keep It Simple, Stupid. When in doubt, go for the short sentence and the simple word.

The concept of a writer's 'voice' is a contradictory one. The reader doesn't want to feel that they're reading an imitation Faulkner or Charles Handy. Nor does the reader want to be overwhelmed with quotations from eminent figures, presented to conceal the timidity of the writer. However, the reader is just as resistant to a writer who obtrudes at every point or whose idea of a 'voice' is to be heavily facetious, nudge-nudging the reader into an unsought partnership.

Facetiousness is a version of tongue-in-cheek humour. It's akin to the kind of remark someone makes that is offensive to another person, but allows the perpetrator to claim the remark was 'only a joke'. It never works in business writing, and is teeth-grindingly awful in creative writing. The facetious is equalled only by the pun in counter-productivity. Addiction to punning is tedious. The *Guardian* newspaper for many years suffered from this in its headlines. Now they've largely detoxed, leaving the problem with the tabloids, which give us headings like 'Celebrity Big Blubber' over a story about a famous whale and 'Plucking Hell' over a report about the removal of excess hair. Puns are the lowest form of wit. Even if they're part of your authenticity, they should be amputated.

Effortful failures to achieve an individual voice are nearly always caused by lack of attention to the reader. The reader is regarded as somewhere between an enemy and a dupe. Either way, the writer is seeking to *put something across* to the reader.

Writers need to trust their readers. Imagine one single target person and set out to interest them. If you're really writing for one person who is liked and trusted by you, your humour or authority or charm will begin to assert itself without overwhelming the text. The same is true if you're writing something calculated to emotionally move the reader. You've seen it on TV, where a presenter starts with that idiotic question, 'How did you feel when your baby was swept away from you by the floodwaters?' and probes with a crowbar down the side of which is written: *Please cry. Tears are good for the ratings*. Bad writing tries to force the reader's responses by use of the emotional crowbar. Don't *tell* us we should be sad. *Show* us why we should be sad.

Having an individual style does not mean spattering your text with the personal pronoun. This is particularly relevant in business writing. A report filled with 'I found' and 'I believe' manages to put the writer centre-stage without adding to his or her persuasiveness. The same is true of the collective personal pronoun 'we.' Get your first draft written, and then search it for those words. Every time you encounter an assertion of personal belief, see if you can turn it into a straightforward assertion.

Instead of:

'I feel it would be best to restrict recruitment next year.'

Try:

'Hiring new staff would not be productive, given the economic outlook for the coming year.'

Above all, remove any references to feelings or beliefs. The reader couldn't care less what the writer feels or believes. The reader must be given the evidence on which to build their own feelings and beliefs. For creative and business writers alike, that requires slavish obedience to this rule:

No assertion without evidence.

Gender comes into play when selecting evidence, similes or metaphors. Men and women write and speak different versions of the English language. Here's an example: 'The candidate fainted.' We immediately assume that the candidate is female. Men pass out or collapse.

Most of the similes and metaphors used by men come from war or sport. They talk about attacking an issue, crushing the competition or operating on a level playing pitch. Women are more likely to use relationship, cooking or childcare examples. Women also tend to talk and write in pictures rather than in concepts. However, if a woman is writing a report for a male Board or a speech for a male speaker, her work will be more relevant if she uses *their* language and selects persuasive evidence from within *their* life experience.

Readers do not require business writing to have an authoritarian tone, but they *do* like the writer to be in charge. That means back-loading any qualifications to the main statements. The rule is:

State and then qualify.

For example:

'The offer should be refused, because…'

Rather than:

'Given that her roof fell in yesterday, and that there was a down-pour, and even though she is generous in offering us the use of her spare bedroom to store files, the offer should be refused.'

The qualifications should always be evidence-based. Perhaps because doctors have to find the evidence from examination of the patient before they come to a diagnosis, the man who uttered the two best pieces of advice for writers of all kinds – especially business writers – was himself a doctor. Somerset Maugham said that the job of a writer was to make old things new and new things familiar. Sounds simple and obvious, but it's often only on second reading that the business writer realises: That's what this report/study/speech is all about. Refresh the familiar or routine, so that readers or listeners notice it all over again, and introduce the unfamiliar, so they come to terms with something new or challenging.

The second piece of advice Maugham gave was to do the first draft in its entirety, and then go back over it in search of the three things – phrases, words, similes – that the writer likes best. And cut them out. Murder your little darlings. Because those clauses that, on rereading, start you purring gently in the back of your throat are likely to be show-offs: sequins stitched onto good plain fabric. Off with their heads…

In fiction, a good editor will help the writer remove self-indulgences. Not always, though. Readers who get hooked on the work of a particular writer invariably find repetitious usages in their work. Walter Macken, an Irish novelist who produced fine historical novels, repeatedly described his favourite male characters as having 'a stomach as flat as a table'. Jonathan Kellerman, psychologist and one of the twenty-first-century's bestselling thriller-writers, tends to have his characters say 'Like I said…' which, while allowing him to restate a clue the reader might otherwise miss, can irritate and distract.

In this regard, the best friend a writer can have is a positive but observant pet reader. That reader can be a colleague, a pal or a mother: someone who's rooting for the writer and who thinks their work is good, but who has enough detachment to spot repetitious phrases and draw the writer's attention to them.

BREVITY

Here's a test for your forensic reading capacity. Put your watch in front of you and see how long it takes you to identify the familiar yarn embedded in the two following paragraphs. Four minutes is average. Anything less is excellent.

Crucial intervention of a third party

Neither the geographical location or the timeline are possible to ascertain in relation to the foregoing circumstances, however one seeks to. This must be noted whilst not serving to obviate the possibility of personal development – albeit at a rudimentary stage implicit herein. Suffice it to say that the circumstances surrounding the individual who may be assumed to be at the nub of the account would suggest a precipitate loss of disposable income (although this precipitate loss is unexplained and is juxtaposed against social conditions of near although not blood relatives so different as to represent a quantum leap) are established both by the vocational calling of the central character and by the palpable dearth of regard demonstrable in the behaviours of those kin towards the subject of the case study. What may be drawn from standard sources, taking into account commonly articulated warnings about the applicability of apocrypha to the quotidian, is that an element of jealousy over relative pulchritude may have been instrumental in the absence of the normal female affiliation one might have expected between the to siblings and their adoptive family member.

The crucial intervention of a third party resulted from a social engagement involving the siblings but specifically excluding the central figure who was on her own as a consequence of their departure when visited by an individual claiming a spiritual relationship with her. She then caused the manifestation and mutation of rodents and vegetables into means of transport into which she embarked having first undergone significant alteration of raiment, the latter involving items for the termination of her nether limbs of doubtful durability but immediate transparency. How could the central figure have undertaken the activity recounted so garbed?

Got it?

It is, of course, the story of Cinderella, though when told with brevity, it begins: 'Once upon a time, a poor little girl named Cinderella was a slave for her stepmother and two ugly stepsisters.'

In one sentence, we have the dramatis personae and enough information about Cinders and the other three to know where we stand. We stand with the poor little girl.

Most people can be brief in the spoken word. When someone waffles on and on, the other people in the room tend to shift around and take deep breaths, or – if they're blunt enough – will say, 'And your point?'

Because writers can't see their readers, they lose that valuable feedback, and often with it, their brevity. Word borrows word. Interest is paid on the borrowings. And a brief exciting story about a prince and a pauper turns into a slab of cement. To retrieve brevity, writers need to obey a number of drafting rules – and then go back through their draft to find and kill redundancies.

See the ten essential drafting rules broken by this version of the Cinderella story opposite. (It breaks a lot more than ten, but these are the most important.)

The value of wordiness

Added words and added syllables do not give added value. Sometimes, they suck the life, the poetry and the pace out of writing. George Orwell demonstrated this by selecting a chunk of the Bible and 'improving' it by adding self-important words. The original, from Ecclesiastes in the King James Version, is:

> I returned, and saw under the sun, that the race is not to the swift, nor the battle to the strong, neither yet bread to the wise, nor yet riches to men of understanding, nor yet favour to men of skill; but time and chance happeneth to them all.

This is Orwell's version:

> Objective consideration of contemporary phenomena compels the conclusion that success or failure in competitive activities exhibits no tendency to be commensurate with innate capacity, but that a considerable element of the unpredictable must inevitably be taken into account.

Ten essential drafting rules broken by 'Crucial intervention...'

Rule 1
Answer the who/what/where/how/why/when questions as quickly as possible.

Where it's broken
It begins with detailed vagueness.

Rule 2
Never begin with a negative: it tends to dispirit the reader. Remember, Dickens could have begun *A Tale of Two Cities* like this: 'It was not the most propitious period for the populace...'

Where it's broken
'Neither'

Rule 3
Keep your twins together: neither is followed by nor; either is followed by or.

Where it's broken
'Neither... or'

Rule 4
Ban jargon – it forces readers to do more work than they may be willing to do. In this instance, it's a term used by sportsfans and let's leave it to them.

Where it's broken
'timeline'

Rule 5
KISS Keep It Simple, Stupid

Where it's broken
'possible to ascertain'
'the applicability of apocrypha to the question'

Rule 6
Use the simple word you know, not the more impressive word you'd like to know.

Where it's broken
'Jealousy' is not the same as 'envy'. 'Disinterested' means having no vested interest; 'uninterested' means not caring.

Rule 7
Tell it straight: 'She worked as a scullery-maid.'

Where it's broken
'the vocational calling'

Rule 8
Don't reverse to your point.

Where it's broken
The sentence beginning 'What may be drawn...'

Rule 9
Don't rely on your spell-checker.

Where it's broken
'between the to siblings'

Rule 10
Keep things clear. 'She' is used to refer to different people in the same sentence.

Where it's broken
'She then caused the manifestation... into which she embarked'

Fowler, the man who produced an invaluable book for writers, always recommended that the simple word or phrase should be preferred to the lengthy, elaborate one. When in doubt, therefore, pick the words on the left, rather than the ones on the right.

Brief	Elaborate
about	concerning the matter of/in reference to/with regard to/with reference to
adjust	make an adjustment to
although	notwithstanding the fact that
because	on the grounds that/due to the fact that
build	construct
consider	take under advisement/take into consideration
contact us	please do not hesitate to contact us
do	accomplish, implement, achieve
encourage	give encouragement to
end	terminate
fix	rectify, amend
for	for the purpose of
has	is equipped with
if	if it should transpire
kill	terminate with extreme prejudice
like	in the nature of
many	a large number of
now	at the present time/at this point in time
pipes/roads/railways	infrastructure
rare	infrequent
roughly	on the order of magnitude of
since	in view of the fact that/considering the fact that/inasmuch as
so that	with the result that
unsatisfactory	less than satisfactory
use	utilise

Sometimes, elaborate phrases creep into a sentence in bundles, padding the simplicity out of it. Here's an example of a sentence padded out of shape:

'During the course of the year 2007, during a trip to the city of Paris, about which we will write more at a later date, we found out that the roads were made out of asphalt.'

Padding removed, it reads thus:

'In 2007, during a trip to Paris, about which we will write more later, we found the roads were made of asphalt.'

The word count drops from 36 to 22. No meaning is lost. But the shortened sentence is easier for the reader to take in in one cognitive chunk.

Intensifiers

The redundant intensifier is one of the great enemies of brevity. This is the word that sets out to add meaning, but fails. Examples include:

absolutely
basically
considerably
comparatively
completely
definitely
extremely
generally
possibly
relatively
very (this is one of the worst offenders)

Intensifiers often end in 'ly' because they are adverbs. Adverbs like to attach themselves to attributions for quotations, like this:

'I'm going to stab you, rape you and cut you into tiny pieces using a blunt kitchen knife,' he said menacingly.

Now, most readers would figure a degree of menace was implicit in that detailed threat, so the 'menacingly' is a waste of paper. Writers who are good at dialogue – at reproducing what a character would actually say in a threatening, exciting, seductive, or amusing situation – don't need to back-announce the tone of the words they have put in their character's mouth.

The Fog Index

One way to avoid inadvertently producing this sort of text is to apply the Fog Index.

The Fog Index is the invention of an Oxford don named Robert Gunning. Gunning's Index allows writers to analyse what they've written to gauge how easy it is to read and understand.

Here's how the Fog Index works. First, pick a paragraph or a page of your work, containing at least one hundred words. Then:

• Count the words in the sample.

• Count the sentences.

• Count the number of words with three or more syllables in them.

• Pick the longest sentence and the shortest and work out the average.

• Divide the number of sentences into the number of words

• Establish the percentage of big words.

• Add the average sentence length to the percentage of big words.

• Finally, multiply the result by 4.

The best total is around 7 or 8. Going above 12 means the writing in the sample examined is too hard for most people to read.

Sometimes, intensifiers make nonsense of a sentence:

'Because it was absolutely unique, it was impossible to make an exact duplicate.'

Think about that. If it was unique, then 'absolutely' adds nothing. An object cannot be more or less unique. Unique is an absolute in itself. Adding 'exact' to 'duplicate' is just as unproductive. The sentence should read:

'Because it was unique, it was impossible to make a duplicate.'

Or, better still:

'It was impossible to duplicate it, because it was unique.'

Needless intensifiers, like *basically* and *fundamentally*, pop up at the beginning of sentences where the writer lacks a supply of transition words or phrases to get from one idea to the next.

To take a thought further
above all
in addition
in reality
to this end

To contrast ideas
despite this
however
in contrast
nonetheless/nevertheless

To compare ideas
common to both is
like
matching this is
similarly

To show time
later
meanwhile
now
this year/next year

Contractions

If you want to make any statement more user-friendly, remember to use contractions. In conversation, we use contractions all the time. They make sentences more brief, more cursive, less formal.

> 'I couldn't do anything, because I didn't have the money, and my mother wouldn't give me any.'

Shorn of its contractions, that sentence turns into something between a witness statement and an ultimatum:

> 'I could not do anything, because I did not have the money, and my mother would not give me any.'

In some writing, contractions are frowned upon as over-familiar and insufficiently formal, but, whenever you can, have the courage of your contractions: your reader will have the sense that you're talking directly to them, as opposed to from the formal distance which so irritated Queen Victoria about one of her prime ministers. She never liked Gladstone because, she said, he always addressed her as if she was a public meeting.

The ultimate hint about brevity, oddly, used to be found on the lids of jam jars: 'Pierce with a pin. Then push off.'

CLICHÉS

The Irish love clichés in their own language. Generations of Irish school-children were forced to learn off lists of *sean-fhocail* (literally, 'old words'). Harvard mathematician and comedian Tom Lehrer famously described gargling as a habit indulged in furtively by a remote tribe who passed it down from father to son as part of their oral tradition. *Sean-fhocail* were the Irish version. Children learned to pad their essays in the Irish language with gems like 'as black as coal' and 'nature breaks out through the eyes of a cat'. (The latter is the Irish version of a leopard's incapacity to change its spots.)

The Irish oral tradition notwithstanding, clichés are bad. Full stop. Bad. Unacceptable. To be culled. To be eliminated.

It sounds easy. It isn't. It's particularly difficult for tabloid TV journalists, who are encouraged to lash clichés into their commentary as a way of 'writing to pictures'. Should the camera catch the attendance at a political conference arriving in a downpour, the reporter will gallantly match the pictures.

'Raindrops were falling on the heads of the LibDems today,' she will begin. 'But the party was not going to let the weather dampen their spirits.'

As the footage shows a procession of delegates making their way to the hotel entrance, the voice will continue:

'It might have looked as if it was raining on their parade.'

Cut to a shot of two of them shaking hands.

'However, for the delegates, it was a hands-on occasion.'

Sometimes, such reports carry so much cliché-traffic, collisions happen.

'The Party Leader demonstrated that, while he's a dark horse, he can paddle his own canoe.'

Politicians have their own frequent-flier clichés. Coming up to an election, they start to talk about what they're 'hearing on the doorsteps'. Never mind that most people, in this century, don't live in homes with doorsteps.

There are those exceptions within politics who use clichés, but confuse them into freshness. Taoiseach Bertie Ahern has a genius for it. He talks about 'upsetting the apple tart' and 'fighting their own canoe'.

Unfortunately, most people who use clichés don't know a cliché from a fresh statement. Indeed, they may believe using a relatively recent cliché will establish them has having cutting-edge wit. (And, yes, 'cutting-edge' is a cliché, too.)

For example:

'The gathering was distinguished by shoulder-pads, streaked hair and Prada bags – and that was just the men.'

The 'and that was just the' device is a cliché. As is, 'Tough job, but someone's got to do it.' As is, 'Now I want to move on with my life.' And, 'She was always there for me.' The cliché is the fast-food of writing. Superficially satisfying, but nutritionally poor.

The great breeding-grounds for clichés are domesticity, sport, war, nature and medicine. Domesticity gives us the impossibility of omelette-making, absent the breaking of eggs; sport provides us with level playing-pitches and a welter of others; war delivers front lines and 'putting the kibosh on the enemy'; nature cherry-picks; and medicine is spectacularly rich in cancer-similes.

Cliché-ridden writing has its comforts. Old-shoe comforts. The writer doesn't have to work too hard, and the reader has an easy time of it, too. Taking on board a new idea, adopting a new policy or embarking on the development of a new behaviour, however, is never helped by clichés. Writing that smacks the reader in the vulnerabilities, or startles them into rereading and perhaps writing down a phrase or two, rarely has clichés in it.

The insidious attraction of clichés lies in their truthfulness. Truisms, by their nature, deliver eternal verities. People in glass-houses *shouldn't* throw stones, and whoever first stated this truth made a hell of an observation. A shut mouth *doesn't* catch flies, and discretion *is* the better part of valour, and it *is* easier to get forgiveness than permission. Conscripted writers (the ones who have to write for business purposes, as opposed to volunteers who can't stop themselves) tend not to be readers, and so, when they first happen on a truism like 'it's not rocket science' they assume it's new and incorporate it into their own document.

Clichés lubricate the onward flow of writing, and so must be permitted to slither into a first draft, but extirpated from the second draft. A dictionary of clichés should be on every writer's desk. (See the Bibliography for our preferred dictionaries.) In addition to a dictionary, books that fill you in on the origins of particular sayings can make the culling process more fun. For example, while we would advise against the 'kibosh' example, it's interesting to note that this is one of the few clichés derived from the Irish language. (See Hiberno-English, Ulster-Scots, Irish-English, Section 5.)

Where there is no alternative to a cliché, it must be used. A writer tempted to employ the term 'couch potato' can always find a better term for the passive reality he or she wants to convey, but a writer faced with the concept of a 'soundbite' may have no alternative. While soundbite is a cliché, it is also a precise descriptor of a TV reality.

A soundbite is what happens when the newscaster reports that a fire has gutted a cat-food factory that employed five hundred workers, which is directly followed by a clip of an interview with the owner. The owner says that the factory has been in operation for thirty years and

Some quite good clichés die off because the context renders them peculiar. Earlier generations would comment on bad weather by saying, 'You wouldn't put a milk bottle out on a day like this.' Once milk was no longer delivered, that particular saying withered on the cliché-vine. The same thing happened to 'You wouldn't know what to pawn,' as the old pawn-shops with their three golden balls closed down.

that the blaze is devastating for his family and for the local community. That clip is what's called a soundbite, and to use the term in describing a news bulletin is valid.

To talk of a 'soundbite culture', by contrast, is a cliché. Soundbites have always existed. 'I came, I saw, I conquered,' is a pretty good example. 'The shadow of fear is longer than fear itself,' is another. 'Soundbite culture' is an easy way of denigrating the times in which we live without actually adding value. It's shorthand – but a stale form of shorthand.

The only time you should use a cliché is when you're serving it up with a refreshing seasoning: a cloud with *no* silver lining or he who lives by the sword survives to a ripe old age. Turning clichés on their heads can illustrate a point in a way that gets the reader thinking.

Never assume that a cliché will be so big and obvious that its excision will be easy. Some clichés are just two words long, and invade an otherwise lively sentence without the writer noticing.

Brief clichés best avoided

any shape or form	full and frank
beggars description	fur-lined mousetrap
the bitter end	goes without saying
blow by blow	golden handshake
bring to a head	high dudgeon
burning issue	last but not least
city fathers	league table
cool as a cucumber	leave no stone unturned
cool and groovy	needs no introduction
crying need	pillar of the establishment
cutting edge	quality time
each and every	sea of faces
economical with the truth	speculation was rife
face up to	sure as eggs are eggs
fan the flames	take the bull by the horns
fair means or foul	this day and age
flash in the pan	win-win situation
foregone conclusion	worst case scenario

SPIN

The true spin-doctor, one who goes out to media and appears on media defending their employer's interests, is an American phenomenon. Some European public relations consultancies have taken on the role of representing their client, appearing in news bulletins to explain their views or actions, but many reject the role, believing that a politician ought to be able to speak for themselves, and that if they do it correctly, their words need no *post-factum* gloss applied by third parties.

However, a key part of business writing is presenting the best possible case for a company or a corporate action, past or future, and this can be described as 'spin'.

Some of the more egregious spin tactics include attacking media for publishing criticisms, on the basis that they should concentrate on the 99 percent of a company's products that perform as they should, as opposed to getting hysterical about the 1 percent that kill consumers. Another is the admission that is so blandly wordy that the reader isn't clear what the topic is, never mind who's confessing to what. A third is painting a picture of the company or individual as saintly, selfless and professional in every word and deed, stashing the acknowledgement of fraud, misrepresentation or pollution in the second last paragraph. Burying the bad news is an old, old tactic, updated with disastrous results by a PR woman working for Tony Blair's New Labour Party, who proposed in an e-mail directly after the 9/11 attacks on the Twin Towers that any government department sitting on stinker news should get it out expeditiously, in order to have it swamped in the inevitably extensive coverage of the terrorist action.

The line at which 'spin' takes over from straightforward communication is thin. Thin – and important. Too often, the desire to put one's company in a good light can lead to spin-doctoring of the facts. Where a company has done something wrong, the first and best service its executives (including its PR or Public Affairs staff) can do the corporation is to ask questions. Getting the facts straight is the essential step towards ethical and effective communication.

The second step is to tell the truth. That should be linked with corrective action. Arguably the best exemplar of these linked priorities were the makers of Tylenol when someone doctored their painkiller with cyanide. At the first death, the manufacturers worked with the police to spread the word that the product had been tampered with and

The term 'spin-doctor' began to figure in print around the same time as 'soundbite' first arrived. A reference appeared in a *New York Times* report, in 1984, of the Reagan/Mondale TV debate:

'A dozen men in good suits and women in silk dresses will circulate smoothly among the reporters, spouting confident opinions. They won't be just press agents trying to impart a favourable spin to a routine release. They'll be Spin Doctors, senior advisors to the candidates.'

Guidelines for spin-avoidance:

Don't lie or set out to mislead
It is misleading to liken a negative outcome to something much less serious, or to present statistics so confusingly that the reader will come, with your help, to the wrong conclusion. Using euphemisms like 'rightsizing' conceals the reality for about thirty seconds and angers the readers: 'D'you think we're that stupid?'

Don't minimise
Executives working for bosses who hate to receive bad news sometimes try to minimise it when writing reports. That's spin, complicated by cowardice.

Don't explain away error
Apologising for corporate or individual error and in the next sentence explaining it away is unacceptable and unproductive spin.

Don't repeat the words of an accusation
This rule applies to print and electronic communication. If your CEO is accused of laying waste to pet cats in his neighbourhood during his formative years, it doesn't help his reputation to issue a press release headed, ' "I never slaughtered cats," says CEO.'

Don't attribute motivation
People inside your company or outside it may be opposed to your policies for all sorts of reasons. It does them no harm if you include vague attributions of malign motivation to them. References to 'those with personal agendas' simply give your document an impotently spiteful tone without nailing your opponents.

not to buy or ingest it. They also pulled Tylenol off the shelves of every pharmacy in the United States within forty-eight hours. At no point in the sorry saga, at the end of which the multiple murderer went unapprehended, did the company make a PR push.

Despite the threat to their market share, they kept Tylenol off the shelves until they had developed a tamper-proof lid, now standard on such products, and a new kind of vehicle, called a 'caplet', which had the easy-to-swallow shape of a capsule, but was filled with solid material into which foreign substances could not be injected.

The consequence of their ethical communication was that Tylenol, post-poisonings, ended up with a larger market share than beforehand and a greatly enhanced corporate reputation. The lesson from the Tylenol episode is clear: reputation risk is ever-present, no matter what your product or service, but a straightforward response putting the customer first can, even in negative circumstances, result in an enhanced, rather than a diminished, reputation.

The grim reality, however, is that, long after Tylenol had been so exemplary in their response to an external threat, some corporations in the same business have resorted to the worst kind of spin in response to an internal threat. It goes like this. A pharmaceutical company comes up with a new treatment. Puts it on the market. Doctors prescribe it. It becomes hugely popular. It earns enormous amounts of money for its manufacturers.

Then lethal side effects surface and it emerges that the drug company knew about them. It was aware, for a while, that hundreds of people have become very ill as a result of taking the tablets, and a fair few have actually died. But the drug company has convinced itself that these are but anomalies, and so does not feel an overwhelming need to tell the regulators or stick one of those off-putting health warnings on each package. They keep it a secret. Their share price stays buoyant.

Eventually, of course, it stops being a secret. When this happens, as it has more than once in recent days, the drug company gets smacked around by the FDA and other authorities, gets class-action lawsuits in droves, gets fined, gets more column inches of godawful coverage than they could ever have imagined, pays out millions if not billions in damages, and is likely to take a hit on its share value.

Between concealment and spin, public sympathy for their travails is limited, because people feel the manufacturer had to have known that such egregious concealment of data was going to damage the public good and kill off a proportion of the citizens. Transparency and open-ness are the way to go. The public's right to know is paramount. The more people know, the more in control they are. Good information flow saves lives and contributes to general well-being.

Is spin necessary to make the truth accessible?

That does not obviate the requirement to clothe the truth, if not in a body-guard of lies (as Churchill once suggested was necessary), then at least in terms that make the truth accessible to those who should know it and change their behaviour as a result. Sometimes, the incapacity to make the truth unthreateningly interesting can be a matter of life and death.

Sherwin Nuland, Professor of Surgery at Yale University, has published an account of a tragedy that might not have been averted by 'spin' but that certainly happened because the central figure was not able to write his findings in a persuasive way.

Nuland's slim volume *The Doctors' Plague* opens in Vienna in 1847, when a pregnant woman arrives at the city's main hospital to deliver her baby. She is directed to a ward run by expert surgeons. Her response is terrified protest. 'No, no,' she begs. 'Please can I go to the other ward – the one run by midwives?' If she goes to the surgeons' ward, she will die there.

She is dragged, screaming, into the surgeons' ward, where she delivers her baby. And dies. As do most of her fellow-patients, because, at that time, mothers delivered by surgeons fully trained in anatomy tended to die in huge numbers. Their deaths, caused by 'childbed' or 'puerperal fever' were characterised by raging septicemia, agonising pain, ferocious temperatures and delirium.

On the other hand, women who delivered their babies under the care of an illiterate midwife had a much better chance of survival. Division One of the Vienna Hospital, where the surgeons worked, had a horrific death rate. Division Two, where the midwives worked, was reasonably safe.

The same pattern followed all over Europe. Between 1831 and 1843, only 10 London mothers per 10,000 died of puerperal fever when delivered at home (by a midwife), compared to 600 per 10,000 in the city's General Lying-in Hospital, where consultants did the job. It was a mystery.

But in the hospital in Vienna was a young doctor named Ignac Semmelweis, who observed what was going on with a fresh eye. He spotted that the key difference between the two wards was that midwives didn't dissect dead bodies, whereas surgeons did. Having dissected a dead body, they went straight to the maternity ward to examine pregnant women. No rubber gloves, no handwashing intervened. Nobody at the time knew about germs, so Semmelweis, when he figured out that surgeons were carrying killer organisms on their hands, called those organisms 'cadaver particles'.

Semmelweis installed basins of a cleanser – chloride of lime – together with nail brushes at the entrance to the 'killer' maternity ward and got surgeons to clean their hands with it before approaching patients. Within weeks, the mortality rate dropped. Brilliant. No need for a communications consultant there, you may say. Unless you wanted Semmelweis's discovery applied forever more in that particular hospital *and* introduced all over the world so it could save millions of lives.

If you wanted both of those outcomes, then someone was needed to grasp Semmelweis warmly by the throat and say, 'Sunshine, this is not going to catch on unless scholarly papers are published about it in the medical journals. You can't write, you say? You're half-fluent in two languages and a bore in both? You're incapable of a coherent written sentence? No problem. Sit down there while I get out my quill. Talk, I'll transcribe and write up a paper for you.'

That didn't happen. In the absence of a clear written account of what was happening, an inaccurate version of Semmelweis's theory got around. The wrong version was easy to dismiss – and dismissing it was a very welcome option for surgeons who did not want to admit that their hands had killed hundreds of their patients.

For Semmelweis, the truth was so inescapably obvious that anyone who failed to apprehend and live by it was evil. He never understood that failing to communicate your truth means you might as well not have discovered it in the first place. He needed to be able to temper his truth to the minds of those who needed to understand it, and to write it – not using spin – but employing neutral, non-pejorative language.

The old city cemeteries of Europe are filled with the bodies of women and babies who died because the man who knew how to save them couldn't communicate his discovery in a persuasive way – and lived before it was possible to hire someone who could.

SLANG

The English language is marvellously promiscuous. It can have offspring of varying entitlements. Four or five years ago, writers who stated that they 'Googled' someone were using informal or slangy language to show that they had used the search engine Google to find information about an individual. By 2005, 'to google' was an accepted mainstream expression.

Some slangy expressions don't make it into mainstream English because they are rooted in a particular trade or sport. So, if, in your writing, you describe someone as 'diving', the reader is likely to imagine someone on a diving board with water below them. However, if you're a sportswriter, you may mean to convey a footballer who threw himself down to win a penalty. This more slangy use of 'to dive' has not yet moved into all the dictionaries.

Slang is a little like cant, the dialect spoken by the travelling people. It allows for communication within a specific community while excluding outsiders. Teenagers adopt slang for this purpose, and it never works when a teacher tries to pick up and use that slang. In the wrong mouth, slang simply sounds odd, just like swearing. Mark Twain's wife was so bothered by his constant swearing that she began to embroider her own genteel conversation with four letter words, to show him how awful they sounded. Her husband was intrigued and delighted, rather than shamed. He said she got the words right, but didn't know the tune. Using slang words that aren't your own has the same effect.

This is exacerbated by the constantly shifting lexicon of slang. The word that is hot (or sometimes cool) this month will be seriously untrendy a few weeks later: not so long ago, it was fashionable to describe anything you did not like as 'the something from hell'. Now, it sounds dated.

Slang is autopilot communication 'Omigod, that handbag is amazing!' does not require the speaker to genuinely flatter the handbag owner by referring to its workmanship or its suitability to the outfit being worn.

Some slang is used inside particular trades or professions. Slangy politicians refer to voters as 'punters'. Slangy gardaí refer to female members of the force as 'banners', the word deriving from the way they were first described: ban garda (female garda). Slangy medics refer to orthopaedic surgeons as 'orthopods' and psychiatrists as 'trick cyclists'; slangy journalists call each other 'hacks'.

Some slang is used by outsiders *about* particular trades or professions: 'beancounters' for accountants and 'briefs' for barristers. Inevitably, sex workers are called a variety of names, one of which gave rise to unintended comedy on the otherwise serious American quiz programme, *Jeopardy*. The question looked for a word that can refer to a garden implement and a sexually active individual. The contestant opted for 'hoe'. What had been intended was 'rake'.

Arguably the best and longest-lasting slang comes from the underworld. We may not still speak of 'cutpurses' but we do talk about doing time in the clink. Clink was a real prison in south London, renowned for its infestation of rats and insects.

The downside of using slang is that it dates so quickly and can give a serious report an over-familiar tone.

BUZZWORDS

Made-up Americanisms and noun-verbs like *author, impact, conceptualise, interface, target, action* and *impact* are out of place in business writing. Excise examples like these:

'Joe Murphy *authored* this report.'

'The MD likes to *interface* with customers. He's big on MBWA.'

'These issues may *impact* negatively on the residents in the area.'

'I would ask you to *action* this as soon as possible.'

'We are *targeting* a wide market for the new product.'

Acronyms like MBWA (Management By Walking About) date quickly and force the reader to do work they may be unwilling to do.

Also to be avoided are words created by adding *-wise*. *Efficiency-wise, timewise* and *statuswise* are uniformly horrible.

Business writing breeds more buzzwords than any other kind of writing, perhaps because insecure executives believe that by borrowing a killer phrase from the latest management book, their work will seem more current.

Consider the following example:

The corporate culture of the Buggins company is to constantly push the envelope and raise the bar. Buggins seeks to recruit those who can think outside the box, our paradigm being proactivity and avoidance of the low-hanging fruit. Our mission is to do just-in-time delivery in a lean and mean way, and our KPIs reflect this. Going forward, the granularity of the company will be assured by hot-desking, focus on core competencies in an holistic manner, and facilitating each member of our staff to grow as a person within a context of participatory decision-making. Buggins operates advanced Customer Relations Management policies and interfaces with our stakeholders on a roll-out basis, while ensuring water-cooler conversations with our valued associates.

Awful, isn't it?

Buzzword Indicator

Pompous jargon pervades English, from corporate-speak to silly legalisms. No more so than with buzzwords. They are the ill-fitting little black dress of business expression – every season and every year they re-cut themselves for a fresh audience. How many of us have made the transition from 'paradigm shifts' to 're-engineered corporations' to 'organisational chokehold'? And although they are somewhat of a party trick, buzzword generators are a potent way of illustrating the prevalence of linguistic gobbledygook.

To demonstrate, pick any word from column one. Follow it with any word from column two and finish off the trio with any word from column three. The combination of these words will turn any boring sentence into one of limitless sophistication and maximum unintelligibility.

Column one	Column two	Column three
integrated	management	options
total	organisational	flexibility
systemised	monitored	capability
parallel	reciprocal	mobility
functional	digital	programming
responsive	logic	concept
optical	transitional	time-phase
synchronised	incremental	projection
compatible	third-generation	hardware
balanced	policy	contingency

But, irony of ironies, even the buzzword generator can elevate itself to further grandiosity. So, for a more radical and technical approach, simply choose any three-character hexadecimal form between 000 and FFF and extract the word corresponding to each character from the table below. For example: B31 = scalable reciprocal flexibility.

(For the non-technical, hexadecimal is a counting method used by programmers. It is a way of representing the internal binary code of a computer. The symbols for the numbers 0 to 9 are the same as those used in the decimal system. The numbers 10–15 are represented by the letters A–F.)

Column one	Column two	Column three
0 integrated	0 management	0 options
1 total	1 organisational	1 flexibility
2 systemised	2 monitoring	2 capability
3 parallel	3 reciprocal	3 mobility
4 functional	4 digital	4 programming
5 responsive	5 time-phased	5 concept
6 optional	6 transitional	6 welfare
7 synchronised	7 incremental	7 projection
8 compatible	8 third-generation	8 hardware
9 balanced	9 policy	9 contingency
A automatic	A tactile	A feedback
B scalable	B pre-processing	B architecture
C intuitive	C hyperbolic	C logic
D modular	D re-entrant	D process
E professional	E boolean	E debugging
F interactive	F recursive	F effectiveness

The serious concern is that the use of this language may reveal much about the attitudes of an organisation. How often have we heard, used or written the following phrases?

on the front burner	workforce optimisation	one-on-one interface
get with the programme	think outside the square	target the skillset
take it under advisement	flat management structure	on the same page
don't reinvent the wheel	massage the data	put this to bed
circular filing cabinet	meanderthal	learning opportunity
let's table that	touch base	soft landing
drop the ball	smithpress the bar	peel the onion
paradigm shift	mission critical	analysis paralysis
shield time	create synergies	head shunting
heads up	ramp up	tee up
Band-Aid	drill down	win-win
uptitling	empower-forced	prolitical
SME (subject matter expert)	CXO (chief executive officer)	SPOC (single point of contact)
FYI (for your information)	KPI (key performance indicator)	PVM (perceived value for money)

Although light-hearted and jocular in an everyday context, at least some of this language is worthy of analysis, particularly when it deals with official roles and responsibilities. Is there, for example, a preferred approach to dealing with issues and people? Certain expressions by their nature demand clarity and explanation within an organisation as a starting point, before dispersing them to outside constituencies. In the meantime, when it comes to the written word, we may have to make a choice between corporate-speak or clarity. And, wherever possible, that choice should be ours.

Reference

J. Randy Gordon, *BusiBUZZ: Business Buzzwords For Survivin' and Thrivin' In The Big City* (Booksurge Publishing, 2006).

STEREOTYPING

The USA may look like a hugely diverse society, but, as far as British and Irish media were concerned, the week after George Bush was re-elected, it was really the opposite. It was home to 51 million religious fundamentalists. Gun totin' religious maniacs, all of them anti-abortion, anti-stem-cell research. Beer drinkin', boot scootin', Bible-totin' unsophisticates, too thick to deserve democracy. Mercifully, most of the individuals so stereotyped did not read the editorials portraying them in such terms.

Disagreement with someone's political views or origins or lifestyle should be part of a stimulating exploration of the complexity of life. More often than not, in the real world, it edges into condemnation and caricaturing of the person, rather than examination of the issue they represent.

The Romans called it *argumentum ad hominem:* arguing against the man. When an eminent figure in Irish public life got caught at it, he called it 'playing the man, not the ball'. This eminent figure allowed his rage over a cleverly articulated mathematical point made by a member of the Opposition to provoke him into calling said member of the Opposition, a man of quiet manners and somewhat nerdy preoccupations, 'the Doctor Goebbels of political propaganda'. Apart from its tautology (he didn't need to mention the political propaganda, since Goebbels is the archetype), so characterising an opponent was inappropriate and distasteful. The perpetrator made a public apology a few days later.

It should be remembered that Goebbels promulgated the notion that a big lie was always more believable than a small one.

Stereotyping usually takes the form of damning an individual by association with a tribe, race or group, all of whom are portrayed as stupid, venal, vicious, inept, crooked, alcoholic, idle or physically repulsive.

In the nineteenth century, Britain's *Punch* magazine surpassed all others in its stereotyping of the Irish, who were portrayed in cartoons as bandy-legged alcoholic toads carrying shillelaghs and talking begorrahs. Nazi Germany did the same to the Jews.

Stereotyping mars the track record of otherwise admirable men, including Daniel O'Connell, who said something so offensive about Jews that Prime Minister Benjamin Disraeli retorted that when O'Connell's ancestors were running around naked and painted with woad, Disraeli's ancestors were priests in the Temple of Solomon.

'Ethnic stereotypes are misshapen pearls, sometimes with a sandy grain of truth at their center. It is true that my forebears were the folks for whom the paddy wagon was named, because of the number of them taken away drunk and disorderly on long-ago Saturday nights. The words Tammany Hall speak for themselves. We are storytellers, accomplished mourners, devout Catholics. And we are none of these. Because all of them are stereotypes.'

Anna Quindlen

Writers, by nature, are observant. They store up every incident for later use. But they must be careful not to generalise from a single incident. It is quite possible, for example, that a Jew might – in the days when Jews were the only group allowed to lend money – extort an unacceptably high level of interest. That would not entitle any writer, then or now, to spread their anger at their impoverishment at the hand of one money-lender over an entire race, any more than it would be acceptable for an English writer who had encountered a profane and intrusive Irish drunk to extrapolate from that singular experience a stance that all Irish people are offensive drunks.

All sex workers do not have a heart of gold. All anaesthetists are not drug addicts. All politicians are not out for themselves. All men are not out for the one thing. All gay men are not camp. All older people are not confused. All women do not become irrational viragoes for three days before their period. It doesn't matter that a writer's most vivid encounter with individuals from any of these groups, races, genders or professions has confirmed in the writer a pre-existing prejudice: it's neither civilised nor logical nor good writing to conflate that experience into a generalisation.

Positive stereotyping is as offensive as negative stereotyping. That's what happens when a writer credits all black people with great rhythm or all Inuit families with the willingness to lend a wife or two. Until relatively recently, thanks to the overhanging influence of classic children's books like *Heidi* and *What Katy Did*, a saintly acquiescence to the trials of life was widely attributed to people in wheelchairs. It drove intemperate unsaintly wheelchair-users nuts.

To avoid stereotyping, a number of rules must be followed.

1. Call people what they call themselves. For many years in Ireland, well-intentioned middle-class members of the settled community called travellers 'itinerants'. While it may have been a better term than some of the slangy pejoratives often directed at travellers, it was nevertheless as offensive as calling an African-American 'coloured'. Travellers call themselves travellers, and that's what the settled community should call them. Gay men and women do not like to be described as homosexual. And, while a gay man may jokingly refer to himself or a friend as 'queer', it is not acceptable for a straight man or woman to use the same term.

When in doubt, ask the person you want to write about to tell you the correct term. Never make assumptions. Jews are frequently referred to in print as 'Jewish' because the word 'Jew' sounds pejorative – to a gentile. To a Jew, it is the correct term.

Within living memory, Ireland was so closed a society that whenever a black man was spotted on the streets of Dublin, most people assumed (correctly) that he was likely to be a student at the Royal College of Surgeons in Ireland. Ireland is now so multicultural that, whether you're writing an annual report, a memo or a feature for a newspaper, the requirement not to offend by description is quite onerous. Nothing is so irritating to a second- or third-generation black Dubliner or Corkonian than to be asked, 'Where do you come from?' and have the answer quickly followed by, 'Ah, I know you *live* there, but where are you from, really?' Writers must be clear on the differences between immigrants, asylum seekers and new citizens. They must be wary of stereotypical statements about immigrants from any one particular country.

Another imperative for writers is to come to terms with proper usage around disability. In the last thirty years people with disabilities have come out of institutions and joined the mainstream population at every age level. Whereas in the past, visually impaired children were educated in one school and children with Down's Syndrome in another, the trend nowadays is to involve such children with their peers from the start, so that their disability cannot become a cause for excluding them, nor can it become so threatening and strange to others of their own age that they shrink from the pupil with the disability.

All of this has moved Ireland quite suddenly away from pity and coercive concern to a quite new view of disability as an *aspect* of a person, rather than as the *definition* of the person. To that end, writers should steer clear of identifying anybody by their disability.

People with learning disabilities should never be described using old, offensive terms. Those with Down's Syndrome, for example, are simply that: the possessor of an extra chromosome that influences the speed of their development and adds up to a recognised syndrome. They are not Mongoloid, a description going back to when observers groped for a way to describe the facial features of the syndrome.

This is sometimes described – by people who don't want to take the trouble to get the terms respectfully right – as 'political correctness'. It isn't. It's taking a moment's care in order to be respectful to others. No more; no less. Once you've accommodated the rule that you shouldn't identify somebody by their disability, it's easy to avoid describing someone as 'a cripple' or 'a spastic'. People are people first, disabled second, which is why people with disabilities prefer to be so described. If you know the name of the disease, put the individual first by writing 'a person with motor neurone disease' or whatever the disability is.

Writers should never use terms like 'victim' or describe someone as 'afflicted with' or 'suffering from' a specific disability. They *have* multiple sclerosis, cystic fibrosis or schizophrenia. At first glance, 'victim' seems a kindly way to refer to someone who has developed an illness, but in the early days of AIDS, it morphed into 'innocent victim of AIDS' to distinguish someone infected through a blood transfusion, say, from someone infected through unsafe sex. This kind of distinction is pointless and punitive. (See The Language of Illness in this section.)

Stereotyping is bad enough, but ignoring a disability completely is even worse. People who are deaf tend to be ignored, because their disability is not visible. It's as if they don't exist, as was made clear when the first cochlear implants were achieved, giving patients who had been profoundly deaf from birth the opportunity to access a limited form of hearing. Newspaper readers were astonished to read letters from deaf people with a negative take on the new surgery:

> We have a language – Irish Sign Language – and a culture of our own [the deaf activists stated]. We do not want to be second-class citizens in the hearing culture, and that's all we can ever be.

Writers rarely fall foul of the deaf community – for the simple reason that so little is written about them. However, disproportionate coverage goes to people in wheelchairs, partly because the wheelchair is used as a general icon to signify disability, thus keeping it at the front of people's minds, and partly because falls, traffic accidents and age put quite a proportion of the population in wheelchairs at some point in their lives. One of the apparently ineradicable descriptions is: 'She has been confined to a wheelchair since 2003.' This is matched by: 'He has been wheelchair-bound since a scrum fell on him in a rugby match two years ago.' Many find these descriptors maddening – no one would describe a person as 'confined to his legs'; wheelchairs are just another form of getting around.

2. Don't be sexist. To ignore the issue of sexism puts the writer at risk of being pointlessly offensive. That offence, in an official or Human Resource document, could lead to a staff complaint or legal action.

Get into the habit of using non-sexist terminology:

executive	*not*	businessman
staff hours	*not*	man-hours
supervisor	*not*	foreman
Chair	*not*	Chairman
workforce	*not*	manpower
spouse/partner	*not*	wife

If you must use a pronoun, choose 'they' rather than 'he or she' or 'he/she', which are acceptable but unwieldy. Just make sure to turn the subject of the sentence into a plural to match the verb.

Not:

The writer should make sure they avoid sexism.

But:

Writers should make sure they avoid sexism.

3. Include with specifics. Majority cultures tend to define others by exclusion. In other words, where the Catholic Church is the majority religion, the temptation is to describe others as 'non-Catholics'. Similarly, where the majority of parents are married, the instinct may be to describe those who are not as exceptions: 'unwed mothers'.

This habit clearly breaks Rule 1 above. But it also sends a message of exclusion. Muslims don't think of themselves as the control group validating the majority. So, when referring to an individual or group belonging to a race or religion or lifestyle other than your own, be specific – and use their preferred term. 'Single parents' describe themselves as such; it's how you should describe them, too.

THE LANGUAGE OF DIVERSITY

The language of diversity makes people uncomfortable. Words such as discrimination, oppression, dominance, subordination, racism and heterosexism thankfully evoke negative responses. When we talk or write in these terms, others will focus on what they mean for them. It is easier to become defensive, argue the semantics of or ignore these interactions than it is to learn how the language of diversity affects all our lives. And because we may have inadvertently absorbed oppressive terminology while learning the English language, we cannot always unlearn it without making a conscious effort.

No text can definitively catalogue 'correct' and 'incorrect' terms, despite the best efforts of sociolinguists to deconstruct the etymology and usage of words. For example, race and gender are classifications that permeate government, culture, religion, societal institutions and even economics. Conglomerates use terms such as 'free' trade, 'aid packages', 'open' markets and 'mutual' agreements. (But who is free to do what and who benefits?) How can we make an apples-to-apples comparison of consistencies, prejudices and realities in a universal context? The fact remains that language is living and evolving and cannot be decreed. At any point in time, diversity means a lot of things to a lot of constituencies.

Until recently – while acknowledging that sexism, racism and homophobia existed – for many Irish people the concept of 'diversity' might have seemed too alien, too American. It related only to problems with black/white integration and social marginalisation. But Ireland has become a culturally and linguistically diverse society with significant visible minorities and large immigrant populations. In February 2006, Bishop Trevor Morrow stated that his local congregation in Lucan was represented by every continent except the Antarctic.

It may never be possible to devise a universal language of diversity. Words may not be transferable, but the guiding principles should be equity and the fair treatment of people. We share our human-ness, and we react the same. All we can do is to challenge the values and assumptions underpinning the things we state or write, and express ourselves in ways that are considered, sensitive and accurate. At the end of the day, perhaps a useful benchmark is that respect is what you say about me.

In the absence of a global language of tolerance, but recognising the need for editorial guidance, the following glossary has been reproduced with the kind permission of Diversity Matters in Belfast. The result of four months' consultation by nine partner all-Ireland organisations, it is an effective and thought-provoking summary of the issues involved.

Age. For most purposes the categories are: those under 18, people aged 18–65 and people over 65. However, different countries, legislation and/or specific organisations can categorise age differently. Any definition used needs to be sensitive to the context in which it is being used, e.g. children and/or youth services or education and lifelong learning. At present, one of the key issues in this area is the consideration of retirement age.

Affirmative action. Although affirmative action in the Northern Ireland context has a very specific definition in fair employment legislation, in the wider intellectual debate it is seen as a tool for change to assist disadvantaged groups. It usually involves measures to redress existing disparities and correct historical imbalances and under-representation, particularly in relation to employment.

Black and minority ethnic communities. The term 'black' has often been used to describe 'visible minorities', which include people of African, Caribbean, South Asian, Chinese and South East Asian origin, etc. The use of this single term was adopted by race equality activists in the '70s and '80s to refer to people who experienced racism because of their skin colour. However, in recent years numerous individuals and groups have objected to the term 'black' as the only term being applied to them as they argue that it does not adequately convey the ethnic diversity that exists within minority ethnic groups. All human beings have ethnicity and therefore belong to an ethnic group. The term ethnic minority or minority ethnic refers to people whose ethnic group is smaller in number than that of a society's majority ethnic population. There is a growing tendency to use minority ethnic rather than ethnic minority as the emphasis is placed on the minority status rather than ethnicity, which is something shared by everyone.

Capacity building. Enabling people, groups and organisations to do things for themselves by building skills, experience and contacts as well as by targeting the provision of resources that are needed, e.g. information, venues, workers and support costs.

Carers look after family, partners or friends in need of help because they are ill, frail or have a disability. The care they provide is unpaid. This does not include caring for children or young people unless the children are also ill, frail or have a disability. Nor does it include paid care workers, personal assistants or people engaged in formal volunteering schemes. (A care worker is provided through a government agency to meet the assessed needs of a person in need of care. A personal assistant is employed directly by the person in need of care.)

Community development. Traditionally, community development would have referred to enabling people to positively participate in identifying and addressing issues of importance in their local communities. In recent years, the model of community development has also been used by people who see themselves as belonging to a community of interest. Community development supports people to identify their own requirements and to organise and initiate actions that address these issues. Through this, people identify and articulate their community's needs and work with others to address them.

Community of interest is a term used to describe a group of people who see themselves as belonging to a community with common interests, e.g. carers, disabled people, older people, the lesbian, gay, bisexual and transgendered (LGBT) community.

Discrimination. In its widest sense, discrimination can be seen as prejudice in action, where an individual or organisation, knowingly or unknowingly, allows behaviour or actions, which diminish the value or rights of others, to flourish unchecked. Under equality law, discrimination has a more specific meaning relating to less-favourable treatment of particular protected groups, e.g. in relation to disability, sex, race, religious belief, political opinion or sexual orientation.

Dependent. This term is used in Section 75 of the Northern Ireland Act 1998 to refer to an individual who relies on support from relatives or friends in order to remain in his or her home.

Diversity is about individual and group relationships. It is not only the acknowledgement and appreciation of what is different in people but the positive value placed on this difference.

Disability is a physical or mental impairment, which has a substantial and long-term adverse effect on a person's ability to carry out normal day-to-day activities.

Disadvantage can be described as a lack of access to opportunities that particularly affects certain groups, in the social, economic, political and cultural spheres of life. Disadvantage has a direct effect on a person's ability to participate in some or all aspects of society. It ranges from being unaware of all the options available to being aware of the options, but being unable to access them.

Equality. When applied to a society, equality describes a state in which people have similar opportunities in social status, income, wealth, opportunities and living conditions. Equality is the absence of inequality and disadvantage currently experienced by many individuals or groups within society. It is often the aspiration of marginalised and excluded groups.

Equality of opportunity is about ensuring that people have access to the same opportunities in all aspects of their life. Promoting equality of opportunity challenges the barriers to economic, cultural, political and social participation on the grounds of age, caring status, disability, gender, marital status, political opinion, race, religious belief, sexual orientation, geography and location.

Equality of outcome. A current concept that moves beyond equality of opportunity. It argues that disadvantaged individuals and groups require additional support to enable them to make the maximum use of available opportunities. Equality of outcome assumes that equality of opportunity and diversity strategies are successful.

Equality proofing is a check carried out on a policy to ensure that any potential discriminatory effects relating to age, caring status, disability, gender, marital status, political opinion, race, religious belief, sexual orientation, geography and location arising from that policy have been considered and that equality will be promoted, where possible.

Empowerment is a process of change in which disadvantaged groups discover their ability to challenge people or factors that disadvantage them. It enables people to gain the experience and skills necessary to act on their own behalf.

Ethnicity is a complex concept with numerous definitions and academic theories that attempt to explain its meaning. In popular usage, ethnicity is often thought of as an attribute of minority groups, but most social scientists argue that everyone has ethnicity, defined as a sense of group belonging based on ideas of common origins, history, culture, language, religion and traditions.

Gender refers to social differences, as opposed to the biological ones, between women and men that have been learned, are changeable over time, and have wide variations both within and between cultures.

Human rights are about human dignity, equality and freedom. There are different categories of rights, e.g. civil and political, cultural, social and economic. There are also different types of rights – some are regarded as absolute and others are regarded as qualified depending on the circumstances and judicial decisions.

Interdependence means that individuals and organisations are reliant on each other within any society.

Institutional discrimination is the collective failure of an organisation to provide an appropriate and professional service or work environment to people because of their real or perceived identity. It can be seen or detected in processes, attitudes and behaviour that amount to discrimination through unwitting prejudice, ignorance, thoughtlessness and stereotyping which disadvantages those with particular identity, e.g. black and minority ethnic communities, the LGBT community, women and people with disabilities.

'LGBT' community. As a direct social reaction to long-established homophobic violence, hatred and persecution lesbians, gay men, bisexuals and transgendered people came together to form what is commonly called the gay community (or the LGBT community).

'...isms' and 'phobias' are attitudes, actions or institutional structures that subordinate a person or group on the basis of their belonging to one group and not another, e.g. racism is often linked to an ideology of racial or cultural superiority underpinned by having the power to carry out discriminatory practices. Homophobia, for example, begins with fear and is the belief that heterosexuality is superior to any other type of sexuality, and is often underpinned by the power to act upon this belief.

Mainstreaming equality refers to the integration of equal opportunities principles, strategies and practices into the everyday work of any organisation. It is the process of ensuring that equality considerations are built into the policy development process from the beginning, rather than being 'bolted on at the end'.

Multiple identity. None of us has a single identity; we all belong to different 'groups' and also have our own unique identity. Belonging to a number of different social structures affects our experience, how we see ourselves and how we see others. It is also the recognition that people's identities may/will change as they progress through life – child, teenager, mother, father; religion, gender, and culture. Our identity is defined by who we are at a certain time and place and the role we play within society.

Political opinion. 'Political' usually refers to practices or institutions that are concerned with government and public policy making. Therefore, political opinion is usually understood to be an individual's or organisation's position on the practices and institutions concerned with government and public policy making. Cases taken under fair employment legislation make it clear that it does not have to be linked to religious belief, nor is it confined to debates about the Unionist/Nationalist divide.

Positive action. The term refers to a variety of measures designed to counteract the effects of past discrimination and help to eliminate stereotyping. Positive action should not be confused with positive discrimination. Positive discrimination generally means employing someone because they come from a disadvantaged group regardless of whether they have the relevant skills and qualifications, and it is unlawful. Although positive action and affirmative action can be regarded as very similar, positive action should not be confused with affirmative action as it is specifically defined in Northern Ireland legislation.

Poverty is often only associated with money, but it cannot be measured by income alone. Poverty can be both absolute and relative. However, any definition of poverty must include access to services and participation in civic society. A definition of poverty must start from the perspective of human rights and a right to live a life that would be considered reasonable in our society.

Prejudice is a preconceived opinion about, or bias against (or in favour of) a person or thing. Prejudice is often based on presumptions regarding the identity, character and/or attributes that a person possesses, such as their skin colour, gender, disability, sexual orientation or accent.

Race. Theories that advocate the classification of people into distinct and separate 'races' have been largely discredited by scientists as not having any biological or genetic evidence to support them. Therefore, despite the outward physical variances in appearances that exist among human beings, 'race' is not a scientifically valid classification system. Racial categories are based on social constructs rather than genetic or biological differences. 'Race' refers to the artificial and arbitrary categories into which society places individuals and groups.

Racism refers to prejudice and discrimination towards individuals and groups on the basis of their skin colour and/or cultural origins. Notions of racial and cultural superiority underpin racism. It can manifest in attitudes as well as behaviour and actions.

Refugee. Someone who has a well-founded fear of persecution for reasons of race, religion, nationality, political opinion or membership of a particular group. A refugee is a person living outside the country they belong to or in which they normally reside who is unable or unwilling to return home for fear of persecution. Whilst someone is waiting for their application for refugee status to be considered by the government he or she is known as an 'asylum seeker'.

Religion or belief. The term 'religion or belief' is not specifically defined in Northern Ireland legislation and comes within the definition of religious belief. This means that religions other than those related to Christianity are also covered in law. The absence of religious belief is also covered, as are philosophical beliefs that are similar to religion.

Sexual orientation means a sexual orientation towards persons of the same sex, persons of the opposite sex or people of both sexes.

Social capital is based on the notion that social networks have value both for those within them and those outside of them. Communities build their capacity to do things for themselves and make links based on common concerns with other communities/organisations. There is then a more powerful potential to access resources and influence decision makers through such increased civic participation.

Social class is the social and economic position of an individual or group within society and is often determined by access to basic life chances, e.g. education, employment, housing and participation in civic society. It is a label given by people to explain the many differences in society.

Social exclusion encompasses not only material deprivation but also, more broadly, the denial of opportunities to participate fully in society. Social exclusion can be deliberate or indirect. A set of processes, including within the labour market and welfare system, by which individuals, households, communities and even whole social groups are pushed towards or kept at the margins of society.

Stereotyping. Simplifying judgements about a certain group of people so that we see all members of that group as having certain (usually negative) traits.

References

Leigh Stephens Alrdrich, *Covering the Community – A Diversity Handbook for Media* (Sage Publications, 1999).

Diversity at Work: The Business Case for Equity (John Wiley and Sons, 1996).

Mind Your Language, Diversity Matters Briefing Paper (Disability Action, Belfast, March 2004) www.disabilityaction.org/publications

THE LANGUAGE OF ILLNESS AND ITS WIDER IMPLICATIONS

The headlines shout, and the story is always the same. A wave of unsettling, unexplained deaths appears in an emerging country. An infected animal or person travels across borders and tugs the tripwire of global epidemic. Hysteria and fear spread, outrunning the disease itself until another catastrophe is averted at the eleventh hour by an agency response or the United Nations. This sequence of events has shaped reports of every infectious outbreak from Ebola in the 1990s to SARS in 2003 to bird flu in 2006. Although unrelated, these diseases are always portrayed in the same way, using a common language and inevitable set of metaphors.

Yet language is more than the manipulation of consonants and vowels. It reflects the culture and attitudes of the media and countries where it is spoken – what is said or written becomes the currency of social engagement. In *The Dynamics of Human Life* Mark Elliot declares that 'language is our only reality'. As writers, we have a responsibility to examine the images and metaphors we use, consciously or unconsciously, when treating sensitive subjects, particularly the issues of health and illness. Because despite the challenge of intelligent discourse, the careless (or deliberate) misuse of language in this context can create a culture of fear and leave the vulnerable open to injury and exploitation.

The language of plague and war

The notion of an ill person waging a war that can be won or lost has become the predominant characteristic of the way we write about sickness. How often have we read that, 'She has lost her battle against breast cancer,' or 'Her struggle with the disease lasted five years'? Today a person has to fight for his life. Those who win the battle are said to have beaten, fought off or conquered illness. But should anybody's body be considered a battlefield?

The dangers of this standpoint were eloquently deconstructed by Susan Sontag in *Illness as Metaphor*, a book-length essay written out of her experience of cancer. She proposed that weighting the disease with meaning only isolated those who suffered from it. By using the dialogue of battle we were in danger of turning dying into defeat.

She further asserted that the language of illness had always been inflamed throughout history, from cholera and Black Death in the Middle Ages to tuberculosis and cancer in the twentieth century, often for political ends. The powerful and healthy could demonise the illness and dehumanise the sufferer. Even in enlightened times – when language should have caught up with science – as medicine makes one disease less terrifying, Sontag suggests that another stands by to take its place as the conduit for plague terminology. For her, this was epitomised by AIDS and the death of her friend, the photographer Robert Mapplethorpe.

In *AIDS and Its Metaphors*, Sontag called for the debate around this illness to rid itself of the Biblical language of plague – which had instantly become the vernacular. AIDS was labelled a curse from God and, as a consequence, the sick were not merely segregated but considered ripe for internment and detention.

Ireland was not exempt. Consider how the same front page in 1991 treated similar illnesses and the likely effect on its readers. The *Evening Press* stated that singer Freddie Mercury had 'admitted' to an AIDS diagnosis shortly before his death from bronchial pneumonia, whereas athlete Magic Johnson had 'announced' the HIV status that led to his retirement from professional basketball. It is reasonable to ask whether sexual orientation informed the choice of verb in each instance. Although the stories had different authors, they were probably read and signed off by the same editor.

This trickles down into common parlance. Court reports in national and provincial media refer to 'reformed' alcoholics or drug addicts, rather than as people suffering from or recovering from these illnesses. Although such writing may be in the context of offences where the actions that led to prosecution are inexcusable, the underlying drivers of the misbehaviour can be open to distortion.

In a broader political context, the language of illness has implications. 'AIDS has banalized cancer,' Sontag wrote in *AIDS and Its Metaphors*. And over the past five years, the latest infectious diseases have done the same to AIDS now that retroviral drugs have made it a chronic condition. A renewed plague vocabulary that goes beyond personal sickness, particularly in the international arena, has announced the re-emergence of cholera, anthrax and even of plague itself. Smallpox, which had not killed anyone in a generation, caused widespread panic and an upturn in the sale of face masks in the wake of 9/11. So is there a danger that by writing and reporting in such a narrative, military metaphors of the type identified by Sontag and others are no longer merely words? Have they become literal exhortations to kit the troops, stop the germs at the border or in the postal sorting office, and send us to war? Are we stating or informing the real agendas?

Perhaps the problem isn't in the scenario. Perhaps it's in the script.

References

Martha Balshem, *Cancer in the Community: Class and Medical Authority* (Smithsonian Books, 1993).

Mark Elliot, *The Dynamics of Human Life* (Paternoster Press, 2001).

Susan Sontag, *AIDS and Its Metaphors* (Farrar, Straus and Giroux, 1988).

Susan Sontag, *Illness as Metaphor* (Farrar, Straus and Giroux, 1978).

2. ENTERING THE WORLD OF STUDY AND WORK

WRITING FOR ACADEMIA

The first point to be clear about is that a third or fourth-level essay is different from an essay at second-level. It's neither a research paper nor an exercise in literary self-expression. It's not merely a report of what numerous experts have said on a particular topic. Its purpose may go beyond presenting the latest findings of tests or experiments. Rarely does it present your personal feelings or impressions. In most instances, it is a reasoned defence of an argument.

Above all, an essay at this level requires that there must be a specific point that you are trying to establish – something you are trying to convince the reader to accept – coupled with grounds or justification for its acceptance.

'In a very real sense, the writer writes in order to teach himself, to understand himself…'

Alfred Kazin

Preparation is key

The first rule of preparation is to contextualise. Establish how what you are writing about matches your larger subject or field. Try to figure out why it was assigned in the first place. How does it fit into the course? To what concepts, theories or paradigms does it relate?

You should have thought sufficiently about this before putting pen to paper to be able to state precisely what you are trying to show. It is not enough to have a rough idea of what you want to establish. Rough ideas are exactly that: unpolished, unfinished and, as a result, unlikely to be understood. You should be able to state in one short sentence what you want to prove. If you cannot formulate your position thus, you are not sufficiently clear about it.

'It is the mark of an educated mind to be able to entertain a thought without accepting it.'

Aristotle

This is where writers tend to make one or more common errors. First, many make poor arguers because they have already made up their minds before embarking on a project. Passionate partisanship can produce brilliant reasoning, but most of the time it diminishes an argument's power by acting as a mental blinder, leading the writer to ignore anything that doesn't fit his or her preconceived argument.

Sometimes writers feel that because their proposal is clear to them, it does not need much arguing. It is common to overestimate the strength of your own position. This is because you already accept a particular point of view. It is yours, after all. But feelings are not the most important consideration. Evidence and logic arrive at the truth, not instinct. It's best to assume your readers are intelligent and know a lot about your subject, but disagree with you. Remain cool and detached.

Another mistake is to think that your case will be stronger if you pinpoint, even briefly, every argument that you have come across in support of your proposition. In academia, this is known as the 'fortress approach'. It's derided in good university departments. It's almost inevitable that the fortress approach will not result in a strong paper. And there are several reasons for this.

First, the more you load on your reader – no matter how clearly expressed – he or she will find it difficult to keep track of so many arguments, especially if they buttress you from different positions.

Second, the ones that will stand out will be the very best ones and the very worst ones. Terrible but true. This is crunch time – the time to discriminate. Only one or two of the most compelling arguments should be developed. Including weaker ones gives the impression that you are unable to differentiate between the shaky and the strong. However galling, you have to accept that your markers or lecturers will know your source material. Only the few geniuses are capable of truly original, lateral thought. The rest of us will have to settle for presenting the already elucidated in a fresh and superbly written way. But there is an upside: selecting one or two arguments will give a paper focus.

At this stage of preparation, you may be tempted simply to reword the best argument you have discovered. You think it is impossible to improve on it. If that's the best you can do, then you may as well photocopy your source document or turn in the library reference code. You don't need to retype someone else's argument.

To avoid this, and to construct your position and present a half-decent academic paper, ponder the topic. Ideally at the desk and not at the bar. Unfortunately, your reader has no access to your musings except by way of what actually ends up on the page. He or she cannot tell what you meant to say but did not, and cannot read in what you would quickly point out if you were debating face to face. For better or for worse, your paper is all that is available and must stand on its own. The responsibility for ensuring the accurate communication of ideas falls on the *writer's* shoulders. You must say exactly what you mean in a way that minimises the chances of being misunderstood.

Stop thinking, start writing

Best to be aware of the pitfalls before you begin. Avoid the following at all cost:

Long introductions. These are unnecessary and of no interest to the informed reader. There is no need to point out that the topic is an important one; you wouldn't be writing about it if it weren't.

Try this exercise. After writing an introduction, save the document, cut the intro and go immediately to the first section. Does it weaken or strengthen your paper? More often, it's the latter. If you feel it necessary, open with a single sentence.

Long quotations. New writers rely too heavily on quotations and paraphrases. Direct quotation is best restricted to those cases where it's essential to establish another writer's exact selection of words. Also, keep paraphrasing to a minimum. This is *your* paper and the instructor is concerned with your thoughts. Keep that in mind, especially when your essay topic requires you to assess someone else's views critically.

Fence sitting. Do not present a number of positions in your paper and then end by saying that you are not qualified to settle the matter. In particular, do not close by saying that commentators have been divided over this issue and you cannot be expected to resolve the dispute in a few short pages. Your instructor knows that. It's probably the reason for setting the question. But you can be expected to take a clear stand based on an evaluation of the argument(s) presented. Go out on a limb. If you have argued well, it will support you.

Begging the question. You are guilty of begging the question (or circular reasoning) on a particular issue if you somehow presuppose the truth of what it is that you are trying to show in the course of arguing for it. Here's a quick example. If John argues that war is morally wrong on the grounds that it amounts to murder, John begs the question. John *presupposes* a particular stand on the moral status of war – the stand represented by the conclusion of the argument. To see that this is so, notice that the person who denies the conclusion – that war is morally wrong – will not accept John's premise that it amounts to murder, since murder is, by definition, morally wrong.

When arguing against other positions, it is important to realise that you cannot *show* that your opponents are mistaken just by claiming that their overall conclusions are false. Nor will it do simply to claim that at least one of their premises is false. You must *demonstrate* these sorts of things, and in a fashion that does not presuppose that your position is correct.

What can you do?

Organise. Before you start to write, make an outline of how you want to argue. There should be a logical progression of ideas – a progression that will be easy to follow. If your paper is well organised, the reader will be led along in what seems a natural way. If you jump about in your essay, you will lose the reader. It will take too much effort to follow you, and he or she may not feel it worthwhile. Use paragraphing to your advantage when fleshing out a theme. Block out your sections, subsections and paragraphs. Keep sub-arguments together. (A sub-argument usually takes one to three paragraphs to develop.) Make the conclusion of the sub-argument the first sentence. It's a good idea to let an outline simmer for a few days before writing the first draft. Does it still seem to flow smoothly when you come back to it? If not, the best prose in the world will not be enough to make it work.

Use the right words. Once you have determined your outline, you must select the exact words that will convey your meaning to the reader. A dictionary is essential. Do not settle for a word that (you think) comes close to capturing the sense you have in mind. Notice that 'infer' does not mean 'imply'; 'disinterested' does not mean 'uninterested'; and 'reference' does not mean either 'illusion' or 'allusion'. Make certain that you use 'its' and 'it's' correctly. Notice that certain words such as 'therefore', 'hence', 'since', and 'follows from' are strong logical connectives. When you use such expressions you are asserting that certain tight logical relations hold between the claims in question – you had better be right. Finally, check the spelling of any word you are not sure of. (See The 1,000 Most Commonly Misspelt Words, Section 6.)

Support your claims. Assume that your reader is constantly asking such questions as 'Why should I accept that?' If you presuppose that he or she is at least mildly sceptical of your claims, you are more likely to succeed in writing a paper that *argues* for a position. Most first attempts at writing essays fall down on this point. Substantiate your claims whenever there is reason to think that your critics would not accept them.

Anticipate objections. If your position is worth arguing for, there are going to be reasons that have led others to reject it. Such reasons will amount to criticisms of your stand. A good way to demonstrate the strength of your position is to consider one or two of the best of these objections and show how they can be overcome. The trick is to anticipate the kinds of objections that your critics would raise if you did not disarm them first. The other challenge is to come to grips with the criticisms you have cited. You must *argue* that these criticisms miss the mark as far as your case is concerned, or that they are in some sense ill-conceived despite their plausibility. It takes practice and exposure to good writing to develop this winning style of argumentation, but it is worth it.

Give credit. When quoting or paraphrasing, always give some citation. Indicate your indebtedness, be it for specific words, general ideas or a line of argument. To use another writer's words, ideas or arguments as if they were your own is to plagiarise. Plagiarism is against the rules of academic institutions and is dishonest. (See Plagiarism, Section 1.) Appropriately citing the works of others also indicates an awareness of at least some of the relevant literature on the subject.

Use the correct format. A standard academic paper has the following parts: the title page; the final outline; the text (or body); of your argument with footnotes at the bottom of each page (or end notes at the end of the main body) and a bibliography. Because attribution is key in academic papers, its proper styling is crucial. End notes and bibliographies are entirely different. End notes sequentially list sources as they appear in the paper. Footnotes do the same, but page by page. The bibliography lists all the sources used in preparing the paper, whether or not they are actually cited in the paper. They are organised alphabetically by author. All papers must have a bibliography. You may use footnotes or end notes, and all papers will have one or the other. Check with your lecturer if your college or institute has a specific house requirement.

Paper-Writing Checklist

Before submitting an academic paper, complete the following checklist:

Introduction

- In the introduction I state the subject of my research and outline the themes I will consider.
- I clearly state my defined proposition.
- If it is appropriate, I have outlined the broad strokes of my argument.

Paragraphs

- I've thought about how my paragraphs are arranged, and have structured them to support my argument.
- I've checked to make sure I tackle one element of my argument before moving on to the next, and I've made sure not to revisit claims unnecessarily that I treated earlier in the paper.
- I have focused each paragraph on a main idea ('mini-thesis'), which is stated in the paragraph's first sentence ('topic sentence'). My sub-arguments and themes are set out in following paragraphs, ideally in no more five sentences.
- Each paragraph has a logical transition from its predecessor.
- I have displayed evidence to support my ideas. This evidence is analysed; that is, I have considered how my data support the topic sentences.

Argumentation and critical thinking

- I have identified the arguments that may be marshalled against mine, and have addressed them through refutation or concession. (See Critical Thinking in this section.)

Quotes and citations

- My quoted material appears in quote marks.
- I have minimised or eliminated block quotes. When I must use them, I have indented them on the left or centred them single-spaced, and not placed quote marks at the beginning and end.
- Each time I introduce evidence that is unfamiliar, I have cited its source with a footnote/end note.

- For each quote, it is clear who the speaker is, and the circumstances in which he or she authored the quote including, where possible, the time, place and context.
- I have established whether I must conform to any house or academic style.
- My footnote or end note style is consistent.
- I have included a bibliography of sources, and begun each reference with the author's name.

Presentation and display

- I have put an appropriate heading and have numbered each page.
- I have used a common, legible typeface – Times, Helvetica or Verdana.
- I have correctly spaced the text on plain, white paper, and have used 2 cm margins.

Editing and revision

- I have proofread the paper for spelling and grammar errors.
- I have re-written the paper at least once, not just cutting and pasting further text, and have identified and eliminated instances of:
  - the passive voice
  - inconsistent tenses
  - subject/verb disagreement
  - misuse of suffixes
  - improper pronoun references
  - comma splices, run-on sentences and sentence fragments
- I have read the paper aloud to myself or to someone else, listening for sentences that do not flow.
- Where possible, I have had the paper read over by a colleague or fellow student.

I have met my deadline, written to the required word count and submitted the paper to the correct contact. My name is on the first and last pages.

Edit boldly. Every first draft can be improved by rewriting. The secret to good writing is rewriting – often. Of course it will not do just to reproduce the same text again. Better drafts are almost always shorter drafts – not because ideas have been left out, but because words have been cut as ideas have been clarified. Many of us are so used to padding our writing that it is hard even to consider cutting the fat. Writing to required lengths is one of the reasons many writers are good at wordiness. It can also serve as a camouflage to reduce one's visibility. Sometimes, though, wordiness just seems to happen, but every word that is not needed only clutters. Clear sentences do not just happen. They are the result of tough-minded editing.

Some final words about proofreading. Do it. Again. After that, have someone else read your paper. Is this person able to understand you completely? Can he or she read your entire paper through without getting stuck on a single sentence? If not, go back and smooth it out. Others can show you awkward phrasing, weak arguments and confusing development. Try hard to find people who disagree with your position. They will do the best job of showing you weaknesses.

In conclusion, don't be content simply to get your paper out of your hands. Take pride in it. Clear writing reflects clear thinking and that, after all, is what you are trying to show.

Reference

Diana Hacker, *Rules for Writers*, www.dianahacker.com

And, now, a warning!
A note on composing with a PC: Be fanatical about saving, backing up and archiving work. Save every five or ten minutes or set your computer to do so. If you're working on a public terminal, keep a copy of your paper on another medium – for instance, online. You can get two gigabytes of free online storage at www.gmail.com. Don't trust floppies or flashdrives to keep your files for long, and absolutely never store all your work in just one place, even your own PC. (Have you heard the urban legend about the PhD student who lost his whole doctoral dissertation – some seven years in the making – when his laptop was stolen from his backpack?) If you don't maintain an up-to-date archived copy, it is a sure bet that your hard drive, floppy or Zip disk will explode just as you go to print out your essay.

CITATION OF AUTHORITIES

It is crucial to cite authorities correctly, not only for aesthetic precision, but because the purpose of a citation is to help find and identify the source of your material. To do this properly and uniformly, it is helpful have a formula or template to distinguish between a reference to a book, periodical or article. No universally accepted format for formatting and documenting citations exists in academic writing. Different disciplines (and even different journals and texts within a discipline) are each likely to have their own partly rational and partly idiosyncratic customs and rules.

You can agonise over whether to use capital letters, commas, points and semi-colons, particularly when dealing with footnotes and bibliographies. However, unless you have to work to a definitive house style, university template or for a legal publisher, simple consistency should be a priority. Having trawled through myriad guides, we offer the following simple formats.

Books

Author or authors; title in italics; date in round brackets; volume number; page number(s).

> S. Pollock, T. Maitland, *The History of English Law* (1911) Vol 1, pp 518, 520-522.

If you have the publisher's details, so much the better and adjust the form as follows:

> C.J. Smitskam, *Flexible Employment Relationships* (Kluwer, Arnham, 1989).

Essays in collections

If a book or journal comprises collected essays by different authors, the title of the essay should be in roman with quotes and the title of the book in italics:

> T. Maitland, 'The Mystery of Seisin' in *Select Essays on Anglo-American Legal History*, Vol 3, p 591.

> Goldberg, 'Concepts of Depreciation' in *Studies in Accounting Theory* (Baxter and Davidson, editors, 1962) p 236.

Speeches

The location and date of the meeting at which a speech was given or a paper presented should follow the title.

> Stacy D'Erasmo, 'The Craft and Career of Writing' (lecture, Northwestern University, Evanston, Illinois, 26 April, 2000).

Web attribution

Follow the paper formula where possible and cite the full http reference at the end of the citation. Do not finish with a period to avoid confusion when cutting and pasting into a web browser.

Bibliographies

Published works should be in one alphabetical list with the author coming first. List the surname first to make it easier to alphabetise. Consistency and navigability are the order of the day in lists:

> Smith, E.; Watts, D.; Bates, F.; *Leadership in Schools*, 'Leading the Way' (Routledge, 1982) pp 11-29.

> Jones, G.H., *Leading the World in Education* (Oxford University Press).

> White, F., *Our Leaders of the Future*, 'Why Headteachers Need to Have Vision' (Journal, 2002) pp 65-70.

Strict academic convention

In history and the humanities, Chicago style is a widely used format, favoured by those who prefer the traditional look of footnotes (or end notes) rather than in-text citations. See *The Chicago Manual of Style* (University of Chicago Press, 2003). A useful Q&A version can be browsed at http://www.press.uchicago.edu/Misc/Chicago/cmosfaq/cmosfaq.html

The *University of Minnesota Style Manual* is considered the benchmark in some institutions, particularly in the preparation of PhD works. First produced in 1979, a revised edition with minor changes was printed in 1989. While offering templates, it still highlights the value of consistency as the overriding approach to styling citations. It can be ordered directly from the university or an abridged version can be found at http://www1.umn.edu/urelate/style/italics.html

CRITICAL THINKING, READING AND WRITING

People don't always act objectively and rationally. We gossip, boast, exaggerate and equivocate. It's no different with the written word. In fact, it's often worse with the written word. A computer screen or blank page cannot debate a point or accuse you of spouting nonsense. When communicating with an audience, in whatever context, we want to validate our knowledge, vindicate our assertions, or sustain and promote our beliefs. This may be about ego. But it may also be about stunted intellectual growth, wasted opportunity and sloppy writing. Just because we are intelligent or have knowledge does not mean we can think critically. The most brilliant of minds may hold the most irrational beliefs or perverse opinions. Critical thinking is about how we use intelligence and knowledge to reach objective and reasoned viewpoints.

Media professionals, in particular, have an obligation to think critically because their statements are broadcast or published and quickly become 'truth' for millions of viewers, listeners and readers. Citizens of almost every nation rely on them for 'knowledge' of politics, business, military activity, crime, medicine and even such subjects as UFOs, faith healing and psychic powers.

Not everyone values the need for critical thinking. Methodical impartiality can be viewed as cold, sterile and, worst of all, boring. Arguments based on critical thinking are not necessarily the most persuasive or appropriate. Perhaps more often than not, the most compelling are designed to appeal to our basic human and emotional needs rather than to our sense of objectivity. For that reason, it is common for highly convincing arguments by politicians, clergymen and sales people, among others, to disregard critical thinking.

But, for many of us, the written word may have to offer solutions, draw up proposals, devise legislation or design advertising campaigns. To be effective writers, we must evaluate research and source material and integrate our comprehension with our prior understanding and experience. To appraise someone else's conclusion, especially if we're using it as the basis of our own offering, involves considering the evidence upon which that conclusion is based. We don't want just any information; we want reliable information. Only then can our writing be truthful.

What critical thinking is not...

First of all, thinking critically is not thinking negatively with a determination to find fault or error. Ideally, it is a neutral, unbiased process for evaluating claims or opinions, either someone else's or our own.

Second, it is not intended to make people think or write alike. Critical thinking is distinct from one's values or principles, which explains why two people who may be equally adept at the process, but who have dissimilar values or principles, can reach conflicting conclusions. There will always be differences in perception and response.

Third, critical thinking does not endanger our individuality or personality. It may increase our objectivity, but it will not change who we are.

Fourth, critical thinking is not a predetermined belief. It can and perhaps should evaluate the validity of beliefs, but it is not a principle in itself. It is a process.

Fifth, critical thinking does not discourage or replace feelings or emotional reaction and will not sanitise or flatten your writing. Emotions give our lives meaning, pleasure and a sense of purpose, functions that critical thinking cannot replace.

Lastly, critical thinking does not blindly support everything based on science. To do so would be irresponsible. For example, it does not take undercover investigation to show that our media culture is full of bogus claims that are used to market everything from vitamin-enriched breakfast bars to breast-enhancement pills.

Critical thinking – a starting point

At the heart of critical thinking is the ability to recognise, construct and evaluate arguments. The word argument does not mean to quarrel, complain or disagree, even though it can be used in that context. In critical thinking, an argument means the presentation of a reason(s) to support a conclusion(s):

Argument = Reason + Conclusion

Many people distinguish between two basic types of argument: **inductive** and **deductive**. Induction is usually described as moving from the specific to the general, whereas deduction begins with the general and ends with the specific. Arguments based on experience or observation are best expressed inductively and arguments based on laws, rules or other accepted principles are best expressed deductively. Consider this example:

Kieran: I've noticed that every time I kick a ball up, it comes back down, so I reckon that the next time I kick one up, it'll come back down.
Terry: That's Newton's Law. Everything that goes up must come down. So if you kick the ball up, it must come down.

Kieran is using *inductive reasoning*, arguing from observation, whereas Terry is using *deductive reasoning*, arguing from the law of gravity. Terry's argument is clearly from the general (the law of gravity) to the specific (this kick of the ball); Kieran's argument may be less obviously from the specific (each instance in which he has observed balls being kicked up and coming back down) to the general (the prediction that a similar event will result in a similar outcome in the future). This is because he has stated it in terms only of the *next* similar event – the next time he kicks the ball.

It is important to recognise whether the form of an argument is inductive or deductive, because each requires different supports. Kieran's inductive argument is supported by his previous observations and Terry's deductive argument is supported by her reference to the law of gravity. Should he so wish, Kieran could provide additional support by detailing those observations without any recourse to books or theories of physics, and Terry could still provide additional support by discussing Newton's law if she had never seen or kicked a ball.

Even at a subliminal level, the appropriate selection of an inductive or deductive format provides a first step towards sound argumentation.

Deductive versus inductive (and where to go from there). Deductive reasoning holds to a high standard of correctness. A deductive inference succeeds only if its premises provide such *absolute* and *complete* support for its conclusion that it would be inconsistent to suppose that the premises are true but the conclusions are false.

Every deductive argument either meets this standard or it does not: there is no middle ground. Some deductive arguments are perfect and if their premises are in fact true, then it follows that their conclusions must also be true.

The standard of correctness for inductive reasoning is more flexible. An inductive argument succeeds when its premises provide some legitimate evidence or support for the truth of its conclusion. Although it is reasonable to accept the truth of that conclusion on these grounds, it would not be completely inconsistent to withhold judgment or even to deny it outright. What if the ball that Kieran kicks lodges itself in a tree? His inductive approach may change as he learns from experience.

Inductive arguments, then, may meet their standard to a greater or to a lesser degree, depending upon the amount of support they supply. No inductive argument is either absolutely perfect or entirely useless, although one may be said to be better or worse than another in the sense that it recommends its conclusion with a higher or lower degree of probability. In such cases, relevant additional information often affects the reliability of an inductive argument by providing other evidence that changes our estimation of the likelihood of the conclusion. Court arguments, where it may be impossible to prove something beyond a reasonable doubt, are a good example.

It should be possible to differentiate these two types of argument with some accuracy. Remember that deductive arguments claim to guarantee their conclusions, whereas inductive arguments merely recommend theirs. Ask yourself whether the introduction of any additional information – short of changing or denying any of the premises – could make the conclusion seem more or less likely; if so, the pattern of reasoning is inductive.

From critical thinking to critical reading

We can distinguish critical reading and thinking in the following manner:

- Critical reading is a technique for discovering information and ideas within a text.
- Critical thinking is a technique for evaluating information and ideas, for deciding what to accept and believe.

Critical reading is active, reflective and analytical. Critical thinking involves considering the validity of what we have read in light of our prior knowledge and understanding. The use of language is highly relevant. The choice of words can confuse, mislead or deceive – from advertisements that guarantee weight loss to politicians promising prosperity for all.

Consider this sentence: 'Parents are buying expensive computers for their children to destroy them.' As defined here, critical reading is concerned with determining whether – within the context of the sentence as a whole – 'them' refers to the parents, the children or the computers, and whether the sentence encourages that practice. Critical thinking would help decide whether the chosen meaning was indeed true, and whether you, as the reader – and maybe the writer – should champion that practice.

By these definitions, critical reading would appear to come before critical thinking. Only when we have understood a text (critical reading) can we evaluate its assertions (critical thinking).

The two in harmony. In practice, however, critical reading and critical thinking work best in tandem.

Critical thinking allows us to monitor our understanding as we assemble source material. If we sense that some assertions are ridiculous or irresponsible (critical thinking), we can examine the text more closely to test our understanding (critical reading).

Conversely, critical thinking depends on critical reading. You can think critically about a text (critical thinking) only if you have understood it (critical reading). Confused? Put it like this. You may choose to accept or reject a proposition, but you must know why.

So why distinguish? If critical thinking and critical reading are so closely linked, why is this still a useful distinction?

The value of the distinction lies in its reminder that we must read each text on its merits, not imposing our prior knowledge or views on it. Although we must evaluate ideas as we read, we must not distort their meaning. We should not allow ourselves to infer a meaning that suits us – or we will never learn anything new. And, if we choose to embody that in our own writing, neither will our readers.

From critical thinking and reading to critical writing

As writers, we have taken on a job. No matter what the subject matter, certain tasks must be done:

- a topic must be addressed
- terms must be defined
- evidence must be presented
- common knowledge must be accounted for
- exceptions must be explained
- causes must be shown to precede effects and to be capable of creating the effect
- conclusions must be shown to follow logically from earlier arguments and evidence

As critical readers and writers, we aspire to assure ourselves that these tasks have been completed thoroughly, comprehensively and consistently. Only when we have decided that our own text is consistent and coherent can we begin to evaluate whether to publish it. Because when we have put pen to paper, others will be the judge of our assertions and conclusions. It is of little use to argue that there is life on Mars because it has not yet been proved that there is no life on the planet, or that David Blaine can levitate a Mercedes just because there are no obvious wires attached to the ceiling.

Critical writing – identify the fallacies

The *non sequitur* **fallacy:** presenting an irrelevant reason or premise that bears no relationship to your conclusion: 'I don't like getting wet, so I'll take up flying.' (It's quite a leap from fear of showers to drowning in a ferry accident on the way to Bertolucci's villa.)

The *ad hominem* **fallacy:** attacking a person's character to discredit the arguer rather than the argument: 'Don't buy Terry and Kieran's book. They're idiots.' (Although we may be hurt, we hope this won't put you off a trip to the bookstore.)

The *post hoc ergo propter hoc* (Latin for 'after this, therefore because of this', often shortened to post hoc) **fallacy:** generalising and propounding the notion that an occurrence or event was caused by a previous one(s): Book sales surge at Christmas time. Burglary rates triple before Christmas. Therefore, higher book sales triple the chances of your home being burgled. (The Irish Book Publishers' Association and the Garda Commissioner will have strong views on such a statement.)

The **false authority fallacy:** citing authorities that are unattributed, irrelevant or without credibility: 'Experts agree that all writers should be adept at critical thinking.' (Which experts?)

The **slippery slope fallacy:** arguing that if one event occurs, then a series of undesirable events will inevitably result: 'Ireland's smoking ban means that the government has established a precedent to control every aspect of our social lives.' (When did the Minister for Health and Children become the Hitler of his generation?)

The **fallacy of emotional appeal:** expressing through pure sensation rather than through logical persuasion: 'If Terry and Kieran don't sell a million copies of this book, their careers are over!' (Our distributors may think so, but we don't necessarily share that view.)

The **fallacy of false dilemma:** restricting the number of options, and omitting relevant choices from consideration: 'If we do not relax rural planning laws immediately, there will be no-one living west of Kildare in 20 years' time.' (Enterprise Ireland, An Taisce and the Construction Industry Federation will have different perspectives.)

The **fallacy of generalisation:** 'Julie Burchill is the best writer in the English language. This is true because two million people read her column religiously.' (And some four billion people might disagree.)

The *ad populum* (or bandwagon) fallacy: appealing to the popularity of a claim as the reason for accepting it and perpetuating communal reinforcement: 'The world is flat because everybody knows it.' (Luckily for science and the Cunard Line, Galileo disagreed.)

Critical writing – avoid the fallacies

Be open-minded yet sceptical. This may appear contradictory but it is not. Being both open-minded and sceptical means:

- seeking out the facts, information and reasoning to support the issues we intend to judge
- examining subjects from as many sides as possible
- looking for the good and bad points of the sides examined
- accepting the fact that we may be incorrect ourselves
- maintaining the goal of getting at the truth (or as close to it as possible) rather than trying to please others or find fault with their views

Arguments are only as strong as their weakest link. Intellectual humility and natural curiosity can be a useful starting point:

1. Research all sides using authoritative sources. After blocking out the initial approaches to your argument, you can research the possibilities, including the sources that will eventually form the basis or your proposition. Building support for your conclusion is dependent on the strength, bias and fairness of comparison. It is hardly fair to recommend that a company purchase Copier A rather than Copier B if you neglect to mention that Copier B can also fax, print, scan and staple.

2. Analyse. When researching, identify the intended and inferential relationships among statements, questions, concepts, descriptions, data or other forms of argument intended to express belief, judgement, experiences, reasons, information or opinion. (Arguments will sometimes have indicators such as 'since', 'because' and 'therefore' to separate the conclusion statements from the reason statements.) After you've analysed this information, the approach to your first draft may appear obvious.

3. Evaluate. Evaluate the validity of facts and information. In a popular culture where speculation and soundbites have become universal, it can be difficult to find unbiased and objective reporting. For example, the mass media has found 'what if' journalism sells very well: 'What if the President did sanction the use of torture at Guantanamo Bay?' 'What if the timing of the drug trials were motivated by shareholder interest?' Even reputable journalists report conjecture in the same tone as simple facts.

4. Anticipate. Before you reach any conclusion, identify its reasonable alternative. With research, you will have gathered information about the obvious choices. You will also need to ascertain the preferences of other people and take account of their knowledge, assumptions and prejudices. It's especially important to consider the view of your readers. For example, right-wing newspapers in the US reported that evangelist Jerry Falwell had blamed comedienne Ellen DeGeneres for the September 11th attacks because her coming-out had vented God's anger on America, whereas the liberal press was outraged at this assertion.

5. Weigh the evidence for all sides and avoid bias. All of us share a temptation to promote positive outcomes between two or more variables, while omitting unfavourable findings. We may to choose to quote studies that say fish oil supplements improve children's behaviour but do not cite surveys that suggest the same supplement offers increased risk of reflux and stomach ulceration. Pragmatically, it may not suit us to offer both sides, but critical writers should be aware of opposing viewpoints both for their research value and for the ability to refute. Generally, the more reliable the source, the greater the weight for the argument.

6. Identify and respond to counterarguments. Identify the counter-arguments (against your position) and decide how to respond to these – whether you will agree with them (concede) or disagree (refute). By claiming that a football injury responds best to magnetic-bandage therapy, you will likely be forced to acknowledge that physiotherapy, acupuncture or anti-inflammatory medication may play an equal or greater part in recovery.

7. Seek out the omissions. A cogent argument is one that is complete, in that it presents all relevant reasoning (evidence) and not just the evidence that supports it. Arguments that omit significant evidence may appear to be stronger than they really are. Sometimes, writers do this unintentionally or carelessly. Often, they do it intentionally. However, in order to bulletproof your proposition in so far as you can, it is useful to determine if you have omitted – or suppressed – important evidence that may surface and be used against you.

Critical thinking, reading and writing – an illustration

Take the ostensibly simple matter of critiquing a biography of Elizabeth I, for example. The author has developed her thinking in the text, has taken ideas and, in some way, represented those ideas in extended form. The role of a reviewer may be to translate the meaning of the author into meanings that a greater audience can appreciate. This process requires critical evaluation every step of the way:

- What's the purpose of the book?
- What is the author trying to accomplish?
- What issues or problems are raised?
- What data, evidence or experiences are given?
- What concepts are used to organise this data and these experiences?
- How does the author view the world or her subject matter?
- Is her thinking justified from our perspective?
- How does she justify it from her perspective?

- How can we enter her perspective to appreciate what she has to say?

A critical reader/reviewer will raise these questions. In this sense, he is simply someone trying to come to terms with the text. So, if he is an uncritical reader or writer, he may not be an effective communicator. Communication, in short, can be considered a transaction between at least two logics. In reading, there is the logic of the thinking of the writer and the logic of the thinking of the reader. In the example of reviewing a book, the journalist reconstructs (and, therefore, translates) the logic of the author into the logic of his thinking and experience. He then writes a review in this context. If this is done responsibly, the end-result is a new creation – the reviewer's view of the book and of Elizabeth I for the first time now exist within the reader's mind. That is no mean feat.

Argument checklist

Having considered this process, a critical thinker may wish to use a checklist when evaluating and composing arguments:

1. Is there any ambiguity, vagueness, or obscurity that hinders my full understanding of an argument?
2. Have I separated the reasoning (evidence) and relevant assumptions/facts from background information, examples and irrelevant data?
3. Have I determined which assumptions are warranted and which are unwarranted?

4. Can I list the reasons (evidence) for the argument and any sub-arguments?
5. Have I evaluated the truth, relevance, fairness, completeness, significance and sufficiency of the reasons (evidence) to support my conclusion?
6. Do I need further information to make a reasonable judgment on the argument because of omissions or other reasons?
7. Is the language excessively emotional or manipulative?

In Conclusion, best to avoid (or at least assess critically...)

Ambiguity. A word or expression that can be understood in more than one way. From the statement 'Lying expert testified at Milosevic trial', is the expert a liar or is he or she an expert on telling whether someone is lying? If the intended meaning of an ambiguous word or expression cannot be determined, avoid guesswork and rewrite.

Assuring expressions. Expressions that disarm you from questioning the validity of an argument, such as 'as everyone knows', and 'common sense tells us that'. Focus instead on facts and reasoning that support arguments.

Emotive content. Choosing words to arouse feelings about a subject to bias others positively or negatively – the Home Secretary using the phrase 'neutralising the opposition' (less negative) rather than 'killing' (negative). Learn to recognise and distinguish the emotive content of language.

Euphemisms. The use of inoffensive terms or expressions to mislead, disarm or deceive when writing about unpleasant realities – referring to a policy of mass murder as 'ethnic cleansing' or the inadvertent killing of innocent people as 'collateral damage'.

False analogies. Making illogical analogies to support the validity of a particular claim – by arguing, for example, that two children sharing the same bedroom is wrong because the sharing of jail cells by criminals can lead to bad or recidivist behaviour.

False implications. Language that is clear and accurate but misleading because it suggests something false. The dairy industry cleverly expresses fat content as a percentage of weight, not of calories. In truth, 2 percent 'low' fat milk really has 31 percent fat when fat is measured as a percentage of calories. Understand not only the facts, but also their relevance and context.

Hedging and weasel words. Language that appears to commit one to a particular view, but because of its wording, allows one to retreat from that view. President Clinton's claim that he did not have 'a sexual relationship' with Monica Lewinski, in which he later explained that 'engaging in sexual acts' was not 'a sexual relationship'.

Jargon. The use of technical language to make the simple seem complex, the trivial seem profound or the insignificant seem important, all done intentionally to impress others. What is the value in referring to an organisation as 'a bounded plurality of role-playing individuals' or to a homeless person as a 'non-goal-oriented member of society'?

Judgemental words. Stating opinions as though they were facts, so your audience does not have to judge for itself. 'The Minister took justifiable pride in extending artists' tax exemption.' Distinguish fact from opinion in any statement or argument.

Meaningless comparisons. Language that implies that something is superior but retreats from that view. An ad that claims a battery lasts 'up to' 30 percent longer, but does not declare that it *will* last 30 percent longer and, if it does, longer than what? Avoid making judgements if it is not exactly clear what is being compared.

Vagueness. Language that is less precise than the context requires. If someone needs to be paid back tomorrow, and the borrower says 'I'll pay you back soon,' the borrower's response was too vague. Be aware of the consequences of imprecise claims based on vagueness.

References

Sheila Cooper, Rosemary Patton, *Writing Logically, Thinking Critically* (Pearson Books, 2006).
Theodore Schick, Lewis Vaughn, *How to Think about Weird Things* (McGraw-Hill, 2005).
W. Lance Bennett, *News: The Politics of Illusion* (Addison Wesley Longman, 2005).

CURRICULUM VITAE COVER LETTERS

A cover letter has one purpose: to get you an interview and boost your chances of landing that job. It may be the most important correspondence of your life.

A cover letter must make waves, interest employers and place you top of the pile. Even in Ireland's days of plenty, personnel managers tell us they receive an average of 45 written applications per advertisement. More if they come by e-mail. The cover letter must sell – by showing what you have to offer the employer.

Plan your cover letter. Take time to plan your cover letter and curriculum vitae. Employers want information to show how you match their needs.

Step back and ask this question before you write: What can I offer? Then find the most relevant, specific achievements or skills you have to make the employer want to interview you.

Of these sample letters, which would compel you to meet Robert Murphy?

---

43 Oak Lawn Drive
Sandyford
Dublin 18

Dear Sir or Madam

In response to your advertisement of July 14th in *The Irish Times*, I wish to apply for the position of relationship manager. Attached please find a copy of my *resumé* for your consideration.

I should be happy to provide further details should you require them and I look forward to hearing from you.

Yours faithfully

Robert Murphy

Robert Murphy
43 Oak Lawn Drive
Sandyford, Dublin 18

Project Manager advertised in
***The Irish Times*, July 14th 2006**

Dear Ms O'Loughlin

Leading Datacom's sales initiative

I would like to lead Datacom's sales team as your new Relationship Manager and bring to your company my seven years of experience working on international corporate clients for Intel International.

My training at Intel helped me become Regional Sales Representative of the Month four times in two years. After my promotion to North-East Regional Sales Manager, we improved training for sales representatives, revamped our marketing strategy and moved into direct selling on the Internet. Turnover has increased by an average of 27 percent year on year.

Many of these ideas apply to Datacom's product range, especially the innovative broadband offerings and group e-search you recently launched in the trade press.

I would be happy to discuss these ideas at an interview. Could we arrange to meet in early July when I return from the International Computer Roadshow in Munich?

Yours sincerely

Robert Murphy
Enclosed: curriculum vitae

The standard-form letter may be easy to knock out, especially if you're making multiple applications, but does nothing to get you an interview. The tailored alternative is harder to write but worth it. We'll use the latter to explain the professional writing techniques you should use.

Paper and letterhead. Type your name and address in a font and type size different from the rest of the letter and you immediately create an attractive, professional letter – and a positive impression. Be wary of using fancy, calligraphic or esoteric fonts that either can't be read easily or mightn't match with the culture/style of your prospective employer. Use high-quality light-coloured paper for your letter and CV.

Your first paragraph. Employers, particularly large companies, want to know what position you are applying for and where you saw the advertisement. The temptation is to list this information in the opening sentence of the first paragraph: *In response to your advertisement of June 23rd in The Irish Times, I wish to apply for the position of project manager.* This may be accurate and to the point, but you need a more powerful beginning – one that makes you stand out. Place the administrative information above the body of the letter or as a reference. This frees you up to write a more-effective opening.

Personalise. Write to a person rather than an anonymous company officer or partial e-mail address. If you don't know the contact name, ring the company and find out.

Personalising a letter goes further than using the name of the reader. Check the use of pronouns, the name of the firm and especially the information in the third paragraph. This shows that the letter is tailored to meet the needs of this employer.

Write a positive, action heading with a strong verb. Use the journalistic technique of putting verbs in your headings. Start your letter by suggesting an action. Here the verb 'leading' as the first word of the heading shows confidence — so important in a candidate for a guiding role.

Use the second paragraph to show what you've achieved. This is a managerial position, so tell how you led your team. If it's for an auditing job, it's what you saved the company. If it's a public relations position, it's the results of a large publicity campaign you organised. By putting this information towards the end of the paragraph, it's likely to be the one piece of information the reader will retain. Once the employer has trawled through those 45 applications, you'll want him or her to remember you.

The power of the third paragraph. Flattery can get you everywhere. But softly does it. In your third paragraph, you should compliment your prospective employer, not by gushing adjectives but by highlighting his or her organisation. It shows you've researched the company. It confirms you've matched skillset to need. It proves your letter is to them and to no one else.

Close strongly, suggesting the next action . You need to take control of the next action. Don't write: 'I look forward to hearing from you.' or 'I am available for interview.' Suggest a date for an interview or say you will ring in ten days to arrange a meeting. Such techniques show your confidence in getting the interview and put you in control of the next step.

List enclosed information at the end. Only include your *resumé* with your cover letter. Don't attach examples of work or references. Confidence is one thing; vanity is another. It's too early in the selection process. Use the business convention of 'Enclosed': to show you have attached your *resumé*. This stops you writing such a weak and obvious sentence as 'Attached please find a copy of my *resumé* for your consideration.'

Electronic applications. For some jobs, you may decide to submit your curriculum vitae and application letter electronically. Many recruitment advertisements request submissions in this format or you may find it expedient to send materials quickly. In such situations you can attach your *resumé* to an e-mail.

If the application letter is an attachment, the e-mail itself should be brief and courteous; it should simply state that you are submitting the attached file in support of your application. Mention the specific position for which you are applying in the subject heading. And make sure you scan your outgoing message for viruses.

When you are applying for a job electronically, never use your current work e-mail as the point of contact. Imagine how your boss would react if he knew you were trawling the appointments pages in work time and sending out curriculum vitae to other organisations. Neither will be the irony be lost on any half-competent personnel manager in your prospective employer organisation. Create an account with hotmail, eircom, gmail or any of the myriad providers and start your job-search from home turf.

Sample curriculum vitae

Print your curriculum vitae on two pages of high-quality white paper, using a legible font such as Times or Helvetica. Do not use coloured paper or inks. Staple the pages in the top left-hand corner and attach the document to your covering letter with a paperclip.

Name	Robert Murphy
Address	43, Oak Lawn Drive, Sandyford, Dublin 18, Ireland
Telephone	084 1234567 **(Mobile)** 01 9876543 **(Home)**
E-mail	robertmurphyexample@eircom.net
Date of Birth	June 27th 1972

Experience

Oct 1999–present **North East Regional Sales Manager**
Intel, Collinstown Industrial Park, Leixlip, County Kildare
Arranging re-seller agreements with providers in North-East Ireland. Four times regional sales manager of the month. Turnover increase of 27 percent year on year

Jan 1997–Sept 1999 **Production Manager**
Messer Legal Eagles, 196, Fitzwilliam Place, Dublin 2
Managing the SAP programme for the company's annual catalogue of digital products. Facilitated the transition of the paper portfolio to proprietary electronic Web and electronic provision

Jan 1996–Dec 1997 **Online Editor/Humanities Researcher**
The Thomas McCreevy Hypertext Chronology, Computer Science/English Initiative, University College Dublin www.ucd.ie/~cosei/
Member of e-publishing and research team of an online chronology site charting the life and work of the writer, critic and former Director of the National Gallery of Ireland, Thomas McCreevy.

Jan 1994–Nov 1995 **Data Copyist**
Microsoft Worldwide Product Group, Sandyford Business Park, Dublin 18
AutoRoute Express (CD ROM), a multimedia travel guidebook and map product containing interlinked articles.

Education

1998–2002 **Dublin Institute of Technology**
Postgraduate diploma in Marketing (Hons) – part-time
Modules included branding, strategic positioning and budgeting

1989–1995 **University College Galway**
BA (Hons) in Computer Science
Specialist study options included: programming, Linux, networks

1983–1989 **Summerhill College, Sligo**
Leaving Certificate Examination 1989 – five honours grades at higher level

Professional Training

2003 **The Sales Training Centre, Excellence House, Ballsbridge, Dublin 4**
Cold-calling, telesales, negotiating, closing skills

1996 **Microsoft Wordwide Product Group, Sandyford Business Park, Dublin 18**
Onscreen editing, MS editorial applications: MS Hyperlink, MS ARIES Editor, and MS RAID

Hobbies and Interests

Literature, language, theatre, film, the visual arts, travel, swimming

Letter layout

Assuming you're successful in your application and have secured your dream job, you may have to show off you perfect business penmanship. And it's (nearly) as much about how you say it, than what you're saying.

5, Maple Grove
Landscape Park
Churchtown
DUBLIN 14

July 14th 2006

Ms Helen Jones
President
SSIA Investment Central
IFSC Rented Office Space
Exchange Place
Custom House Docks
DUBLIN 1

Dear Ms Jones

In business letter formats, there are block formats, indented formats and modified block formats, and who knows how many others. To simplify matters, we are demonstrating the block format on this page, the most common design in current use, and the most mis-styled despite the prevalence of word-processor letter templates. For authoritative advice on all of the variations, we recommend *The Gregg Reference Manual* (McGraw-Hill, 2001), an excellent reference tool for workplace communications.

When you use the block form to write a business letter, all the information is typed flush left, ideally with one-inch margins all around in single-space paragraph format. First, provide your own address, then skip a line and provide the date, then skip two lines and provide the inside address of the party to whom the letter is addressed. (You may have to adjust appropriately if you are inserting the letter in a windowed envelope. A matter

of trial, error and persistence.) If you are using a letterhead that already displays your address, do not retype that information; just begin with the date. For formal letters, avoid abbreviations where possible.

Depending on space and the placement of logos on the paper, skip another three or four lines before the salutation, which may or may not be followed by a colon. (It has surfaced in recent years. We don't like it, but it's your call.) Then write the body of your letter as illustrated here, with no indentation at the beginnings of paragraphs. Hit one return between paragraphs to provide white space and clarity.

After writing the body of the letter, skip two lines and type the closing phrase without commas, unless you have strictly punctuated every line from your address down. Leave five more blank lines, and then type your name and title (if applicable), all flush left. Sign the letter in the immediate space above your typed name. Now, does that look professional or what?

Yours sincerely

John Doe
Administrative Assistant

MEMO WRITING
with the assistance of Aviva Cohen

Nothing gives a better insight into the culture of an organisation than its pattern of memo-use. Hostile, defensive, paranoid companies sprout memoranda the way a dead body sprouts maggots, whereas memoranda tend to be thin on the ground in happy, trustful, communicative companies.

A memorandum or memo is a legitimate internal communication when used to remind a colleague of an action to be taken or a decision made. The Latin term *memorandum* literally means 'reminder'. In many offices memos have been replaced by e-mails. They have a lot in common; both are short messages that are often ignored or misunderstood.

Whenever you send an e-mail or memo outlining and wait in growing frustration for a response, you need to look first at your own writing before you attribute the problem to the recipient. (This is an axiom of good writing. The buck stops with the writer, not the reader.) In this section we explain how to deliver clear and concise communications through memoranda.

In an effort to be 'thorough' and 'professional' we often include far too much information. After explaining the background, the efforts we have already made and anything else we can think of, we finally get to the point. By this stage it can be too late. Your reader has lost the will to read through to the end of your memo.

Like all good business writing, a memo has to be brief, accurate and relevant to the reader. A memo can be one short line or as long as it needs to be, but it should never be longer than one page. And – again in common with all good business writing – it should start at the end and with the recipient: what must happen as a result of this memo, and what's the best way to get that achieved by the recipient?

The first sentence in your memo must convey the main idea so if the recipient remembers nothing else, you can be sure that at least they will remember what's in that first sentence. A typical memo follows the shape of a triangle. The key point should appear first. The evidence follows in order of importance. You should restate the key point at the end of the memo.

It's important to agree a formula for memoranda within a company (see Delivering a Brand in this section), but working within that formula should not iron flat the writer's personal style. It may follow a pattern, but it's still the transference of understanding from one mind to another. Hence, while operating within the formal constraints of the structure, there is no single best way to write a memo. It does not have to be solidly formal. It should sound personal, and it should be tailored to the needs and style of your audience. Below is an example of a typical layout. Variations on this theme could include your company name and logo, 'c.c.' or 'copy to', 'enclosures' and even instructions on how to file the memo.

Like other written business communications, a memo can include bullet points, the name of one or many recipients and a closing statement such as 'Please contact me if you would like any further information.' It is usual for the sender to retain a copy of the memo for his or her records.

Don't get into the habit of including phrases that turn an effective communication into a generic: phrases like 'Please do not hesitate to contact us.' If you wouldn't say it, face-to-face, to a friend, you should hesitate before you say it in print to a colleague.

Finally, proofread your memorandum. Typos send two messages:

• that you don't respect the recipient
• that you don't take care of the details of your own job

Memorandum

To: Subject:
From: Reference:
Date:

The main point
The most important information
The evidence that supports that information
More of the evidence that supports that information
Finally repeating the main point as you reach your conclusion

Signed
Title of Signatory

In this section, we focus on *Action Minutes* because they are most commonly used in a business context. However, two other forms of minutes are sometimes required.

Resolution Minutes are usually used when time is extremely short or where the participants wish to remain anonymous. Here you should record only the resolutions and the actions.

Narrative Minutes detail the discussions to a much greater extent than Action Minutes. They record the name of the speaker and his or her contribution. Narrative Minutes are often used in voluntary organisations where the minutes serve two functions: they record the business of the meeting and they acknowledge the good works of the committee members. Narrative minutes are also useful when recording complex discussions such as the proceedings of the European Parliament. Here, we need to understand more than the conclusions, we need to understand the views of each speaker.

MINUTE WRITING

'He who controls the minutes, controls the meeting.'
Disgruntled executive (attrib)

What people call 'minutes of a meeting' varies wildly. At one end of the spectrum, transcripts are produced that include a detailed record of every comment, every cough and splutter. Sometimes the secretary also tries to do a little emotional manipulation, directing the readers as to how they should feel about what they are reading:

'John made a valuable contribution…' or
'Jane presented an excellent report on…'

Writing the minutes of a meeting is a straightforward task. They should be brief and to the point. It does not require a stenographer, a great knowledge of the subject or the ability to comment on the value of each contribution. It does help if the Chair of the meeting knows what he or she is doing. The Chair should introduce each item on the agenda and facilitate a timed discussion. Then he or she should summarise, reach agreement on the actions and confirm who will take the action if any is required. When the Chair performs his or her role well, the minutes almost write themselves. If the Chair is not running an efficient meeting the secretary may need to seek clarification before writing the minutes.

Remember, the minutes must be accurate, clear and complete because they can be used to settle disputes. They can also be used in legal proceedings. Always write them as soon as possible after the meeting – before you forget what your notes meant. Also ask the Chair to read and confirm the minutes before you circulate them to the other committee members.

How to structure the minutes
The content of the minutes will follow the order of the agenda. This allows you to set up a loose template for taking notes. It is becoming increasingly common to take notes directly onto a laptop during meetings. This saves time and helps to avoid misreading tired or rushed handwriting.

Beginning the minutes

- title
- name of the group holding the meeting

- type of meeting; is it a regular meeting or one called for a specific reason?
- date, place and time of the meeting

Attendance. Check the terms of reference in your organisation. In some places you have to record the name of each attendee. In others you only record the names if there are fewer than a specified number. This is important if a quorum operates.

You should also record the name of the Chair and secretary. If the usual officials are not present you should note this, record their apologies if appropriate and record the names of their replacements.

Matters arising. Always circulate the minutes in advance so that the committee members can let you know if they disagree with the content of your minutes. This gives you time to double check any disputed items. It also allows for an official sign-off.

Opening statement. Take a note of these elements:

- when the Chair called the meeting to order
- that they read the minutes of the previous meeting
- that they did not read the minutes of the previous meeting
- whether the minutes of the previous meeting were agreed or amended

Reports. List any reports that were read and approved. At the end of the minutes take a note of the reports that are due for the following meeting and who has agreed to prepare them.

Motions. List the motions; these usually take the form 'I propose that…'. Note whether the motions were carried forward, defeated or proposed. Name the attendee who proposed each motion and who seconded them. You don't have to record motions that were withdrawn.

Summarise the discussion in your own words. Note the decision and the action taken. Record who has volunteered, what they have agreed to do and when they will report back.

Resolutions. Take a detailed record of any resolutions that were accepted. You have to record each resolution word for word. However, you need only a simple statement of resolutions that were rejected.

Ballots. Record the subject of all ballots. Note the number of votes for and against.

Discussions. Summarise the discussions briefly, again in your own words. Note any objections and disagreements. Here, you could follow headings such as: 'Topic, Discussion, Action Taken'. Where the committee has not agreed any further action, note this as 'Item Parked'. In this case the headings would follow the format: 'Topic, Discussion, Item Parked'.

N.B. Not all meetings require the same elements. If it is your first experience taking minutes for a new committee don't assume that their requirements are the same as your last experience. Make sure that you get proper terms of reference.

Points of information. There may be occasions when it would be difficult to read the minutes because some of the discussions require specialised or technical knowledge. In this case it is acceptable to create a new document to accompany the minutes called 'Points of Information'. You can also use Points of Information to include anything that you believe to be relevant but is not an action item, a resolution or any other formal structure. For example, you could include a proposed resolution that was rejected and the reasons for its rejection.

Ending the minutes. Take a record of everyone who has volunteered to report back on something for the next meeting. State their name and exactly what they have agreed to do; list as a series of action points if appropriate. Make a note of any agenda items agreed for consideration at the next meeting, or any current items carried over for future consideration.

Record the time the meeting was adjourned. Also note the time, date and venue of the next meeting.

Type your name as the secretary of the minutes and sign. Type the name of the Chair and ask him or her to sign also.

WRITING AN EXECUTIVE SUMMARY

All business writing boils down to a relationship with a specific audience. Nowhere is this more true than in the executive summary. Whether you're presenting a business case, making a sales pitch or offering analysis, you're aiming high. You're tailoring your piece to the highest-ranking official you want to inform and whom – in an objective way – you want to influence. The reader who is interested in the bottom-line deliverables, not in the details. Your goal is to get the message to someone who has the authority to act but is so busy that he or she will probably delegate anything time-consuming. If your reader likes the summary, he or she will pass it to assistants or colleagues and ask them to read the whole document.

A good executive summary means that you mean business.

What does it look like?

- It's no longer than 1,000 words, ideally no more than two pages, and preferably one.
- It's laid out in an appealing style and used a judicious mix of formatting techniques, lists and subheads. You've banished grey blobs of text.
- You've written sentences with first-person plurals, few to no abbreviations and no acronyms or titles.
- You've omitted technical terms and jargon.
- Your short, pithy sentences flow with a good rhythm and contain evocative phrases and images.

So what does it say?

Within a word count limited to 1,000 words, it's impossible to include extensive support data, but the executive summary still makes a strong, concise case for supporting the actions of the main report. It sticks to the substance – the issues, problems, strategies or processes to which they apply. Most importantly, it concentrates on recommendations, on who should take action, what benefit will ensue and what alternatives are available. It doesn't recount task activities nor refer to the report contents. In fact, it doesn't even mention the report. The executive summary is a stand-alone document. Note the expression 'stand-alone'. It can be read in a single pass in under ten minutes.

How do you write an executive summary?

You do not cut and paste from the original report. That makes for a stilted summary, and even, sometimes, a fatal error. But you do read over the entire document several times before you type as much as a comma, noting the points you want to promote along the way. Start your executive summary with a sentence that puts the problem in a nutshell, that presents the nature of the task in fewer than 25 words. Follow this with an illustrative statement that supports your assertion. Develop this idea concretely with either (short) quantitative or qualitative findings that show your reader the extent of the problem. Indicate the implications of failure to act. Nothing captures the reader's interest like a warning.

Sample executive summary

Libre Services:
A non-proprietary model for delivery of Internet services

Executive Summary
March 28, 2006

The Internet has created an enormous new offshoot of the software industry: the **Internet services** industry. This industry has become a key medium, not just for day-to-day communications and productivity, but also for the expression of information and ideas.

However, this vitally important new industry exists entirely in the form of the traditional proprietary software model. Within the general software arena, the free software movement is well established as an alternative to proprietary software. But as yet, the free software movement has no formal presence within the Internet services domain.

We are a group of engineers with a vision for the future of Internet services. We believe that the free software movement as we see it today is just the beginning, and the next major evolutionary phase of free software is its strong emergence into the Internet services arena.

We believe that the intellectual property ownership mechanisms of patents, copyright and trade secrecy, as they exist today, have almost no legitimacy at all within this arena. At bottom these ownership mechanisms are business constructs, intended to provide competitive advantage in a commercial context. That they do. But they do so at great cost to the broader society. Some of the societal costs are obvious; others are more subtle and indirect. But the costs are real, and very far-reaching. They include:

- A crippling of the software-engineering profession. These ownership mechanisms cut directly across the engineering freedom of action that is the foundation of the software development process.

- The loss to the public of the technical benefits of unrestricted engineering development.

- In the case of Internet services based on commercial providers, the compromising of a number of important civil liberties, including personal privacy, freedom of information, and freedom of speech.

- A severe distortion of the competitive business environment.

- Eventual loss of governance of the Internet to purely commercial interests.

Instead of the proprietary software model, we are advocates of the free software movement, in which software is treated as a communal resource, freely available for reuse by anyone. Our ultimate vision is a completely open software industry, in which **all computing and communications are based entirely on free software.**

We are proposing a radically new, completely non-proprietary model for the delivery of Internet services. We call this the **Libre Services** model.

Libre Services are an extension of the principles of free software into the Internet services domain. They are Internet services that may be freely copied and reused by anyone. They are a communal resource, not owned by anyone, freely available for use by society at large. Any company, organization or individual can reproduce and host any Libre Service, either for their own use, or for commercial or non-commercial delivery to others. The Libre Services model exists in relationship to the proprietary Internet services model of AOL, MSN and Yahoo, in an analogous way to how GNU/Linux exists in relation to Microsoft Windows.

This is a radical departure from the existing commercial model, with societal benefits that are equally radical and far-reaching. The Libre Services model provides a range of critical **freedoms** that are entirely absent from the proprietary model:

- The freedom of the engineering community to engage in unrestricted creative development, building new and better Internet services for the benefit of the public.

- The freedom of any group or community to operate their own Libre Services, according to whatever principles they see fit. Since they are no longer subject to the actions of a commercial service provider, this guarantees a range of critical civil liberties: privacy, protection against government monitoring, freedom of information, freedom of ideas, freedom of speech.

- The freedom of the business community to participate in the Internet services industry, without any intellectual property barriers standing in the way. Libre Services transform the closed industry of today into a truly open industry, creating major new business opportunities and industry growth.

Libre Services are the right way to deliver Internet services to the user. Our goal is to establish Libre Services as a non-proprietary alternative to the existing proprietary services industry.

In this article we describe the Libre Services concept, and how we intend to turn it into a reality. A key component of our bootstrapping strategy is a project-based model for collaborative participation. We have defined a set of independent, self-contained projects required to move this initiative forward. This allows efficient, coordinated collaboration on multiple bootstrapping tasks in parallel.

Versions of this article

The ideas presented in this article are intended to be accessible to a wide audience, including both technical and non-technical readers.

To accommodate different levels of reader sophistication the article is available in two alternative versions: a General Version, and a Technical Version. It is also available as just an Executive Summary, and in a Presentation Format.

- **General Version.** This version includes background information and explanatory material for a non-technical audience. If you are unfamiliar with the software industry and the principles of free software, this is the recommended version.

- **Technical Version.** A condensed version for software engineering professionals. If you are already familiar with the software industry and free software, this is the version to read.

- **Executive Summary.** A summary of the key ideas of the article.

- **Presentation Format.** The main ideas in the form of a PowerPoint presentation.

All versions are available in several different file formats (HTML, PDF, PS, plain text) at: http://www.freeprotocols.org/libreConcept/accessPage.html

Some tricks of the trade

If it's for a sales pitch, mention the customer's name three times as often as your company's name. And don't forget about technology. If you're presenting the document in electronic form, use the linking functions in Microsoft Word. Make it easy for the reader to click to more information deeper in the main document, the information that you want them to read but can't include in a paper format.

Next, present the three to five major findings. You may have more or fewer, but going beyond this range suggests you may need to rethink your definition of 'major'. What did you discover? Focus on actual results, rather than on the process by which you arrived at your findings. Present these in either descending or ascending order of importance. Use bullet points and subheads. Keep your words crisp, clean and to the point.

After this, shift the focus to your conclusions. Here you can put the problem in its broader context. For instance, you can compare your findings with those gained by other studies, if such information is appropriate and available. By now your reader should be clear about your choice of solutions. Then present your recommendations. If you've followed this template you'll have established firm ground for what you're suggesting. One of the most persuasive means you can use to connect your conclusions to your recommendations is to show clearly why you dismissed alternative options. Now get specific and apply the journalist's rule for a good lead: **Who** should do **What**, **Where**, **When**, **Why** and **How**. Kipling's six serving men. Set your recommendations off with more bullet points so that they stand out. At the end, tell your reader about the benefits of your recommendations.

WRITING PRESENTATIONS

You know the old joke about the Kerryman, who, when asked for directions, says 'If I was goin' there, I wouldn't start from here'?

A presentation is much the same. It doesn't start with writing. It starts with research and analysis. These are the key questions:

- Who's going to be present?
- How much do they know about the topic?
- What must they know when the presentation is finished?
- What's their attitude likely to be before the presentation?
- What attitude should they have after the presentation? (Or: what changes in behaviour or management should they commit to after the presentation?)

A business presentation is not about entertaining people. That may be an added bonus, but the main objectives must always be to inform and persuade. Accordingly, the presenter should first identify what changed attitude or behaviour should result from the presentation, and then work backwards, selecting the arguments and information that will generate that change.

Bad presentations start from what the speaker feels he or she wants to say. Good presentations amount to communication-by-objectives.

When you have worked out where you're going and – in sequence – the essential steps to going there, it's time to prepare your speaking notes in the way that best suits you. Obvious? Not really. Generic approaches to public speaking assume that there's one perfect method that must be employed by every speaker. Of course, if you think about it, this means speakers are not only interchangeable but irrelevant: a taped presentation would be just as useful as a human presenter who's been yellow-packed, and a handout would be faster and more effective than either.

Presenters matter. An impelling presenter can make even ostensibly boring material fascinating. An empathetic presenter will scratch an audience where it itches. A presenter who likes the people being presented to and believes in the material being presented can turn a routine business presentation into an enlightening pleasure.

The individuality of a presenter is precious. The very fact that one presenter *looks* quite different from the previous presenter tends to wake up a group. If all presenters wore a presenter uniform, boredom would increase and more people in the back row would nod off. Yet many presenters adopt a 'uniform' of systems they believe apply to everybody.

The classic example is the myth of cards. The myth proposes that holding a script in your hand is bad, whereas holding cards is highly professional. This ignores the growing tendency for presenters to transfer their entire script onto dozens of playing-card size oblongs of card. They're still reading. It's just that their hands are moving faster, thereby distracting the audience.

Let's address, not the props, but the performance

Pivotal to good presentation is eye contact between the presenter and the audience. Eye contact is crucial to all good communication. Put a big smiley-face drawing in front of a three-month-old baby, and it will immediately seek out the eyes in the picture. When we like or love someone, we listen to them watching their eyes. When we fear or dislike someone, we avert our gaze.

Presenter eye contact should be easy and natural. The presenter needs to engage with all of those present at the beginning, and then glance at individuals throughout the talk, as particular points are made. They may also glance down at their monitor or notes, in order to remind themselves of an upcoming point or of details supporting the point currently under discussion. Anything that significantly reduces a presenter's eye contact with an audience is bad.

A lethal obstacle to eye-contact is a densely written script, faithfully read *at* a group. If fidelity to text is the issue, why not hand the script to everybody, ask them to read it and then have a discussion about it? The presenter's physical presence should deliver something over and above the words on paper. Therefore, the words on paper should be minimal. Few presenters can read as well as news-readers on TV can, so they should not position themselves as corporate news-readers. Trigger words will allow most presenters to explain, rather than read, their point.

Imagine, for example, that the presenter wants to talk about delayed gratification.

Scripted, the input might read thus:

A psychologist in the 1970s did an interesting experiment.
It involved four-year-olds. And marshmallows.
The four-year-olds were put in a room.
The experimenter told them that they could ring a bell at any time.
As soon as they rang the bell, they'd get a marshmallow.
But if they *didn't* ring the bell and waited for 15 minutes, they'd get *two* marshmallows.
Some children couldn't wait. They rang the bell after 5 minutes – and got one marshmallow.
Some of the children *did* wait. For 15 minutes, they waited. And got two marshmallows.
The interesting thing is that, years later, it emerged that many of the children who couldn't wait, the children who had to have the marshmallow *right then*, grew up to be bullies and drug addicts.

On a card, the trigger words might be:

• psychologist, 1970s, experiment
• 4-year-olds – marshmallows – bell

- 15 minutes = 2
- bullies, drug addicts

Remember, what's written on a card should not be full sentences. Pick the most emotive words ('bullies') and stick them on the card. A downward glance will then trigger the point to be made about bullies. Make sure the card is big enough to obviate the audience thinking you're about to deal them all a poker hand, and made sure the hand-printed words on the card are big enough to read without effort.

PowerPoint-itis

If fidelity to a script – or a script divided up into dozens of cards – militates against eye contact with the audience, even worse is fidelity to a script on PowerPoint, particularly if the main screen is behind the speaker. The speaker frequently turns their back on the people being addressed in order to find out what they're supposed to be saying.

Presenting one's rear-view to an audience is rude. But it's a symptom of a different problem: PowerPoint-itis. PowerPoint-itis is now endemic in the business world. Diagnosis of sufferers is easy. The symptoms of the ailment are floridly evident.

They *start* with PowerPoint, not with the audience or the objective.

They are at their most comfortable in front of a screen, inputting bullet-points.

Their PowerPoint-itis infects everything they write. A chronic sufferer, writing a letter of sympathy to a bereaved friend, is likely to describe the beloved dead thus:

- always in good humour
- would lend his lawnmower
- upset when his Labrador died
- fine husband and father

None of which establishes the essence of the man the way a couple of stories about him would. So why is PowerPoint so omnipresent? According to corporate speechwriter Steve Zousmer, writing in the *New York Times,* the reason is corporate contagion: 'Executives use slides because other executives use slides.'

PowerPoint-itis is progressive. In the early stages, those infected suffer occasional bouts. As the condition worsens, however, the bouts become a continuum, and to suggest making a presentation without

PowerPoint becomes unthinkable. Final-stage sufferers would infinitely rather do a presentation stark naked and painted in woad than make one without PowerPoint 'support'.

That last word matters. For too many speakers, PowerPoint is an improvement that makes things worse. It is a support that is unsupportive.

When a presenter's first PowerPoint screen appears, the alpha waves in the brains of the audience flatten. Subconsciously, their brains make the decision that this is entertainment and that interactivity will not be called for until the Q&A session at the end. Unless they have a real and present need to concentrate on the material, the fact is that PowerPoint use will diminish, rather than increase, their attention.

Edward Tufte, a Yale Professor specialising in communication, maintains that the convenience of PowerPoint for speakers is costly to content and audience alike. The evidence that these intrinsic limitations can inhibit, rather than enhance understanding was provided by the PowerPoint presentation made in NASA before the catastrophic re-entry of the Columbia spacecraft. The key screen from that presentation delivered data in so PowerPoint a manner that its deadly message was not understood. Have a look at it.

Review of Test Data Indicates Conservatism for Tile Penetration

- **The existing SOFI on tile test data used to create Crater was reviewed along with STS-87 Southwest Research data**
  - **Crater overpredicted penetration of tile coating significantly**
    - ◊ **Initial penetration to described by normal velocity**
      - Varies with volume/mass of projectile (e.g., 200ft/sec for 3cu. In)
    - ◊ **Significant energy is required for softer SOFI particle to penetrate the relatively hard tile coating**
      - Test results do show that it is possible at sufficient mass and velocity
    - ◊ **Conversely, once tile is penetrated SOFI can cause significant damage**
      - Minor variations in total energy (above penetration level) cause significant tile damage
  - **Flight condition is significantly outside of test database**
    - ◊ **Volume of ramp is 1920cu in vs 3 cu in for test**

Cognitive Style of PowerPoint, www.edwardtufte.com

The first and most obvious problem with this particular slide is that it has immeasurably more data than could easily be read. Power-Point has poor resolution. That's why so many users end up truncating and abbreviating their ideas in order to make them readable in bullet points. In the NASA situation, the room where the presentation was made was crowded to the doors, with people straining to see the screen. Visually, it did not deliver a clear and deadly message.

The second issue is the title, which, by its wordy passive style, wrongly delivered a sense of reassurance. Then comes the differentiation of the points. Four different levels of identifier are used, from a dash to a diamond to a big bullet. This is further complicated by the parentheses at the end of one of the points.

Having seen the presentation, the NASA officials made no further effort to address the threat of the damage caused to the wing of the spacecraft on take-off. Professor Tufte attributes this inaction partly to the way the PowerPoint presentation dampened clear expression and thought. The Columbia Accident Investigation Board's report on the disaster was just as blunt:

> The Board views the endemic use of PowerPoint briefing slides instead of technical papers as an illustration of the problematic methods of technical communication at NASA.

The endemic use of PowerPoint *anywhere* reduces the efficacy of the communication involved. The best communications technology ever invented is a human being. Humans have expressive faces, and from birth are trained to pay attention to the faces of others. They have hands that can, through gestures, emphasise or dismiss different aspects of a communication. Presenters who read their presentations off the screen behind them are reducing the efficacy of their best communications assets.

Of course, some presenters use PowerPoint reasonably effectively. Without doubt, some subjects require the visual presentation of complex data, and PowerPoint can help in such presentations.

The technology, nonetheless, is an adjunct, an addition, rather than the essence of any presentation, and businesses should not buy into the belief that if someone hasn't prepared a PowerPoint, they are lazy and likely to do a poor exposition. Some American corporations are now consciously limiting the use of the technology, believing that it tends to train executives out of the capacity for sequential thinking: they begin to see everything in bullet-point form.

'These costs result, from the *cognitive style characteristic of the standard default PowerPoint presentation*: foreshortening of evidence and thought, low spatial resolution, a deeply hierarchical single-path structure as the model for organising every type of content, breaking up narrative and data into slides and minimal fragments, rapid temporal sequencing of thin information rather than focused spatial analysis, conspicuous decoration and Phluff, a preoccupation with format not content, an attitude of commercialism that turns everything into a sales pitch.'

Edward Tufte

When you choose to use PowerPoint, the technology should not be resorted to until the shape of the presentation has been established. The speaker should block out the sequence of argument and illustration. If necessary, they should write out the entire presentation, so that they can see the organic sequence of their thought in print before it gets blocked into PowerPoint bullets.

Then, and only then, should the writer/presenter ask the question: *What, out of this content, should be visualised for the benefit of the audience?*

Too many writer/presenters give not a thought to the audience, relying instead on PowerPoint prompts for themselves. If a slide does not carry value for the audience, it shouldn't be included. Speakers should find some other way of clueing themselves into what's coming up next. Where technical slides are necessary to illustrate a process or demonstrate progress in an appealingly visual way, by all means include them – and when the audience has finished with them, put up a 'buffer' slide: some general and undistracting visual such as the speaker's name and title.

How to be interesting, understandable and memorable

Create a good beginning. It can be a statement, like 'Animals are dying in agony every day just so that rich women can buy shinier lipsticks.'

It can be a joke, but humour at the top of a script should be used with caution. If the witticism bombs, it tends to make the speaker less confident and the audience more tense.

It can be a statistic, like 'Twenty years ago, the average soundbite lasted 30 seconds. Today, it lasts no more than 10.'

It can be a quotation: 'Experience is not what happens to you. It's what you *do* with what happens to you, according to one writer.'

It can be a story: 'A sower went out to sow his seed…'

It can be a question: 'We are richer than at any time in the past. We are living longer, healthier lives. Yet the percentage of the population that considers themselves happy has been steadily declining since the middle of the last century. How can this be? Why should the luckiest generation in human history be so miserable?' (Be careful about asking questions: the dangers of rhetorical questions are discussed in Writing Speeches in this section.)

Get to the point. It's important that the audience knows, fairly quickly, why they're there. Is it to buy in to a proposition? Change a behaviour? See an issue in a different light? Join a movement? Buy a product?

Avoid speaker-clichés. Public speaking has its own set of clichés. There's the one about an earlier speaker using his data the way a drunk uses a lamppost: more for support than illumination. There's the hoary assertion that you never get a second chance to make a first impression. Or the one about a picture being worth a thousand words. There is the maddening waffle speakers put around the Q&A: instead of saying 'It's now time for questions,' they give the 'last but not least' guff and say they will be *very* happy to take questions.

Keep sentences short.

Use first-degree words.

Use active, not passive, verbs.

Cut redundancies: *Basically, essentially, fundamentally, very* redundant words should *really* go.

Rehearse out loud: Words that look good on paper can sound vile when spoken aloud. Gustave Flaubert used to stand on his balcony speaking his sentences aloud before committing them to paper.

WRITING SPEECHES

This section deals specifically with the writing of speeches, rather than presentations. A speech tends to be made without PowerPoint, in a situation where the audience interaction with the speaker is important, and where most of those attending don't know the speaker personally. Presentations, on the other hand, tend to be supported by PowerPoint. Although the personality of the speaker is relevant in presentation, the material is often delivered to colleagues within a company or to fellow specialists at a conference, as opposed to strangers.

Speeches are made by politicians, by fathers of brides and by business people. We'll leave wedding speeches to another book, but speeches for politicians sometimes have to be drafted by business executives. When, for example, a Minister is visiting a company plant, his or her Department may ask for 'speech material' or 'speaking points' from the host company. In which case it is much better to provide a full speech. They may tinker with it, but with luck, some of the original material will survive, whereas sending them nothing other than data cedes the shaping and tone of the speech in its entirety to a civil service writer who may have little insight into, or interest in, the particular corporate entity.

Drafting a speech for a politician is just one of the situations where a business writer must write for a speaker other than themselves, and it demands a sequence of actions, starting with research. The writer must, first of all, get to know the speaker. Interviewing the speaker is ideal, but not always possible. A taped chat with a public speaker can elicit:

- their length of sentence
- their pet references, whether in sport, music or literature
- their attitude to the topic
- their level of knowledge about the subject
- their pet hates in scripts written for them
- what they want to leave in the minds of the audience

Length of sentence matters because, if you're writing a speech for an asthmatic smoker, any sentence longer than 16 words is going to cause them difficulty. Stylish, accomplished speakers, on the other hand, will not only manage longer sentence, but will be able to inflect and play with single word sentences:

My response to that proposition?
Anger.
Real anger.
Frankly, it maddens me.

Speaker preferences provide the texture and weave of a good speech. A man whose leisure time is dominated by golf will be well served by a speech replete with references to famous golfers and will happily mimic a golf-grip if the script calls for such a gesture. Contrariwise, a speaker with no interest in history will not comfortably handle a speech shot through with stories about great battles or the failure of the *ancien régime*. Sometimes, speech-writers project onto their speaker an interest the speaker doesn't have. A classic example was a speech written for a businessman who was not a reader. The speech was littered with quotations from poems and plays and novels. The speaker, who loved the speech and was determined to impress the audience, got through it without a mishap, until the end, at which point he announced that he would conclude 'with a quotation from Oscar Wilde's 'The Ballad of Reading Goal', thereby humiliating himself and discomfiting the audience.

Attitude to the topic speaks to the authenticity of the speaker. If someone is no more than vaguely benign towards the natural environment, it's not productive to craft them a man-the-barricades diatribe about the hole in the ozone layer. On the other hand, if the material is fresh and exciting, the speaker may be seduced into greater engagement with the topic.

Level of knowledge matters because if the speaker pretends greater understanding than they actually have, the question and answer session after the speech may show them up. It isn't hard to introduce authoritative material for such a speaker. The writer may insert phrases like 'I was startled to learn, just this week,' or 'as experts, you know that…'. Don't render your speaker spurious by scripting him into being more of an expert than he really is.

Pet hates in scripted material are worth teasing out in advance of submitting a first draft. Some speakers hate encountering funny stories at the top of a speech. Others loathe speeches that include foreign phrases. While one speaker will be quite happy to spend the first two minutes of their speaking time addressing virtually everybody in the audience by their formal title, another will refuse to acknowledge mayors and bishops and will always want to begin with the simple 'Ladies and Gentlemen.'

President John Kennedy had superb speechwriters, but, as his presidential campaign progressed, became more confident at speaking off the cuff. He would stand up and jettison the prepared speech that had already been handed out to the press. The journalists, of course, were working against deadlines, and would file a story based on the printed material in front of them. When JFK delivered a quite different speech, often without covering any of the key paragraphs in the text, the journalists got in trouble with their editors, who wanted to know why their report didn't match the radio or TV broadcasts. Which, in turn, caused the candidate's press officer, Pierre Salinger, enormous difficulties.

> Finally [Salinger later said], I developed the policy of putting out a prepared text of only one or two pages, and he would dutifully make good on those pages. *Then* he would ramble. He knew he was better extemporaneously, and it took him a while to realize that he was generating considerable ill will among the press because we were passing out speeches that he didn't give. After a while, Kennedy became almost sophisticated about the process. He would say to me, 'Go talk to the boys

and find out what it is in the speech that they particularly like, and then tell them I'll be sure to say that.'

What to leave in the minds of the audience depends on context. If it's an after-dinner speech, the speaker may want to leave no more than a sense of enjoyment and a couple of relevant anecdotes. If it's a visiting multinational president or a Government Minister, they may want to lay down markers about possible changes in policy. If it's an inspirational speech, the speaker will want to leave the audience, not just with a new zest for their life or career, but also with a few specific steps they can take to funnel that zest into long-term change.

This last is arguably the most important requirement. Leaving something in the minds of listeners who, unlike students in school or university, are unlikely to make notes, demands that the key points (ideally three, no more than four) are made, illustrated and if possible repeated in different forms in order to get them stuck into the long-term memory of those listening. Without specific, visualisable and preferably singular examples, even the best speech will be forgotten quickly.

Meeting the person who will deliver your speech in advance of writing it allows you to clarify all of these issues and to prevent the speech becoming generic.

If you get to interview them, the questions to ask (assuming you already have the basic biographical details) would include:

- favourite book, poem, song, film, sport, public figure, kind of clothing
- what frightens, amuses or annoys them
- who's been most influential in their lives or on their thinking
- what they do when they're not being 'official'
- worst/best experiences in life
- any pets and which kind

Make notes, while they talk, of how they dress and – if you're in their office – what's on their desk.

When you get home, analyse the content of your notes. What analogies do they use? As stated earlier, sporting or war analogies tend to dominate the discourse of men; relationship and domestic analogies dominate the discourse of women. What examples do they use? What stories do they tell? How do they describe themselves?

In effect, you are profiling the speechmaker in order to write a speech so closely tied to the person, so fingerprinted by them, that nobody who hears it will ever believe they didn't write it themselves.

Knowing the audience

Since communication always starts with the audience and the audience's needs, a good speechwriter (or speechmaker) checks out the following in advance:

- who's going to be there
- what they already know/feel about the topic
- what they want from the speaker (The organiser can usually give this information.)
- how long they want the speech to be (Very few speakers can hold an audience longer than 20 minutes. General rule: write the speech 20% shorter than the time allocated: speakers at conferences always overflow. The one who doesn't is loved by everybody.)

Divide any audience into three sections where ideological or other change is part of the speechmaker's objective:

The converted. People who already agree with the speaker's position or argument.

The unconvertible. People who are permanently opposed to that position or argument.

The floating voters. People who haven't made up their mind or know nothing about the issue.

The speechwriter should not waste too much time reinforcing the already converted, but of even more importance is not seeking to convert the unconvertible.

The best place to start writing a speech is to begin at the end. Ask yourself the question: 'If they remember nothing else, what's the one statement they *must* remember?'

That proposition goes at the start, in the most interesting and challenging way you can write it.

The materials sourced by a speechwriter depend on the subject being addressed. We would warn against reliance on dictionaries of quotations. In fact, we would warn against dictionaries, full stop.

The speechwriting process
1. Researching audience and audience needs
2. Sourcing materials
3. Drafting
4. Editing
5. Rehearsing
6. Final rewriting

G.K. Chesterton said persuading a triangle to break out of its shape destroyed it: the individual whose identity and self-esteem is bound up with a set of beliefs cannot afford to relinquish those beliefs in response to a speech.

The two deadliest openings to a speech are these:

'The dictionary defines "ethics" as….'

'Let us begin with an observation made by the great Greek playwright Euripides, in his play, *The Medea…*'

Don't begin your writing task by searching for tedious definitions or for quotations.

Do begin it – and continue to write it – in simple, accessible, person-to-person language. It is tempting to be more formal when you are dealing with corporate clients or government officials. Tempting, but a mistake. Every obscure or conceptual term you employ will require the listeners to translate it into pictures or stories they can understand, because, in the spoken word, that's how understanding moves from one head to another. The first time you include jargon, obscure terminology or purely conceptual language in a speech, the audience may make an effort to explain it to themselves, but if you keep doing it, they won't continue to do your work for you. Instead, they will drift off into consideration of their life outside the speech, and you – and the speaker for whom you write – may have lost them permanently.

Using stories, repetition and the visual

Never underestimate the contribution to be made by story. Stories play a crucial role in every culture: the Norse Sagas, the Celtic Legends, the Greek Myths. Stories have a beginning, a middle and an end. They have an internal logic and an external purpose. That purpose is often to hammer home a moral lesson or posit a behavioural change.

Repetition of a phrase or an image can be a powerful rhetorical device. Churchill constantly repeated key phrases like 'We will fight them on [the beaches, the streets].'

The device trains the listener's ear. The listener, like someone hearing a song played on the radio a number of times, begins to internalise the rhythms of the repetition and is much more likely to remember at least some of the propositions following the phrases.

Inarguably the best example of this is Martin Luther King, Jr's 'I Have a Dream' speech:

> I say to you today, my friends, that in spite of the difficulties and frustrations of the moment, I still have a dream. It is a dream deeply rooted in the American dream.

When President Ronald Reagan addressed veterans of the Normandy invasion on June 6, 1984, his speech was heavily reliant upon story:

'We stand on a lonely, windswept point on the northern shore of France. The air is soft, but 40 years ago at this moment, the air was dense with smoke and the cries of men, and the air was filled with the crack of rifle fire and the roar of cannon. At dawn, on the morning of the 6th of June 1944, 225 Rangers jumped off the British landing craft and ran to the bottom of these cliffs. Their mission was one of the most difficult and daring of the invasion: to climb these sheer and desolate cliffs and take out the enemy guns. The Allies had been told that some of the mightiest of these guns were here and they would be trained on the beaches to stop the Allied advance. The Rangers looked up and saw the enemy soldiers who were standing at the edge of the cliffs shooting down at them with machine guns and throwing grenades. And the American Rangers began to climb…'

> I have a dream that one day this nation will rise up and live out the true meaning of its creed: 'We hold these truths to be self-evident: that all men are created equal.'
>
> I have a dream that one day on the red hills of Georgia…

The level of singing repetition in even this short extract of King's speech would not be safe to incorporate in a speech written for a white European CEO or a Government Minister. It is rooted in the liturgies of the churches of the Southern States of America, King's formative terrain. This is why it's so important to meet and profile your speaker before you write for them. It is your job, as speechwriter, to develop sentences – some of them deliberately repetitive – which fit comfortably into your speaker's mindset and mouthset.

However, one reality applies no matter where your speaker comes from, and that is the importance of the visual. A good speech makes the audience imagine the people and places about which it was written. The process of painting pictures in the head tends to make the topic more easily remembered.

A speechwriter in the habit of writing simply, pictorially, and in logical sequence can produce a speech at short or no notice.

Peggy Noonan, Reagan's speechwriter, has written an account of how quickly she wrote the stunning Presidential speech on the *Challenger* disaster:

> I was on the phone with a friend. The TV a few feet away was, as always, on, at the moment tuned to CNN, which was covering a space shot live. The shuttle was going up. I was laughing at something the person on the other end was saying when Nancy Roberts came rushing in.
>
> 'Something happened to the shuttle. They think it blew up.'
>
> 'What?'
>
> The TV screen is blue with a trail of white smoke. Pieces of something are falling through the sky…I press a plastic button on the IBM word processor; the screen lights up, the buzz begins…

Noonan, having turned on the IBM, turned out the speech in one draft for delivery roughly an hour later.

Internal logic

A good speech does not leap from one subject to another. It may have illustrations, but it is held together by one coherent theme. It is not an assembly of random items.

In Ancient Rome, speechwriters would draft their speeches in their

Jesse Jackson provided a good example of picture-making in his presidential campaign speech of May 1988:

'Most poor people are not on welfare. They work every day. They take the early bus. They work every day.

'They care for other people's babies and they can't watch their own. They cook other people's food and carry leftovers home. They work every day.

'They are janitors running the buffing machines. They are nurses and orderlies wiping the bodies of the sick. A loaf of bread is no cheaper for them than it is for the doctor. They work every day.

'They put on uniforms and are considered less than a person. They change beds in the hotels. Sweep our streets. Clean the schools for our children. They're called lazy, but they work every day. They work in hospitals. They mop the floors. They clean the commodes, the bedpans. They work every day. No job is beneath them. And yet when they get sick they cannot afford to lie in the bed they've made up every day.'

homes. They would write – and talk out – their first point while standing in the hall. Then they would move into a room for the next point, and into the atrium for the third. They would repeat this a number of times, so the flow of their house became associated in their head with the flow of their speech.

A more modern version of this is the memory game, whereby a participant is given 50 items in sequence, with breathing time between them, and is then asked to go through the list in sequence. The person who does it floors the other participants, but the method is replicable by all. Let's say the start of the list goes like this:

boat
pen
hat
espresso machine
keys
newspaper
feather

The person who wins the memory game starts at the front door of their home, and envisages a child's toy boat sitting on the lintel of the front door. Stepping over it, she sees a pen on the hall table. Halfway up the stairs is a rainhat. At the top of the stairs, she has to step over a red Espresso machine, in the shadow of which is situated a bunch of keys. A newspaper, rolled up, has been jammed in a closed bedroom door, and a feather has been stuck into the keyhole of the door.

You can see that, once you have involved yourself in this vivid visualisation, it is relatively easy to remember those seven items in sequence – and (assuming your house is big enough) to recall three or four times as many items.

When *learning* a speech, this 'mental walk-through' device can be helpful. When *writing* a speech, push yourself to weave a logical single thematic thread throughout and to cut away digressions and distractions from that central thread.

Rhetorical questions

A characteristic of a speech with poor internal logic is that it is linked using rhetorical questions, like the famous one used by Sean O'Casey's character in *Juno and the Paycock*: 'What is the stars, Joxer? What is the stars?'

In that play, Captain Boyle doesn't expect a response to his question. It is simply a way of getting him to the next thing he wants to say. Rhetorical questions, dotted throughout a speech, become tedious:

- But what are the implications of the fuel surcharge?
- Given the globalisation of the market, how can we address this deficit?
- When will this move from worrying to catastrophic?
- Where do we go from here?

The tedium of repeated rhetorical questions is matched by the danger that some irritated audience member will start giving the wrong answers to the questions.

Limit yourself to one rhetorical question per speech. They are dubious links. They usually happen when the speech is too diverse in its propositions: trying to sell too many ideas.

Links

Links should be minimal. Here's an effortful clunky link:

'Having outlined our corporate history, I will now turn to the most immediate challenge on our horizon: the fire at the back of the room.'

What the speaker should really be saying is:

'The back of the room is on fire.'

Too many reminders of what has already been covered ('having said that' or 'I referred earlier to') become speedbumps in the path of onward progress, and convey a self-satisfied dogmatism.

Using the personal

The speech should be personal, but not weighed down with the personal pronoun.

'I hate taking off my shoes at airport security,'

can be generalised to reduce the self-reference:

'It's so dreary to have to take off our shoes at airport security.'

The Q&A rule (Keep Yourself Offstage) may seem to conflict with the need to be personal and to take ownership of your material when delivering a speech, but it doesn't. The person delivering the speech will not gain in authority or ownership by gratuitous self-reference:

I think
I feel
I always say

Nor will they be served by parading their successes. If personal stories are told, the writer should try to ensure that they are self-derogatory stories, showing the speaker making a mistake or learning a painful lesson.

Making sure examples can be instantly understood

Finally, at the scripting stage, make sure that every data point adduced is understandable at first hearing, remembering that the audience for a speech can't pause, chew a pen, do sums in their head, and say 'Eureka!' as they might if they were *reading* the material in their own time.

If the speech, for example, describes a room as '24 metres long by 11 wide', the majority of the audience will hear the words, but not grasp, in any real way, the meaning. They must be given an example of a similar-sized space with which they are familiar:

'The main room is about the size of a tennis court.'

The rule is: lead people to the unfamiliar through the familiar.

It's all about the timing

When you've finished your first draft, check the word count. People speak at differing paces. A fast speaker will deliver as many as 170 words a minute. A slow speaker will hit 120 words in the same time. So a speech containing 1,200 words will make a perfect ten minute oration for the second speaker.

At this point, the ideal format for the speech has to be married, sometimes with difficulty, with the preferences of the speaker. You will remember we identified how the speaker uses material as one of the key characteristics with which you must be familiar.

Many a speechwriter has listened to something they wrote being delivered faithfully, but with such passionate ownership that the speech-writer finds themselves bizarrely agreeing with propositions they wrote. On the other hand, there are politicians and managers who transfer trigger words to cards and proffer to an audience the *essence* of the original speech, without using the words as scripted. A huge problem for writers of scripts for other speakers is when the speaker won't stay in the time allocated to them, because they believe a substantive speech must go on for at least 45 minutes. Brevity can terrify. Handed three pages of brilliance, a speaker may believe they won't be taken seriously if that's all they have to offer. It's worth reminding them that when Abraham Lincoln made the 700-word Gettysburg Address, he followed a speaker who had prated on for more than two hours. Nobody remembers the earlier speech, whereas the great phrases of the Gettysburg Address, to this day, stick in the mind, even after a single hearing or reading.

Whereas government ministers rarely get to look at a speech even a day in advance of delivering it, business speakers tend to prefer to have the draft speech at least a week in advance of its delivery, in order to become familiar with it, edit it and, if necessary, have it retyped in a way they find particularly easy to read. Learning speeches by heart is rare these days. Although Winston Churchill was able to memorise speeches by reading them aloud once or twice, most public speakers today have never developed that capacity, and don't see the need for it.

Revising by committee

Now when you, the scriptwriter, send the first draft of your work to the speaker, be aware that he or she is likely to share it with other people, and every one of those people will believe they can improve it. If you can, arrange for a communal reading involving all the individuals who may want to tinker. Outline for them the sequence of the argument and the reason for the illustrations. Then lay down one condition: they are to undertake their first reading of the speech *without a pen in their hands*. A reader with a pen in hand distracts themselves from the flow of the prose by making notes and corrections. That's for the second reading. The first is to get a flavour, a sense, an impression of the overall impact of the speech and so is best done without a pen.

Take notes of all suggested changes. Later, you can decide whether or not you want to incorporate them. If you don't incorporate them, let the person know why.

One of your readers is likely to come up with an abominable piece of advice that has the durability of an ice-hockey puck. It's been around for more than 50 years and it surfaces again and again. It goes like this:

• tell them what you're going to tell them
• tell it to them
• tell them what you've told them

Layout tips

Writers who generate speeches for other people to deliver need to work hard at making those speeches user-friendly.

• A serif font, like Times New Roman, should be used, as opposed to a sans serif face like Arial. Serif fonts draw the eye of the reader onward and make it easier to lift the sense off the page for delivery to the audience.

• Speeches should never be typed in capital letters throughout. Continuous capitals are difficult to read and elicit a dogmatic monotone from the orator.

• Paragraphs should be short, with plenty of white space between them. This allows speakers to more easily locate themselves in the text: a glance down will lead them to the next main thought they want to express.

• Big margins allow the reader to make notes on the page.

• Finish sentences on the page on which they begin. Run-on sentences, which start on one page and finish at the top of the next, are difficult for experienced orators and impossible for newcomers.

• Never staple speeches together – the reader should be able to discard pages as read.

• Scripts should be in 14-point print. This is big enough for glance-down hoovering up of material, but not so big that only one paragraph will fit on a page.

• It's easier to read print from matt, rather than shiny paper, and from cream or yellow, rather than bone-white paper.

Following these instructions when writing a speech requires the writer to utilise the first paragraph as a device to set out the key points that will be made throughout the speech. Thereafter, the points are made. The final paragraph then reiterates all the key points.

In theory, it makes sense: it gives the audience a clear sense of what's coming and provides them with a reminder at the end.

In reality, it was dated 50 years ago: TV moved public discourse away from that kind of predictive formality, because TV is driven by the desire to *attract and hold* viewers, whereas this approach assumes the audience is passively acquiescent to being lectured at.

Business writers of speeches should err on the side of normal human communication. Those present should be addressed as individuals, rather than as an obedient collective.

Imagine what would happen if your speaker were to go home one evening and say to their spouse, 'I'm going to deal with the kind of day you had, then I'm going to have dinner and tell you what kind of day *I* had, and then I will summarise the key emerging issues from our conversation.' The spouse would not be a happy spouse. We don't do that kind of structured didacticism in real life.

'You wouldn't believe what happened to me today,' we say, and get launched on the most exciting, infuriating or delightful happening of our day.

Public speaking should follow the same pattern. Your speaker must start with so interesting a point that the audience is engaged, then move so logically that they don't need advance warning of each point. The conclusion should be Aesop-fashion. It should give the moral, the direction, the desired end result, rather than simply revisiting points already made.

Bringing your text to life

When a semi-final text has been agreed, get your speaker to go through it aloud. Only by hearing them articulate your words will you find out:

- which sections sound overly 'written'
- which words challenge the speaker
- where repetition works – and where it's just irritating
- where signs indicating a pause need to be inserted

The giveaways of seepage from written to spoken word are phrases like 'the following point'. Nobody would ever talk of 'the following point' to another human being sitting in front of them, but speakers

And don't forget…

- to keep the speech on a flash drive. Speakers lose speeches on the way to the conference and need them e-mailed at the last moment.

- not to print the speech on both sides of the page.

- to make sure the pagination is clear and double-checked. A speaker who finds page 7 printed twice may be terminally thrown by the experience.

- that business audiences are likely to buy the same books you buy. So a quotation from Charles Handy or some similar writer may not be as exciting and new to them as you might expect it to be.

will happily say it to 200 human beings sitting in front of them. They shouldn't. Nor should they say idiotic things like 'as I said above'.

One of the great pleasures of speechwriting for others is watching members of an audience actively seeking out a copy of the speech after it's been made. One of the agonies of this kind of work, by contrast, is watching members of an audience reading page 11 of a script when the speaker is only on page 3. For your own sanity, to improve the attention vouchsafed the speaker, and to remove the distraction caused by the rustling of turning pages, insist that copies of the speech are issued only after the speech itself has been delivered.

WRITING A PRESS RELEASE

Writing a good press release starts with an understanding of the home you hope it will find: the news pages of a paper. Here's a news report, from the front page of the *Guardian*.

Calls grow for £15bn pension payout

The government is under renewed pressure to pay up to £15bn in compensation to workers for lost pensions after a scathing report by a Labour-dominated committee of MPs.

The public administration select committee found that the administration select committee had misled employees over the security of occupational pension schemes and had since been more concerned with denials than compensation.

The committee gave its full backing to similar conclusions reached by the parliamentary ombudsman this year and said the minister's rejection of the ombudsman's findings raised 'fundamental constitutional issues'.

At the end of three brief paragraphs, the reader knows the story. In fact, at the end of *two* brief paragraphs, the reader knows the story. The last bit adds background – which is why it's placed at the end. The first two paragraphs answer the key questions represented by Kipling's 'six serving-men' (page 1):

- Who? (government)
- What? (is pressured to pay up)
- When? (it is assumed the committee reported yesterday)

- Where? (Britain)
- Why? (because they codded their own staff)
- How? (pay up and look lively about it)

Because a press release aims at ending up in the sort of space occupied by that news story, it must read the way such a news story reads. It must have

- a good headline
- answers for the key questions in the first paragraph
- active verbs and first-degree words
- short sentences

The headline on a news story is like a free sample. It gives the news editor a flavour of what the overall story is about. If the headline does not grab the news editor, they may read the first paragraph, but they will do so with diminished enthusiasm.

This is a poor headline:

INFRASTRUCTURAL UPGRADE ENABLED BY EU ALLO-
CATION OF £300,000 FOLLOWING CAMPAIGN RELATED
TO PERIPHERAL AREAS POLICY DIRECTIVE

It's a poor headline, first of all, because of length. It's at least twice too long. The words are long, too. You'll listen to ordinary people talk for a long time before you hear words like 'infrastructure' or 'policy directive'. Headlines should always be in the language of the reader, not the writer.

In addition, 'Enabled by…' is an indirect, passive way of saying something; its past tense makes it historic rather than newsy; it is inhuman. Above all, the reader cannot visualise what the story is going to be about. The headline acts as a disincentive to the reader.

This, on the other hand, is a good headline:

NEW ROAD CUTS TRAFFIC JAMS IN HALF

It's short, uses simple, vivid language and is active. It has a human interest hook implicit within it, since most of us have been stuck in traffic jams. It's in the present tense, so it's newsy.

When you're writing a headline, remember that the obligation is on you to attract the reader. It's pointless to say, 'But they *should* be interested in this.' There are no 'shoulds' in mass media. You have to

These examples may help you to remember what to aim for when coming up with a headline:

BAD: Man bitten by dog
        (passive, past tense)

GOOD: Dog bites man
        (active, present tense)

attract and persuade people to read your story: they have a million and one alternatives.

Assuming you craft a great headline, the next task is to get the key details into the first paragraph. This is because another, bigger story is always lurking, ready to compete with your release. If that bigger story surfaces, the sub-editors must edit your release, and the quickest way is to simply chop off the end of it. The story in your press release, accordingly, must be understandable, even if what follows the first paragraph is amputated. It must answer the who/what/where questions.

To answer those questions, the opening paragraph might be along these lines:

> 'The new road from Littletown to Bigtown, due to open tomorrow, will cut traffic jams in half, according to Littletown Council. The Council said today (Friday, 3rd April, 2002) that the new road would eliminate the delays between the two centres.'

Even if nothing else is printed, the reader has learned the essentials.

One of the problems press-release writers face is when they are handed impenetrable material and asked to 'get it into the media'. The following sentence, for example, with its 67 words, would never work in a release:

> 'Through publication of mass media publicity opportunities while ensuring correct presentation of visual identification materials, it is possible to highlight opportunities available to potential beneficiaries of Structural Funds through the portrayal of successful projects already extant and at the same time alert members of the general public to the role played by the Member States together with the European Commission in the process of developing the regions.'

It would be much more easily understood if it were broken into five or more sentences. (It would also help if it used first-degree words, like 'logos', instead of 'visual identification materials'.)

A shorter sentence version might read like this:

> 'Successful projects are the best way to show what Structural Funds do. Potential beneficiaries get to see what opportunities exist. And the general public learns how the Commission and Member States are helping disadvantaged regions. These projects would be publicised in all media to make sure the message reaches everybody. The

10 DON'TS for Press Releases

DON'T type your press release in capital letters.

DON'T type your press release in italics.

DON'T type your press release on both sides of a page.

DON'T fail to proof-read your release – or, better still, have it proofed by someone else.

DON'T use clichés.

DON'T use padding ('with regard to', 'in the context of').

DON'T send it late (some provincial papers stop taking copy much earlier in the week than you might think – check with them).

DON'T send it to the wrong person – or to the right person with their name wrongly spelled.

DON'T use bold type to emphasise points in your release.

DON'T open quotation marks and forget to close them.

DON'T believe that one size fits all. Sending different types of press releases to different media is a good idea. A story presented as a radio script and written in the spoken word has a much better chance of getting on radio than the same story presented in the written word.

Structural Fund logo would always be used so people remember the name.'

The typical layout of a press release is a variation on the example below. While it's acceptable to include a coloured logo at the top of a press release, when submitting it (as most are now submitted) on e-mail, be wary of the seductive visual options on your computer. The deputy features editor of a national broadsheet recommends:

> Personally, I'd say forget all colour – no italics and just a bold, underlined headline – and contact details at the bottom in bold. If a client is trying to get an editor to read more than the first 25 words of their press release, they should just write it straight. I'd probably also suggest one par to every sentence. Ariel 12 point is my preferred font, but if the content is good, 8pt wingdings won't stop a good editor from gettin' the gist.

As you've seen, it's useful in some cases to include an indicator to the recipient as to when it may be used. For example, if you were releasing a major report, you might send it to a journalist on Tuesday the 1st, but embargo it for Thursday the 3rd. That would give the journalist sufficient time to read through the report, master the detail and write a story, while ensuring the story did not appear until Thursday.

By contrast, it might suit you to distribute a press release in the morning, but, in order to ensure that the evening paper does not use it, you might put, in the upper left hand corner, 'Embargo until 9 pm, Thursday 3rd'. That means only the morning newspapers and radio stations can use it.

(Be warned, however. Newspapers have been known to break embargoes. If you have a story that must be kept secret until a particular day, you may be better advised not to send it out in advance under an embargo, but to keep it safe until the last moment.)

In 90% of cases, there are no such complications, and what goes in the left-hand corner of a press release is 'For Immediate Release'.

For Immediate Release
26 April 2009

Headlines and Sensational Writing Vital, says PR Guru

Punchy headlines and sensational writing are vital for press releases, PR Guru Terry Lyons today (Friday, 26 April 2009) told a conference in Dublin organised by the Institute of Chartered Accountants in Ireland. Ms Lyons suggested that releases with long sentences and formal, institutional language often fail.

'Press releases about serious and important issues often become heavy and dull,' she stated. 'As a result, newspapers don't use them.'

Ms Lyons, known as the Hype Priestess because of her pre-eminence among publicists, went on to tell those attending the conference that lack of follow-through often doomed press releases. If a release lands on the wrong desk, she pointed out, only a follow-up phone call will ensure that the right journalist actually receives it.

Following her speech, ICAI announced that she will be hosting a series of press release workshops in the town hall at the weekend. The workshops are free to volunteers working on community development projects.

ENDS

Further information from:

Josey Buggins (Ms)

Tel: 0374 82039 (W)
055 2938 293 (M)

In a press release, quotation marks pull the eye of the reader. Quotes give greater variety to what would otherwise be a straight presentation of details. Keep the attributions simple. Don't have your spokesperson riposting, snorting or opining.

It's important that the recipient of the release knows where it finishes. Putting ENDS in the middle of the line after you have finished, but before you put in the source, is one way of making that clear.

No newspaper will give a moment's consideration to a press release that does not come on a letter-headed sheet indicating the organisation's name and address. In addition, at the end of the release, the news editor needs to know who sent this particular release and where can they be reached *right now* if a detail needs to be clarified or an element elaborated on. So press officers should include their mobile phone numbers and their home numbers. (Make sure whoever is at home on that day knows there is a chance of a call from media and is briefed to cope with it. A news reporter with a fast-approaching deadline who encounters a chatty four-year-old may be less than happy about it.)

CORPORATE COMMUNICATIONS AND CREDIBILITY: THE BOTTOM LINE

Warren Buffet once said he would never invest in a company he didn't fully understand. He also claims he keeps his sisters Doris and Bertie in mind when penning the annual report of his investment company, Berkshire Hathaway. They're not experts in finance, so he asks himself if they'll understand what he's writing.

Call it corporate messaging, brand identity or a writing standard, it's possible to put a value on clear expression. Plain speaking strikes a chord with the reader. Unambiguous communication can help a company win trust, enhance the bottom line and avoid bad press. Over the past decade, as scandals have rocked the business world, it's become essential for companies to build credibility with customers, communities, the press and the public. In a worst-case scenario, those relationships – and that credibility – will pay off in times of crisis.

Even from a general public perception, it seems plausible that successful companies tend to have a bias towards simplicity, allowing a

According to a 2005 *Financial Times* report, one-third of London City analysts – investment specialists – couldn't tell whether the chairman's statement in a selection of annual reports was positive or negative. In another *Datamonitor* survey, three-quarters of a consumer sample said they would be more interested in saving if they could understand what financial-services companies were telling them. A scary thought if translated to post-SSIA Ireland.

good story to tell itself, whereas failing firms are more likely to disguise bad news with vagueness and euphemisms. Have you noticed that when commenting on poor results, a lot of media managers are guilty of saying very little at very great length? Ironically, such obfuscation often lengthens the media life of such a story.

In an era of corporate enforcement, paper communication has taken on an even greater significance. Since the passing in the US of the Sarbanes-Oxley Act in 2002 – which requires chief executives and chief financial officers to attest personally to the veracity of their firm's accounts – it has become crucial for senior managers to keep tabs on what they're signing, lest the words they verify return to haunt them. Honesty is now the only policy.

Your company's writing objectives

Be it on your website, in your annual report or a company memo, begin by asserting your immediate purpose. Tell your reader what you're setting out to do and how you intend to achieve it. Whatever template you select for a house style, whether it's from this book or the *Chicago Manual*, never patronise your audience. And ban the following from all written material:

- expressions such as 'going forward', 'geographies' and 'platform' (the new 'solution', apparently)
- words that have become meaningless through overuse such as 'deliver', 'significant', 'driver', 'facilitate', 'enable'
- vagueness and blandness, unchecked punctuation and careless grammar

An example: Shell has taken flak in recent years, and not just in Ireland, for its commercial activities and corporate objectives. Although it has launched serious communications counter-offensives, how's this for a piece of unmitigated garbage from its *Meeting the Energy Challenge* report:

> We are also talking real partnerships: Shell and others in the private sector innovating affordable locally relevant solutions; local customer and civil society groups being deeply involved in local energy distribution approaches that ensure both access for the poor and conservation; and governments, often with limited administrative capacity, that nevertheless create a policy environment that both keep energy affordable for the poor consumer while ensuring the energy producer the return necessary to stay in business.

So now you know. Or don't. Small wonder the group suffered a media crucifixion. Why would anyone engage positively with a company that is too arrogant or self-serving to explain itself in plain English?

A plan and a message

A communications strategy needs a message – a strong, concise assertion that defines the company's top goals. It should mirror any mission statement and be geared towards customer expectations. This message should be used whether an employee is talking to a business reporter, writing a news release about corporate expansion or delivering a speech at a local prize-giving. Every employee, every client, every customer and every shareholder should know that message – and, in an ideal world, believe it – because your corporate communications are inextricably linked to your most important market tool – your brand.

Delivering a brand

In most markets, there's relatively little to choose between products and services in purely functional terms. So a strong brand – what a product or service stands for – is of real value in providing differentiation. It can:

- justify a price premium – people will pay more for a name they trust
- attract talent – who would you rather work for? Skoda or Mercedes?
- win new business – or help you extend into virgin territory

Brand identity goes further than logos, colours and typefaces. It reflects a company's philosophy and determines how it communicates. That said, it's important that quality visuals support the written channels and be implemented across the public spectrum – website, intranet, publications, newsletters, events and media relations – and even in stationery, business cards, PowerPoint presentations and merchandise.

But brand and its delivery (with their implicit or subliminal guarantees) must be more than lip-service. No matter how strong a brand is, it's surprisingly easy to damage. A single lapse in quality of service, for example, may change a customer's view of it forever. And, over a period of time, a lack of consistency in the way a brand is presented and communicated can dilute its strength.

'As we continue to move towards a marketing model that does not seek to simply "talk at" but instead "engages with" consumers, we recognise that it is the consumer who is now in control of the communications process. In a world where effectiveness is no longer measured in coverage alone, it is clear that the answer is not simply to continue to pump up the volume.'

Stephen Stynes, MD,
TecBrand Marketing

The physical manifestations to consider – your identity applications:

- brochures
- merchandise
- letterheads, compliment slips and envelopes
- business cards and address labels
- faxes and memos
- e-mail and styling

Do nations (and corporations) have navels? Should we all talk the same English?

Since the penning of the Old Testament, the pursuit of a perfect or universal language was seen as the key for resolving the earth's religious, political and economic divisions. It didn't work. We don't all speak Esperanto. (No-one speaks Esperanto.) It was as if there was a realisation that language is a constituent element of a nation along with its territory, annals and myths, and its collective solidarity.

But the past 30 years have turned a new blank page. Modern societies are the first in history in which literacy is near universal and employment is at full capacity. Commerce and business have become the culture of continents. (Our book reflects this.) Although a seamless business language has never been universally agreed, transnational organisations and marketplace relationships have standardised corporate communication.

Take our membership of the European Union, for example. When Europeans were asked about their foreign language skills, 53 percent said they could speak at least one European language as well as their own. Some 26 percent said they could speak two foreign languages. Over 40 percent of Europeans already considered English their primary second language. Overall, the most–spoken first foreign language in Europe is English (33 percent) followed by French (10 percent). In the EU at least, the international language of business is English. And there's a bland Canary Wharf/Wall Street tone to it. It's almost as if a fate similar to the Tower of Babel must be avoided or no-one will sell anything to anyone.

As the number of online, telephone and classroom business-writing courses testifies, people will pay high prices to learn English. Conversely, our education system acknowledges the value of multilingualism and has encouraged students to become fluent in French, Spanish and German (while almost having to bribe them to learn Irish). In the 2006 Leaving Certificate exams, students could sit papers in 14 languages.

Two arguments can be raised against the standardisation of English. Firstly, it would lead to a tremendous impoverishment of Shakespeare's mother tongue. It would shift to fit an international Internet role, becoming the jargon of new technologies. Second, and perhaps more importantly, any language uniformity – be it business or otherwise – is a threat to diversity and heritage.

A balance is needed. Day-to-day business writing implies the

Over 70 percent of Europeans agree that every EU citizen should be able to speak one EU language in addition to his or her mother tongue. Almost 80 percent of this group agree that this should be English. However, this desire to facilitate communication is counterbalanced by a perceived threat to national identity. So, 63 percent of Europeans think that EU enlargement implies the absolute necessity of better protecting their own language.

Eurobarometer, *Europeans and Languages*, February 2001

manipulation of messages and contacts with a large number of sometimes anonymous partners. You want your communication to be skillful, not just phonetic. Everyone needs a baseline competency. But not one that is bland, homogenised and featureless.

So if you're formulating or working to a corporate style perhaps it's worth considering the lexicon. When did it come into existence? Do you reflect geographic areas or ethnicity – both yours and your target market's – when writing? Are you afraid to use your own idiom in its expression?

Going all Big Brother, is it worth asking if there's anything sinister about your corporate dialect? Has it been designed in some upstairs language lab and driven from the top down? It's more likely that it evolved through daily practice – the words adopted by brand managers which that spilled over to all employees.

We cannot answer these questions. We do not advocate that you navel-gaze and become defensive about every comma. Rather, we suggest that the international business arena is a multifarious cosmopolitan space, open to people coming and going, where getting to meet each other – in writing or in person – is the most common feature. However, we do believe you don't have to sacrifice the Irish vernacular or your own 'voice' to enter it.

WRITING TO A DEADLINE

Throughout this section we've shown how writing is easier when you break a project down into steps. It's a straightforward process of planning, researching, drafting, revising and polishing.

What about situations in which you don't have the luxury of time? What about writing an essay question in an exam or an on-the-job composition where you have only minutes to produce a letter or memo? What about a situation – like this one – where you have literally five minutes to commit your thoughts to paper with an editor baying for blood over wasting her time?

Any writing task, no matter how hurriedly it must be done, will go more smoothly if you stick to the three basics of the process: plan, draft and revise. Even if you have only a few minutes to craft a document, allow yourself some of that time to think about who you're writing to, what you need to say and the best way to present your material. Then draft your paper. Do give yourself even a couple of minutes to revise. PC editing is quick and painless. Use a spell-check program (taking account of its limitations and our advice on the subject) to prune embarrassing spelling or typographic errors.

If you don't have access to a computer, remember that people wrote by hand (including your authors) long before computers became ubiquitous. If you must compose with pen or pencil, you can still write effectively, perhaps more so because by necessity it will take longer and you'll have time to self-edit.

3. PC WORLD

USING THE INTERNET FOR RESEARCH

When researching anything on the Internet, start with a sceptical frame of mind. Always remember the way the characters in old spy movies used to warn each other about getting into the first cab that appeared: it was bound to be filled with electronic bugs, headed for sub-machine-gun fire, or on a good/bad day, seductresses. Similarly, on an Internet search, when you find an answer to a question, do not simply accept it. Check where the answer comes from. Evaluate the site where you found it to make sure it can be trusted. See whether the same answer pops up elsewhere. If it does, try to find out whether they simply copied the data from the first place you found the answer. Look for a bibliography on the site. If possible, try to corroborate your answer in a book. The problem with data on the Internet is that it can be placed there by anyone and may be more a reflection of their prejudices than a recounting of fact.

Wikipedia demonstrates the problems and benefits of easily accessible Web information. Wikipedia is a free encyclopaedia accessible to all. It can also be added to by all – and it is. It now contains millions of entries. So you can look up almost anything on it, from the Dublin Port Tunnel to Chuck Norris, whereas the Encyclopaedia Britannica is unlikely to hold much data on either topic. However, what's in Wikipedia may be entirely factual, or it may not. This is because the people who created Wikipedia have an editorial policy that encourages contributors to cite reliable sources for their information, or risk having it removed. That policy is not without flaws.

At last count, Wikipedia had some 4.6 million entries compiled by 13,000 active contributors. Some of the writers are experts; some, inevitably, are lunatics. So take its content with a pinch of salt.

The death of Kenneth Lay, the discredited Enron chief, prompted Reuters to monitor its reporting on Wikipedia. Over the space of 30 minutes, Lay's entry was edited five times and his death had four causes: suicide, heart failure, nervous strain and God's vengeance.

It's a chicken-and-egg scenario. Many Wikipedia users are its creators and understand its limitations. This online encyclopaedia is not an authoritative research tool, but a work in progress that by definition will never be finished. Treat Wikipedia as a first draft. It may not be the truth but is a useful, populist pointer towards it.

One line in Wikipedia's instructions to contributors demonstrates how shaky the sources of data can be:

> Sometimes a statement can only be found in a publication of dubious reliability, such as a tabloid newspaper. If the statement is relatively unimportant, remove it. If it is important enough to keep, attribute it to the source in question. For example: 'According to the British tabloid newspaper *The Sun…*'

Quite apart from the insult to 8 million *Sun* readers, the statement makes it clear that unreliable information will get through. It is therefore important that writers recognise that, while Wikipedia is one of the better information sources on the Internet, its offerings need to be verified.

Search engines processing the most searches at time of writing:
Google
Yahoo
MSN
AOL

Search engines – how to. Start by picking a large search engine. This is significant because, like surgeons doing particular procedures, search engines work better the more often they get used. They tend to build a profile of what the right answer to a search request is depending on which links are clicked on from the results they produce. So, the more often a search engine is used, the more useful its answers tend to be.

Then abandon the idea of asking it a question. Computers don't really like the complexities of grammar and the nuances of meaning that a proper question can present. There used to be a site known as *Ask Jeeves* that boasted you could actually ask its helpful butler questions. But what it did was scan the question for key words and search for connections to them, which is pretty much what every other search engine does. It has since dropped the *Jeeves* element and rebranded itself as ask.com, and is a perfectly serviceable search site.

(It is important to note that there are some exceptions to the 'don't ask it a question' rule. Google will convert currencies and properties for you if you ask it nicely – like 'How many metres in an astronomical unit?')

The best approach is to take your question and remove all the little words like 'what', 'how', 'it', 'the' and reduce it to a series of key words. So, rather than type in 'Where do I find out about renaissance art produced in France?' just type 'renaissance art + France'. Have a look at the answers produced and then fine-tune your search depending on the value of the first offers. It might be, for example, that the initial responses to your art query makes you realise that what you were really looking for was information on sculpture. So add that and search again.

One thing to be conscious of is that the search engines will give you two kinds of answers: the ones that are produced by checking the words you type in against previous searches and the contents of millions of websites, which the industry like to call 'organic' answers; and sponsored answers, meaning the ones companies pay to have included. Usually, the term 'sponsored' will be clearly visible so you can tell which is which.

Specialist search engines. Finally, if you try the big guys like Google and are not satisfied by their efforts, it may be time to try the specialists. Entertainingly, you can find these quite easily by typing 'specialist search engines' into one of the big guys. The search methodology for these engines is no different. The advantage is that a more specialist engine is less promiscuous in its offerings. Hence, if you are in a classical painting search engine and you type in 'Madonna and Child', you won't be directed to a certain pop star's sites.

Searchengineguide.com
Beaucoup.com

WRITING E-MAILS

In the first quarter of 2006, 171 *billion* e-mail messages were sent on their electronic way daily. Despite the presence of software filters designed to catch SPAM as it arrives, a huge proportion of those messages were unsought and useless to the receiver.

However, e-mail is now the main tool for many executives when they want to brief, query or confirm an issue with another executive. In addition, it's widely used for scheduling, collaboration and file-transfers.

Executives can make the best use of e-mail by taking the time to proof and edit. Some writers of e-mails do this when the e-mail is headed for an important client, but don't bother when it's internal. Sending a badly spelled, rambling e-mail to a co-worker wastes their time and, even more offensively, suggests they are less important than external readers. Brevity is the soul of wit – and the heart of a good e-mail. Of course it takes time. Writers should remember Mark Twain's observation: 'I wrote you a long letter because I didn't have the time to write you a short one.'

Sending them to the right person. Your e-mail programme will helpfully fill in a name if you give it the first few letters of one it remembers. Make sure it's the right name. Misdirecting an e-mail can result in a continuum of embarrassment, starting with a red face and ending with a court case.

A texting time of it
According to a Pew Internet and American Life Project report in July 2006, there's increasing migration from e-mail to text. In a professional environment, text contact is a variable commodity. If you must use text for business purposes, keep messages brief, ideally spelling words in full. Web texting offers greater scope than breaking a nail on tiny telephone keypads, even if it chains you to an office PC or wireless laptop. For example, vodafone.ie has a script box for 160 characters. Two advantages: the web facility allows you to type complete words and you can punctuate properly. If you need more space, it's better to communicate by telephone, e-mail or letter.

Should you find yourself with a constant need to text, it might be wise to invest in a BlackBerry, the all-in-one wireless gadget capable of handling voice, e-mail and SMS messaging – in short, your office in your hand. The keys are bigger and in QWERTY layout. But, remember, you'll never be alone again…

The six rules of e-mail

1. MANY READERS DON'T LIKE ALL CAPS. IT'S HARD TO READ AND SEEMS LIKE YOU'RE SHOUTING!!

2. Use punctuation its hard to read stuff that doesnt have any commas capital letters periods or apostrophes and remember. ur not wrtng a txt msg u no

3. Usee yur spall chacker. Its annyang to try to reede constent misstakes.

4. When forwarding an e-mail, copy and paste what you want to send into a new e-mail and then send it off. This is especially true if you had to dig through tons of layers to get to the heart of the message.

5. Avoid embedding sounds or using 'stationery' in your messages. They take longer to download, can clog company servers and may annoy the recipient. And he or she may have to reformat the text (especially with colour) when replying to make it legible.

6. Remember that attachments over 50k are infuriatingly long to download when you don't have broadband. They may cause your recipient's connection to 'time-out' or the e-mail may be blocked. Keep your files and attachments manageable.

Sending them only to the right person. Promiscuous cc-ing of e-mails is a bad habit of the insecure and imprecise. Don't copy or forward your messages to people who don't need them.

Changing the topic line. When the first e-mail in a sequence is transmitted on Monday, the topic line may be relevant. By Thursday, the issue may have morphed into something completely different, and constantly reusing the original topic line can confuse and irritate. Sometimes, changing the topic line can be desirable for other reasons, such as when the topic isn't business. One man, sending his brother an e-mail headed 'Golf in Mt Juliet', received a fast response ticking him off for the phrase because all e-mails in the brother's company were circulated to a large management group. The sender, suitably humbled, headed the next e-mail '2nd Annual Viagra Users Conference, Mt Juliet'.

Personalising the general. It may save time to send one e-mail to several recipients simultaneously. However, it may make the mail more productive if a few words are included to indicate to each person what action is sought from them.

Keeping it clean. Do not put anything in a business e-mail that is sexually harassing, personally libellous or damaging to a company. The litmus-test is the oldest in the world: *Would I like my mother to see this?* If your mother is a raunchy old broad who loves salacious, slanderous gossip, then an alternative is to ask yourself: *Would I be happy to hear this read in open court by the barrister representing the person who's suing me?*

Avoiding e-mail ADD. The constant arrival of e-mails in your inbox tends to induce a type of Attention Deficit Disorder whose main symptom is assuming that because something is new, it must matter. Confine your visits to your inbox to a set time of the day; accustom your colleagues, customers and family to expecting responses from you at that time; and train them gently by indicating (ideally in person, not by e-mail) that they don't need to mail you every time they sneeze.

Preventing run-on. E-mail 'run-on' happens when you forward an e-mail to someone else because they need to know about something in the latest letter from a correspondent, but you don't check the sequence of letters that have led up to it and to which you're now making your recipient privy. If there's something distracting or insulting to the recipient in one of those letters, it will not be helpful. Check the tail of the comet before you forward correspondence.

Remembering e-mails, unlike relationships, last forever. Several court cases have established that, while one side may delete a sequence of e-mails, and may further instruct the excision of the mails from their Recycle Bin, they may still lurk in the undergrowth of the hard disc. In addition, the recipient may retain them. Finally, they may surface on a flash drive. Moral? Don't ever write a contentious e-mail in a what-the-hell frame of mind, convincing yourself that it'll be gone by morning. E-mails have a longer half-life than enriched plutonium.

Learning better ways to e-mail. An excellent advice website is:

www.ft.com/e-mailoverload

VERSIONING AND BACKING UP... OR SAVING YOUR FILES FOR A RAINY DAY

Let's face it, there's nothing sexy about hard drives. But as we load more and more crucial information and digital mementos – whether e-mail, music or photos – onto PCs, we need a way to back up those files in the event of catastrophic damage that no amount of praying will fix. Because if you use a computer regularly, one of the following events will occur:

- an application will crash
- your computer will crash
- a plug will come loose from the wall

Start by saving files

Save as often as you think about it. There is never a reason not to save. Save every time you take a drink, the phone rings, a commercial comes on or you stop to think. Make this a habit until it becomes second nature. A reminder:

- in any program, go to the File menu, select Save
- in most programs, Ctrl-S for PC or Command-S for Mac

You can set almost every program to save files automatically. Use the Help function to enable this. Advanced advice for PC users can be found at www.microsoft.com/windowsxp/using/setup/learnmore/bott_03july14.mspx and Mac experts can try www.quark.com/service/desktop/support for sophisticated auto-save solutions.

Then back up those files

In addition to saving files, you'll need to copy them to a location other than your hard drive to protect you in the event of disk (and heart) failure. Copy your important files to CD and/or compress your files and e-mail them to yourself or a friend.

CDs – not just for music. CDs are a cheap and reliable way to make back-ups. You have two main options: CD-R and CD-RW, the difference being you can write only once to a CD-R.

Use CD-Rs when you want to make an unchangeable archive of your work. Label the CD with the date you performed the back-up and lodge it somewhere safe. If you get into the habit of doing this once or twice a week, the cost of buying CDs will pale beside the reassurance that you are protected from most mishaps.

Use CD-RWs for day-to-day back-up. These cunning disks allow you to erase and rewrite up to 1,000 times, so if you use your disk daily, it should last about three years. We suggest using two disks lest you lose one.

E-mail attachment. Another way of protecting your sanity is to save and attach files as an e-mail to yourself, having ensured your network or server offers you the space. This method also has the advantage of storing multiple versions of the same file at varying stages of progress and being able to find them by the date on which the e-mail was sent.

Best practice. This habit should scale with the importance of the contents of the disk. If you modify your files once a day, you should back up at least every two days. If you are working constantly on an assignment for five or six hours a day, you should back up every day. A maximum of 15 minutes' archiving over the course of a week is all it takes.

Sing off the same hymnsheet

Any amount of hardware and software products will allow you to over-write, auto-recover and record file changes. For retrieval purposes, most company networks save data hourly. However, care is needed if you are sharing documents to ensure that everyone is working/reworking the correct material – saving documents by name and date is a sensible option. Decide how many previous versions of your data need to be retained. Within documents, Microsoft Word allows the user to track changes. Files can be locked and write-protected with access to relevant users only. Take a pragmatic look at your information requirements and decide whether a simple procedure or an external solution is warranted.

Cyberstyling

Use this style for the following words:

Amazon.com (company trademark as opposed to Web address)
America Online (AOL)
CAD (computer-aided design)
CD-ROM (should be set in small capitals where possible)
cookie
databank, database
diskette
disk (in reference to computers)
DES (data encryption standard)
DOS (disk operating system)
DSL (digital subscriber line)
domain
DVD (digital video disc)
e-business
e-commerce
e-mail
FTP (file transfer protocol)
GSM (global system for mobile)
ICQ (phonetic for I seek you)
IM (instant messaging)
JPEG or JPG (joint picture experts group)
MPEG (motion picture experts group)
PDA (personal digital assistant)
PDF (portable document format)
POP3 (post office protocol)
SMTP (simple mail transport protocol)
TCP-IP (transmission control protocol – Internet protocol)
URL (uniform resource identifier)
WAP (wireless application protocol)
WiFi (wireless fidelity)
WWW (caps – worldwide web)
XBRL (extensible business reporting language)
XML (extensible mark-up language)

Computer terms are also usually lower case, with one or two notable exceptions:

desktop
dotcom
laptop
online
the Internet
intranet
the Net (to avoid confusion with internal network systems)
the Web
website
worldwide web

Cyber-terms are also lower case:

cyber-attack
cyber-soccer
cybernetics
cyberspace
cyberwars

When referring to the following computer products, use:

Adobe PhotoShop
Apple Macintosh, Apple Mac
BlackBerry
eMac
Excel
iMac
InterNIC
iPod
PageMaker
PowerPoint
QuarkXpress

4. NUTS AND BOLTS

ABBREVIATIONS, ACRONYMS AND INITIALISMS

What's an abbreviation?

An abbreviation is the form to which a word or phrase is reduced by contraction and omission – a letter or letters standing for a word or phrase of which they are a part. Some examples: USA for United States of America or IRA for Irish Republican Army.

What's an acronym?

An acronym is a pronounceable word formed from each of the first letters of a descriptive phrase or by combining the initial letters or parts of words from that phrase. Some examples: NATO for North Atlantic Treaty Organization and MODEM for MODulator/DEModulator. Sometimes the acronym becomes the standard term and the full form is used only in explanatory contexts.

Do not confuse acronyms with anagrams, which are words or phrases the letters of which can be rearranged into other words or phrases. These are more likely to be found in the Crossaire and Simplex crossword puzzles in *The Irish Times* than in business writing.

What's an initialism?

An initialism is an abbreviation consisting of the first letter or letters of words in a phrase (for example, CIE for Coras Iompar Éireann), syllables or components of a word (TNT for trinitrotoluene), or a combination of words and syllables (ESP for extrasensory perception). They are pronounced by spelling out the letters one by one rather than as a solid word.

Although these definitions should leave little room for confusion, they are not totally unambiguous. The following statements may add some clarity:

- All acronyms are abbreviations, but all abbreviations are not acronyms.
- Some abbreviations are initialisms.

In other words, acronyms are a subset of abbreviations.

It can be helpful to consider the differences in pronunciation. An abbreviation that is formed from the first letter or letters of words in a phrase and pronounced letter by letter is an initialism. An abbreviation formed from the first letter or letters of words in a phrase and pronounced as a word is an acronym. If you're completely bewildered by now, just consider everything else an abbreviation. This table may explain:

Abbreviations, Acronyms and Initialisms			
Type	**Formed**	**Pronounced**	**Examples**
abbreviation	by contraction and omission of any given number of letters of a word or phrase	as a word or full phrase	etc, inc, info, Mac
acronym	from the first letter or letters of words in a phrase	as a word	NATO, UNESCO, Benelux, radar
initialism	from the first letter or letters of words in a phrase	letter by letter	HTML, IMF, TV, UN

Styling

Some style guides suggest using periods with acronyms or abbreviations – for example, the U.K. for United Kingdom. Practice varies, but in modern usage it is increasingly common (and much simpler) to omit them.

On the subject of periods or full stops, we suggest not using them with acronyms or abbreviations. This would include academic awards and degrees (eg, BA, MA, MPhil, BPhil, PhD, for example). We would also omit the full stops in abbreviations such as eg, ie, etc, Dr, Mr, Mrs, am, pm.

Increasingly, abbreviations, acronyms and initialisms are appearing in newspapers with only their first letter in upper case. To our knowledge, there are no such words as Siptu, Nato and Isme. Avoid this practice unless you're certain an organisation has rebranded itself in this way. Log on to official websites to check.

Usage

When using an acronym such as IBEC, spell out the terms the first time round, with the acronym in brackets: The Irish Business and Employers Confederation (IBEC). Thereafter, use the acronym by itself, knowing your readers can turn back to the first reference if they've forgotten its import.

When in doubt, use the entire term:

customer relationship management	*instead of*	CRM
key performance indicators	*instead of*	KPI
business process outsourcing	*instead of*	BPO
strengths, weaknesses, opportunities and threats	*instead of*	SWOT
Public Private Partnership	*instead of*	PPP
Cork University Hospital or		
Children's University Hospital, Temple St.	*instead of*	CUH

Exceptions are HR, MBA, and PR.

CAPITALISATION (AND WHEN NOT TO...)

Capital (upper case) letters have three uses:

• to give emphasis as in official titles and words
• to distinguish proper nouns and adjectives from common ones
• to highlight words in headings and captions

Overcapitalisation is common and it's often used incorrectly for emphasis. Apart from making text look grandiose and self-important, overcapitalisation slows down reading and typing speeds, and hurts your eyes. Typographically, the trend in modern English is towards fewer capitals. As a rule of thumb, when you're in doubt or feel something looks patently ridiculous, use lower case.

Which is all very well, but how do you strike a balance when writing in the commercial environment where people are sensitive to their roles

Acronyms are bundles of initials purporting to convey meaning. They sometimes succeed.

IBM, for example, conjures up for most readers a corporate entity, brand and product range which would not be invoked by International Business Machines, the company's full title. It will take some time before KFC achieves the same status. Older consumers know it – and will continue to refer to it – as Kentucky Fried Chicken.

Not an acronym, merely an excrescence, is 'etc', one of the most insulting usages in the English language. Not that it actually belongs in the English language: in its unabbreviated form, it's et cetera and, therefore, a Latinism. We mention this only because many people assume it's 'ek cetera'.

Etc indicates to the reader that the writer knows a bunch of stuff over and above what is listed, but can't be bothered to share it. We believe if an author or journalist knows more than he or she is telling, it's time to shut up about it, rather than put a little flag down to alert the reader that they're being dissed.

On the subject of abbreviated Latin phrases, let us issue a warning about eg and ie. They don't justify the effort the writer has to make to get the punctuation marks around their feet right. Use the modern equivalents: 'for example' (or 'for instance') and 'that is'.

and titles? You can hide behind the weight of *The Economist Style Guide* with this answer: 'The general rule is to dignify with capital letters organisations and institutions, but not people.'

The following are acceptable conventions:

1. Use initial capitals for proper nouns and names: The Office of the Director of Corporate Enforcement.

2. Capitalise the names of books, films and other major works: *Scary Movie 4*. A general guideline is to capitalise the first word, all proper nouns and key words, including pronouns. Another style, favoured by many historians, is to capitalise only proper nouns, the first word of the title and the first word following a colon: *A history of Reginald Smith: The life of an explorer*. Use one style consistently – it is not helpful to reproduce capitalisations exactly as they appear on the book jacket (which will only cause you to panic when you find a title in all caps).

3. In headlines, capitalise first words and all words apart from prepositions and conjunctions of more than five letters: 'Leading from the Middle'. Headings and sub-headings within publications should be treated in the same way as sentences; there is no need to use capital letters for any words other than the first word and any proper nouns.

4. Always use lower case for rough descriptions or references:

- the census (National Numeracy Strategy)
- the framework (Leadership Development Framework)
- the programme (the NPQH programme)
- the Northern Ireland education department (Department for Education and Skills in its full form)

The one important exception is 'the College' when referring to academic institutions with College in their names.

5. Capitalise Satan but not the devil.

6. Use upper case for definite geographical places, regions, areas and countries: The Barrow Walk, Bible Belt, Cotton Belt, The Hague, the Highlands of Scotland, the Leinster Way, the Middle East, the Midwest, the Nore Valley, South-East Asia, Western Europe.

7. Use upper case for cities: Guatemala City, Ho Chi Minh City, Kuwait City, New York City, Panama City and Quebec City, even though 'City' is not part

It's in the use of short forms that uncertainty arises. Short forms are usually written in lower case when used in a non-specific sense, when they're preceded by a possessive, demonstrative or other type of adjective, and when used adjectivally or in an adjectival form:

'We have formed a committee to consider the matter.' (non-specific)

'The committee meeting was held in The Westin this afternoon.' (adjectival)

'Our committee held its monthly meeting this morning.' (possessive)

of their names, as it is in Mexico City, Dodge City, Kansas City, Quezon City, Oklahoma City or Salt Lake City. This stops the reader confusing the name of the city with the name of the country, province or state.

8. Use lower case for seasons of the year in running text: 'The next edition of this book will be printed in summer 2007.' But use upper case for seasons in the title of a publication: 'ICAI Syllabus: Winter 2006-2007'.

9. Use capitals for particular buildings even if the name is not strictly accurate: the Chrysler Building, the Empire State Building, the Foreign Office, Liberty Hall, Government Buildings or Christ Church.

10. For awards and decorations, use upper case: Nobel Prize, Pulitzer Prize, Medal of Honour, Victoria Cross, Knighthood, OBE, MBE.

11. Use lower case for points of the compass: east, west, north and south. 'The level of precipitation in the north-west of Ireland exceeds that of the south-east.' (See Punctuation, The hyphen, in this section.)

12. Terms are capitalised when used as titles, but should be lower case when referring to the office or appointment: 'Former Tánaiste and Minister for Health and Children Mary Harney'. (Also note no commas in her official title in this instance.) But, 'deputy Lord Mayor Robert Murphy' (lower case d).

However, to confuse matters somewhat, when short forms of government entities stand for the full title and are intended to carry its full force, they are usually capitalised: 'The Minister's position on the privatisation of Iarnród Éireann remains unchanged.' 'The Government reversed its decision on decentralisation.' (The old British convention was to capitalise government in this case, but *The Guardian* and other style guides have stopped doing this – in America it was never correct.) Likewise, use capitals when referring to the Opposition or the Leader of the Opposition (both in the UK House of Parliament and when referring to the party or person eyeballing the Taoiseach across the floor of Leinster House).

The principles here are similar to those for academic attributions. Consistency is imperative. To make life simple, when organisations, government departments, official bodies and office-holders are referred to by anything other than their precise title, use lower case.

13. The following are capitalised: Act, Article, Bill, Chapter, Constitution, Convention, Court (when referring to a specific court such as the High Court, Supreme Court or Central Criminal Court), Directive,

For example, choose lower case for the archbishop of Dublin unless used before the name of the person who holds the office.

'Archbishop of Dublin Diarmuid Martin addressed the congregation in the Pro-Cathedral on Sunday.'

'The Church of Ireland archbishop, Dr John Neill, led the prayers in Saint Patrick's Cathedral.'

Capitalise Archdiocese of Dublin or the Tuam Archdiocese, but use lower case if it stands alone – for example, an American archdiocese has filed for bankruptcy in the light of recent litigation. Any noun preceded by an indefinite article should be lower case.

In general usage, capitalise titles of office or rank when identifying the people involved:

'Pope Benedict XVI visited Germany in May 2006.'

'Prime Minister Tony Blair reshuffled his cabinet today.'

'A visit by Her Royal Highness Princess Anne is planned.'

but:

'The prime ministers of the seven countries attended the summit.'

'The princess attended the Horse Show.'

Titles used in direct address are capitalised.

'Tell us, President Clinton...'

'A question for you, Professor...'

Member States, Part (as in Part III of the 1967 Act), Regulations (when specifying an EU Regulation), Schedule.

14. Use upper case for historical periods or events: Art Deco, Art Nouveau, Bolshevik Revolution, Black Death, Bronze Age, Civil War, Cold War, Cultural Revolution, Great Depression, Middle Ages, Renaissance, Restoration, Russian Revolution, Thirty Years War, War of the Roses.

15. Use upper case for political terms: Bolshevik, Communist, Congress, Crown, Dáil, Democrat, European Commission, European Parliament, Maastricht Treaty, Parliament, Republican, Senate, Tory, Treaty of Rome, Whig, Versailles Treaty, Warsaw Pact.

16. Use upper case for trade names: Band-Aid, Caterpillar, Coke, Hoover, MasterCard, Pepsi, Rogaine, Teflon, Unislim, Valium, Viagra, Visa, Walkman, Xanax. (Interestingly, rayon is not a trade name but Nylon is.)

GRAMMAR

People sometimes describe grammar as the rules of a language. But no language has rules because – apart from Esperanto – no language was invented. Languages were started by people making sounds that evolved into words, phrases and sentences. What we call 'grammar' is simply a reflection of a language at a particular time. Grammar is about speaking and writing well in the dialect of the day.

Beginning a sentence with 'And' or 'But'
Writers get worked up about whether 'and' or 'but' can be used at the beginning of a sentence. Here's what R.W. Burchfield has to say on the subject in *The New Fowler's Modern English Usage*:

> There is a persistent belief that it is improper to begin a sentence with And, but this prohibition has been cheerfully ignored by standard authors from Anglo-Saxon times onwards. An initial And is a useful aid to writers as the narrative continues.

The same is true of the conjunction 'but'. A sentence starting with 'and' or 'but' will naturally highlight its transitional function. If you're worried you'll diminish the quality of your writing with a more-casual approach, ask these questions: Will the sentence and paragraph function just as well without the 'and' or 'but'? Should the sentence in question be connected to the previous sentence?

If the 'and' or 'but' still seems appropriate, use it.

Beginning a sentence with 'Because'

The idea you shouldn't begin a sentence with 'because' also retains a mysterious grip on people's sense of writing proprieties. Maybe they're afraid such a sentence could well end up as a fragment:

'Because e-mail now plays such a huge role in our communications industry.'

Indeed, this does look suspiciously like a sentence splinter (see Grammar, Sentence errors, in this section). However, when the 'because' clause is properly connected to another idea, there's nothing wrong with it:

'Because e-mail now plays such a huge role in our communications industry, the postal service would like to see it taxed in some manner.'

Non sequiturs

This term comes from the Latin for 'it does not follow'. If you're being strict and formal, a non sequitur occurs in text when an action or decree described is unrelated to the preceding event or thought. It is logically, temporally and spatially incoherent. In plain English, your writing doesn't add up. An example:

'Worn elegantly around Uma Thurman's neck, the Hope Diamond was worth $80 million.'

Would it have been worth less – or indeed more – if she'd worn it around her wrist or ankle? Perhaps the writer meant:

'The Hope Diamond, worn elegantly as a necklace by Uma Thurman, was worth $80 million.'

It's still clumsy but it makes sense. (Incidentally, the diamond is variously valued at anywhere from $200,000 to a quarter of a billion dollars and generally lives in the Smithsonian Museum.)

On the subject of showbiz excess, another non sequitur:

'Uma now lives in Hollywood; she must only be a size 4.'

Does this mean the lovely lady will be banished to her New York brownstone if she creeps up to a size 6? Or could the writer's train of thought have been more clearly expressed?

'Uma now lives in Hollywood, where it's fashionable to be a size 4.'

Non sequiturs don't just happen within sentences. You can make whole unfounded leaps over the space of two or three:

'Some believe the Coalition is dogmatic and anachronistic in its views. The refugees should be allowed to stay in the cathedral until their status is established.'

A reader may make the link between the first and second sentence in the development of the writer's argument. Or he may not because, on closer examination, there's no real transition and the second sentence doesn't offer any reason why the refugees should be allowed stay in the cathedral. A slight rewrite clarifies matters:

'Some believe, because the Coalition has been dogmatic and anachronistic in its views, the refugees should be allowed to stay in the cathedral until their status has been established.'

The golden rule of writing applies:

What have I written? What does it mean?

Politically correct pronouns

How do you write a sentence in the age of political correctness and keep the gender open? Consider this (feminine) example:

'In today's classroom, the student often finds herself swamped with huge reading lists.'

Use a plural:

'In today's classrooms, students often find themselves swamped with huge reading lists.'

Lose the personal touch:

'In today's classrooms, the student is often swamped with a huge reading list.'

Replace the third-person pronoun (he or she) with the first person (I or we) or second person (you):

> 'In today's classroom, we students often find ourselves swamped with huge reading lists.'

Get regal:

> 'As a student in today's classroom, one often finds oneself swamped with huge reading lists.'

One can write in this manner but one may find oneself sounding ridiculous and affected. One should use this form as a last resort. (See A List of Usages in this section.)

A sticky area is when dealing with modifiers – in this instance, 'every':

> 'Every student who passes this course will find their writing has improved.'

Correct grammar would dictate that the singular modifier 'every' of the noun 'student' should be followed by a singular pronoun:

> 'Every student who passes this course will find his or her writing has improved.'

However, as with split infinitives, you can relax this rule if there is a danger that a sentence will become clumsy. The use of the plural pronoun their following the singular case is becoming more accepted in business writing:

> 'Every writer should be careful with their spell-checker functions.'

Sentence errors

There are three major sentence errors – comma splices, fusions and fragments. They distract your readers and impede their ability to follow your train of thought. But once spotted, they're easy to repair.

The comma splice (AKA the seamstress). This occurs where a comma with no conjunction joins two independent clauses:

> 'We have five extra monkeys arriving on Monday, we need more nuts.'

Removing the comma doesn't help the reader; it results in a run-on sentence. But the zookeeper has a few corrective options.

Parts of speech – a reminder

noun: name of a person, place or thing

pronoun: a word that takes the place of a noun

verb: a 'doing' or 'being' word

adjective: describes or gives extra meaning to a noun

adverb: describes or gives extra meaning to a verb

phrase: a word-group that acts as a part of speech (such as an adverb) and does not contain a verb

clause: a word-group that contains a verb and expresses a complete thought

sentence: a collection of words that makes up at least one clause, which begins with a capital letter and ends with a full stop, question mark or exclamation mark

sext: a collection of sentences designed to achieve a purpose

'Anyone who can improve a sentence of mine by the omission or placement of a comma is looked upon as my dearest friend.'
George Moore

Change the comma to a semicolon:

'We have five extra monkeys arriving on Monday; we need more nuts.'

Write the clauses as separate sentences:

'We have five extra monkeys arriving on Monday. We need more nuts.'

Insert a conjunction after the comma:

'We have five extra monkeys arriving on Monday, and we need more nuts.'

Make one clause dependent on the other:

'Because we have five extra monkeys arriving on Monday, we need more nuts.'

The fused sentence (AKA **the runaway**). This joins two or more complete sentences with no punctuation. Fused sentences look and behave like comma splices – but because no comma is involved they are harder to spot. When reading or sounding out sentences, try to be aware of the independent clauses. When you see two or more in the same sentence with no punctuation you've caught a runaway:

'My grandmother refuses to go to bed early she's a gamey old broad she thinks she's going to miss out on some of the action.'

Can be rewritten (more respectfully) as:

'My grandmother refuses to go to bed early – she thinks she's going to miss out on some of the action. She's a fabulous woman.'

The sentence fragment (AKA **the chopper**). These are incomplete sentences – usually chunks of text that have become disconnected from the main clause. They're missing a subject, a verb, or both. If you're suspicious, read the text and ask these questions: Is there a verb? If not, supply one. Is there a subject? If not, supply one.

'Author of *Midnight's Children*, the Booker award-winning novel.' (no subject or verb)

'Salman Rushdie is the author of *Midnight's Children*, the Booker award-winning novel.' (with a subject and verb)

Split infinitives

The split infinitive rule was invented in the 19th Century by classically obsessed scholars who wanted English to be like Latin and Greek (whose one-word infinitives cannot be split). As a result, most readers have been trained to recognise split infinitives as a mistake. But modern English is becoming less prescriptive and doesn't see them as violating some real law of language. Indeed, a split infinitive may be the most graceful and rhythmic way to say something. What if Captain Kirk had said, 'Boldly to go where no man has gone before.' So, you can split infinitives, but only occasionally, because many people will think you're making an ignorant mistake. *Merriam-Webster's Collegiate Dictionary* puts it well: 'Split them when you need to… The objection to the split infinitive has never had a rational basis.'

Subject and predicate – living in harmony

Subject-predicate disagreement happens when singular subjects are used with plural predicates and vice versa. For example:

'Whether I study for my Prof 2 exam or go drinking are decisions I have to make.'

Which, in the cold and sober light of day, should read:

'Whether I study for my Prof 2 exam or go drinking is a decision I have to make.'

Or, taking a more subtle illustration:

'Agreement within the Coalition and the passing of the Bill is necessary for any real change to take effect.'

Should read:

'Agreement within the Coalition and the passing of the Bill are necessary for real change to occur.'

The following is a common mistake:

'The manager, and the team, have decided not to appeal the referee's decision.'

Your MS Word spell-check will have spotted this because it should be:

'The manager, and the team, has decided not to appeal the referee's decision.'

In this case, the manager is the subject. The team is an ancillary subject and for the purpose of grammar is effectively ignored. But if they are joint subjects with equal weight in the sentence, then you should write:

> 'The manager and the team have decided not to appeal the referee's decision.'

Tenses

A confession: your authors have in their time been humiliated by merciless editors who spiked our stories for bad grammar or handed back proofs scored so red they looked liked they'd mopped an abattoir floor. Tenses were usually the source of such anger and despair.

We learned (and continue to learn) that some writers and readers are like musicians who have been classically trained. They're purists. Others love the jazz age with its fluidity and improvisation and are more forgiving. The younger ones who didn't have grammar battered into them by the brothers and nuns live in the age of staccato rap. They don't give a damn as long as they get the message across. Which is fine and dandy once we all understand the basic sequence of notes and phrases. Sentences are like musical composition. If someone has to ask what's going on and whether it's a verse or a chorus, you and your tenses are in trouble.

Put simply, tenses allow you to express notions of the past, present and future. They define the actions of verbs and ground them in relation to time. The trick is to construct sentences with simple, logical verbs.

Depending on who you ask, there are myriad definitions and categories of tenses. To keep it simple, let's group them so:

Perfect tenses tell us that an action has been completed:

present perfect	I have read
past perfect	I had read
future perfect	I will have read

Progressive tenses tell us that an action is still continuing in the past, present and future:

present progressive	I am reading
past progressive	I was reading
future progressive	I will be reading

And here's where it gets technical…

present perfect progressive	I have been reading
past perfect progressive	I had been reading
future perfect progressive	I will have been reading

Despite their complexity, these classifications are useful because they show the movement and transition of a verb. It's in reporting – describing one or two steps back in time – where most problems arise.

At the risk of sounding like Dr Who, the moment a word is spoken or a deed has been done, it exists in the past. When you're reporting something in straightforward terms, use the past tense for attribution. We all know what the past tense is: he did; she said; the company lost; the division won. The present tense can be appropriate in business communication because it energises and adds brio, but you need to be careful integrating it with past material. Once you start a paragraph, keep the tenses consistent in context and logical when referring back in time.

Taking extra care with tenses that relate to what's gone before is important not only for the beauty and elegance of language (which may seem too much to care about on a screaming deadline), but also for precision and the sake of your reader. If you write, for example, that: 'He has been in Mountjoy for 10 years,' you're giving the extra information that he's still banged up because the tense implies continuation. And you may not want to do that. If you use the ordinary past tense – 'He was in Mountjoy for 10 years' – you're saying he isn't there anymore (and, depending on your next sentence, may be roaming the streets doing good works or breaking into your car).

Use the simple past tense when whatever you're writing about is over and done with. A recent theatre programme proclaimed:

'Now one of Ireland's leading playwrights, he is a former director who has worked with Hilton Edwards, Donal McCann and Maureen Potter.'

As he no longer works as a director and as those thespians are no longer alive to be worked with, it should have read 'who worked with'.

Reported speech – a word or two or three. When you're quoting someone or from source material in written work, the verb 'said' is the governing verb and, therefore, controls the tenses of any subordinate verbs. Note that 'said' is in the past tense. The same applies to words such as 'reported', 'claimed' or 'demonstrated'.

Because you're writing about past actions, the tenses of subordinate verbs must be changed. So the present is changed to the past, the perfect to the past perfect and the future to the conditional. This is called following the sequence of tenses:

'She announced she would cap her investment at 5 percent.'

And not:

'She announced she will cap her investment at 5 percent.'

'He said he thought the bombing was immoral.'

And not:

'He said he thinks the bombing is immoral.'

There are always exceptions. You may notice not all newspapers use the sequence of tenses, although it is grammatically correct. Their house styles take the view that, although attribution normally will be in the past tense, verbs within the attributed statement may very well be in present tense. They would argue, for example, that someone's opinion, expressed to a journalist on a particular day, still stands:

'He said he thinks the budget favours the wealthy.'

In business writing, you may cite current documents in the present tense:

'The company's annual report shows that strong rental yields accounted for the growth in profitability.'

However, to let yourself off the grammatical hook, the (quite literally) timeless and useful phrase 'according to' may be used when writing about data, statistics or statement of fact.

'According to the company's annual report, strong rental yields accounted for the growth in profitability.'

That

'That' is used as a conjunction to connect a subordinate clause to a preceding verb. (For that/which, see A List of Usages in this section.) It's sometimes called the 'expletive that'. Indeed, the word is often omitted to good effect, but its very ease of omission leads some editors to lick their biros and strike out 'that' everywhere it appears. In the following sentences, we can happily lose the 'that' (or keep it, depending on how the sentence sounds):

'John knew [that] he was about to be fired.'

'She definitely felt [that] her fellow employees hadn't supported her.'

'We hope [that] Marsha doesn't get eye-strain reading this text. '

As a rule, if a sentence feels just as good without the 'that', if no ambiguity results from its exclusion and if the wording is more efficient or elegant without it, we can safely leave out the 'that'.

There are three circumstances in which we should retain the conjunction 'that':

- when a time element intervenes between the verb and the clause: 'The director said yesterday that production in this department was down 50 percent.' (Note the position of 'yesterday'.)
- when the verb of the clause is delayed: 'Our annual report revealed that some losses sustained by this department in the third quarter of last year when compared with the previous time-frame activities were worse than previously thought.' (Note the distance between the subject, 'losses', and its verb, 'were'.)
- when a second 'that' can clear up who said or did what: 'The CEO said that Isobel's department was slacking off and that production dropped dangerously in the last quarter.' (Did the CEO say that production dropped or was the drop a result of what he said about Isobel's department? The second 'that' makes the sentence clear.)

References

The Economist Style Guide, 9th Edition (Profile Books, 2005).

Theodore Bernstein, *Dos, Don'ts & Maybes of English Usage* (Gramercy Books, New York, 1999).

Randolph Quirk and Sidney Greenbaum, *A University Grammar of English* (Longman Group, 1993).

Lynn Quitman Troyka and Doug Hess, *Quick Access: Reference for Writers* (Simon & Schuster, New York, 2006).

William A. Sabin, *The Gregg Reference Manual* (McGraw-Hill, New York, 2001).

Bill Walsh, *Lapsing into a Comma* (Contemporary Books, New York, 2000).

PUNCTUATION

'My attitude toward punctuation is that it ought to be as conventional as possible. The game of golf would lose a good deal if croquet mallets and billiard cues were allowed on the putting green. You ought to be able to show that you can do it a good deal better than anyone else with the regular tools before you have a licence to bring in your own improvements.'

Ernest Hemingway

Punctuation marks are signals to your readers. In speaking, we can pause, stop or change our tone of voice. In writing, we use marks of punctuation to emphasise and clarify what we mean.

The apostrophe (')

Cue the most troublesome punctuation mark in English. No other keystroke causes so much bewilderment, or is so often misused. On the one hand, shops offer pizza's, video's, greeting's cards and ladie's clothing; on the other, they offer childrens shoes, builders tools and artists supplies.

The key rule is simple. Use apostrophes to show possession. Place the apostrophe depending on whether the subject is singular or plural:

the reader's need	the readers' needs
the author's opinion	the authors' opinions
the library's budget	the libraries' order lists

The apostrophe is also used in writing contractions – shortened forms of words from which one or more letters have been omitted. In standard English, this generally happens with a small number of conventional items, mostly involving verbs. Here are some examples, with their uncontracted equivalents:

it's	it is *or* it has
we'll	we will *or* we shall
they've	they have
can't	can not *or* cannot
he'd	he would *or* he had
aren't	are not
won't	will not

Consider content, context and audience when deciding if the use of contractions is appropriate – it can make formal writing seem less considered.

Possessive plurals are worth a word or two. Note the placing of the apostrophe:

two institutes' findings
four years' experience
previous years' figures

(The Hugh Grant and Sandra Bullock rom-com, *Two Weeks Notice*, should have been written as *Two Weeks' Notice*. Warner Bros must have thought this might confuse us.)

If you're wondering how to use an apostrophe when attributing ownership to more than one person or company, consider them as one unit of speech and place the apostrophe on the last word:

'Ginger Rogers and Fred Astaire's choreography revolutionised the art of dance.'

When a year is written in an abbreviated form it should take an apostrophe – The '98 Rebellion, for example. This is fine in certain set or historic expressions. However, don't put apostrophes before the 's' in decades: the 1970s or '70s, not the 1970's.

And, lastly, some words about the cardinal sin. Do not confuse it's with its. It's is a contraction of it is, whereas its is a possessive pronoun. It's important to get this right before your company issues its annual report.

The colon (:) and the semi-colon (;)

Colons and semicolons have a few basic rules that are easy to master. They draw particular attention to the text that follows.

In essence, a colon separates two logically related clauses, fulfilling the same function as words such as namely, that is, as, for example, because, as follows and therefore. Here's a case in point:

'The baker sold all shapes and sizes of pastry: I should like to be a baker.'

Another function of the colon is to lead from an introduction to main theme:

'The question is universal: what is the secret of a happy life?'

A colon will lead the reader from cause to effect:

'It started to snow: racing was abandoned.' (Note the use of lower case after the colon.)

The colon can help bring you from a general statement to a specific example:

'Birmingham has some excellent restaurants: Simpson's in Edgbaston has two Michelin stars.'

You can position the colon after a complete statement in order to introduce one or more closely related ideas, such as a series of directions, a list, or a quotation or other comment illustrating or explaining the statement:

'*The Sunday Times* has myriad sections: news, sports, news review, arts, homes and gardens, and two glossy magazines.'

'The strategies of corporatist industrial unionism have proven ineffective: compromises and concessions have left the labour movement in a weakened position in the new "flexible" economy.'

You can also use colons between closely connected sentence elements, although this should be done sparingly:

'The focus group results point to only one conclusion: indifference.'

If you're feeling brave and literary, *Fowler's Modern English Usage* suggests using colons for 'gnomic contrasts':

'Man proposes: God disposes.'

In the essays of mere mortals, however, colons are used most frequently to introduce quotations. They add emphasis to the text that follows in ways that the use of a comma may not. If you do use a colon, be sure that the quotation is not integrally connected to the grammar of the introductory sentence:

'In the *Apology* Socrates says: "The unexamined life is not worth living." '

Colons can also be used after the salutation in a business letter:

Dear Ms Swan:

We don't like this trend. (See Curriculum Vitae Cover Letters, Section 2.)

Colons are always used between chapter and verse in biblical references:

Genesis 1:18

Colons are often used between the hour and minutes in time notation:

'It began snowing at 5:15 pm.'

Some writers think that because semicolons look like fancy commas, they can be used any time they need commas but want a decorative or formal effect. This is a mistake. Commas and semicolons have different grammatical functions.

Semicolons have only two purposes. First, they allow you to connect two independent clauses in a single sentence:

> You can do this to achieve a more flowing style; the semicolon tells your reader that he has encountered a grammatical break, but implies there is a close connection between the two independent clauses.

(Using a full stop to separate two independent clauses has a more conclusive effect. It forces more of a pause on the reader's part. That's the beauty of full stops. They keep sentences short. They convey energy. They bring the reader with you.)

Their second purpose is to replace commas when you write lists or a series of text with internal commas (that is, where commas occur within one or more items). In such cases, separating the items with other commas is confusing so you can use the semicolon to make a sentence more readable:

> 'Hobbes's *Leviathan* has many memorable passages: his audacious view of human beings as mere mechanical constructions; his evocation of a brutish, savage state of nature; his establishment of a binding, permanent social contract to protect individuals; and his refusal to place any limits on the power of a duly established ruler.'

That long sentence is an example of the colon and semicolon working in harmony. If Hobbes's thoughts had been punctuated with commas alone, the text would have been impossible to read. (It's tough going as it stands.) A simpler example might be:

> 'The original members of The Shadows were Terry Smart, drums; Ken Pavey, guitar; Norman Mitham, guitar; Ian Samwell, bass; and Cliff Richard, guitar and vocals. Hank Marvin and Bruce Welch were later additions to the group.'

The comma (,)

The comma is sometimes viewed as a weak, slightly lame form of punctuation. This is a tad unfair. It's useful for separating the structural elements of sentences into manageable, almost conversational, segments.

The rules as set out here are those found in traditional handbooks; however, in certain rhetorical contexts and for specific purposes, as with most things in life, these rules may be broken.

1. Use commas to separate two or more co-ordinate adjectives that describe the same noun. Co-ordinate adjectives are adjectives with equal – 'co'-ordinate – status in describing the noun; neither adjective is subordinate to the other. This is an easy, simple textbook, for example.

You can decide if two adjectives in a row are co-ordinate by asking the following questions:

- Does the sentence make sense if the adjectives are written in reverse order?
- Does the sentence make sense if the adjectives are written with the word 'and' between them?

If you answer yes to these questions, then the adjectives are co-ordinate and should be separated by a comma.

Here are some examples of co-ordinate and non-co-ordinate adjectives:

'He was a difficult, restless child.' (co-ordinate)
'They lived in a white minimalist house.' (non-co-ordinate)
'Your sister has an easy, happy smile.' (co-ordinate)
'She often wore a gray linen suit.' (non-co-ordinate)

2. Use commas to separate three or more words, phrases or clauses written in a series.

'Bunreacht na hÉireann established the legislative, executive and judicial branches of government in Ireland in 1937.'

'Chartered Accountants are expected to be ethical, honest and fair in their dealings.'

'The prosecutor argued that the defendant, who was at the scene of the crime, had a strong revenge motive and access to a lump hammer, was guilty of assault.'

Note that there are two schools of thought on including a comma before 'and' in a list: in the example above 'legislative, executive, and judicial' would have been equally correct, but we prefer to include it only when it's necessary for clarity.

3. Use a pair of commas in the middle of a sentence to set off clauses, phrases and words that aren't essential to its meaning. Place one comma before to indicate the beginning of the pause and another at the end to indicate the finish of the pause. To help decide whether a sentence element is essential, ask yourself if you leave out the clause, phrase or word, does the sentence still make sense?

> 'That Tuesday, which happens to be my birthday, is the only day when I'm free to travel to New York.' (clause)
> 'This restaurant is a blaze of colour and music. The food, on the other hand, is bland and tasteless.' (phrase)
> 'I appreciate your time and trouble. In this case, however, you seem to have over-exerted yourself.' (word)

4. Commas separate independent clauses when they are joined by any of these seven coordinating conjunctions: and, but, for, or, nor, so, yet.

> 'The game was over, but the crowd refused to leave.'

> 'The editor explained her question, yet the authors still didn't seem to understand.'

> 'Yesterday was filing date, so she stayed late to complete the tax return.'

5. Use commas after an introductory clause, phrases or words that come before the main clause. Starter words that may be followed by commas include: after, although, as, because, if, since, when, whereas, while.

> 'Because she didn't study, she failed the exam.'

> 'If you are ill, you ought to see a doctor.'

> 'When the rain stops falling, we'll mow the lawn.'

6. Use a comma near or at the end of a sentence to separate contrasted co-ordinate elements or to indicate a distinct pause or shift.

> 'He was merely ill informed, not stupid.'

> 'The chimpanzee seemed reflective, almost human.'

> 'The adviser seemed innocent, even gullible.'

7. Use a comma to shift between the main discourse and a quotation.

> 'John muttered, "I'll see you tomorrow then." '

' "I was able to complete the assignment," she answered, "despite your unreasonable deadline." '

'In 1848, Marx wrote, "Workers of the world, unite!" '

8. Take care with comma placement around names.

'Abso Ltd chief executive officer Marilyn Murphy said her company would weather the difficult economic conditions for small businesses.' (no commas)

'The chief executive officer of Abso Ltd, Marilyn Murphy, said her company would weather the difficult economic conditions for small businesses.' (two commas)

'Abso Ltd's chief executive officer, Marilyn Murphy, said her company would weather the difficult economic conditions for small businesses.' (two commas)

In the first example, the company and position title act as adjectives describing Marilyn Murphy, in much the same way as a shorter personal title such as Ms or Mrs would. So you don't need commas. In the second and third examples, the definite article (the) is either used overtly or is implied, making it possible for you to read over her name with commas around it while the sentences still make sense.

It is never correct to use one comma with a name:

'Abso Ltd's chief executive officer Marilyn Murphy, said her company would weather the difficult economic conditions for small businesses.'

This would interrupt the meaning of the sentence. When it comes to names and titles, use two commas or none, but never just one.

Some words of warning:

1. Don't use commas to separate the subject from the verb: 'A five-year-old car, is now subject to an NCT before it is deemed roadworthy.' (incorrect)

2. Don't put a comma between the two verbs or verb phrases in a compound predicate: 'We laid out our text books, and began cramming.' (incorrect)

3. Don't put a comma after the main clause when a dependent (subordinate) clause follows it – except for cases of extreme contrast: 'She failed her exam, because she didn't study.' (incorrect)

'She was still quite upset, although she had passed the other four modules.' (correct)

The dash (–)

Use a dash to emphasise a point or to set off an explanatory comment. Don't overuse dashes or they'll lose their impact:

'To some readers, our pointers on grammar may seem obvious – even simplistic.'

'In terms of public perception – that is, in terms of garnering support from state legislators, parents, donors and university administrators – English departments are primarily places where advanced literacy is taught.'

You can use dashes for an appositive phrase that already includes commas:

'The Bennet sisters – Elizabeth, Jane and Kitty – left Mr Darcy's house after the dance had ended.'

Dashes function in some ways like parentheses (being used in pairs to set off a comment within a larger sentence) and in some ways like colons (being used to introduce material illustrating or emphasising the preceding statement). If you're wondering whether to use brackets or dashes, comments set off with a pair of dashes appear more important to the main sentence than do comments in parentheses. And material introduced after a single dash will seem more emphatic than text introduced with a colon.

The ellipsis (…)

An ellipsis is used to mark the omission of words. It is three full stops; a fourth full stop is not required. Whenever possible, use the correct symbol for the ellipsis (Alt+colon on a Mac and Alt+Ctrl+full stop on a PC) rather than hitting a full stop three times. This makes them consistent and spaces the points correctly. It also ensures they can't split across lines.

The exclamation mark (!)

Known in the trade as a bang or a shriek mark or a screamer, it's used at the end of a sentence or a short phrase that expresses strong feeling.

Hyphens (-), En Dashes (–) and Em Dashes (—): The Difference

Most of us weren't even aware of the distinction between the hyphen, en dash and the em dash until the arrival of word processors when software programs allowed us to use marks of punctuation that once had been available only to professional printers.

The hyphen is the shortest of the three and is used to combine words. The en dash is slightly longer than the hyphen but not as long as an em dash. (Harking back to days of yore, it is the width of a typesetter's letter 'N' whereas the em dash is the width of the letter 'M'.)

The en dash is the mark of punctuation we think of as a 'normal' dash in regard to a sentence; it is used to create a strong break in the structure of a sentence, whether within or at the end of it. A colon and a dash are often interchangeable, though the colon is more formal, and the dash can be used in pairs to set off a phrase or clause.

An em dash is used in exactly the same grammatical way as an en dash – but always use a space on either side of an en dash. The em dash is always closed up against the words on either side of it—never spaced.

Remember, when using a hyphen don't use a space either before or after. The only exception is with a suspensive hyphen. (See Punctuation, The hyphen, in this section.) Confusing the dash with the hyphen makes a sentence impossible to read.

'What a horrible topic for an essay!'

'Johnny, don't touch that case book! It's out of date!'

'This deadline is killing me. Help!'

Examples like these are okay in writing that tries to represent ordinary speech – novels or screenplays. But exclamation marks can look out of place in formal writing. Using them in business communication will give your work a breathy, almost childish, quality. Overuse them in any context and you risk looking like a drama queen or someone who laughs at her own jokes (and expects the reader to get the punch line). And never use two or three of them in a row.

In journalism, screamers are the mark of the amateur, connoting 'Look how clever/funny I'm being.' In creative writing, they may – may – be used at the end of a quote, if that quote is the character's last howl at the moon as he leaps off a cliff. Putting them in prose is regarded as naff.

The full stop (.)

Use a full stop at the end of all sentences that are not questions or exclamations. We suggest that you don't need them for headings (whether in text or tables), sub-headings, bullet points or captions. We also advise against inserting full stops in abbreviations or acronyms. *The Economist Style Guide* says of full stops: 'Use plenty. They keep sentences short. This helps the reader.'

The hyphen (-)

'If you take hyphens seriously, you will surely go mad!'
The Oxford Style Manual

They make look the same, but hyphens are not dashes. In fact, they *shouldn't* look the same. Dashes are longer and, depending on house style, used with a space each side. If you're using a typewriter or primitive e-mail programme, type two hyphens one after the other to distinguish. The purpose of hyphens is to link two or more words or word-parts that have to do the job of one. They're useful to give meaning and clarity to text but they can't rescue an over-ambitious attempt to shoehorn meaning into a 37-word sentence. So choose the right words and use hyphens to help the reader see as quickly as possibly which words belong with which. Here's an example of how hyphens make a sentence easier to read:

'Our much loved head mistress was sixty six years old when she retired.'

'Our much-loved head-mistress was sixty-six years old when she retired.'

Use hyphens in the following instances:

1. For ethnic groupings: Anglo-Indian, Greek-Cypriot, Irish-American.

2. For ancillary points of the compass: north-east, south-east, south-west, north-west, north-north-west.

3. To avoid ambiguity: re-creation (as opposed to recreation), a fine-tooth comb (as opposed to a fine tooth-comb).

4. To form compound adjectives (modifiers): balance-of-payments advantages, half-hearted attempt, well-known author. But, never use hyphens with 'ly' adverbs. Here's an easy way to remember: 'The well-dressed man loved the scantily clad lady.'

5. To form nouns from prepositional verbs: build-up, get-together, shake-down.

6. To form some compound nouns: brother-in-law, jack-of-all-trades, sergeant-in-arms.

7. To separate identical letters in most instances: book-keeping, pre-eminent, shell-like.

8. With a prefix when the main word starts with a capital letter or number: un-American, mid-October, mid-1980s.

9. With certain titles (as taken from *The Economist Style Guide*, the authority on this subject): attorney-general, director-general, field-marshal, lieutenant-colonel, major-general, secretary-general, vice-president, under-secretary. But *not* deputy director, deputy secretary and general secretary.

10. With compound numbers: forty-five, fifty-six, sixty-six.

11. With fractions: one-half, two-thirds, three-quarters.

12. With special prefixes: self-control, re-enter, co-ordinate.

A note on the suspensive hyphen. When writing a series of almost-identical compounds, you can sometimes delay the complete term or compound until the last instance, allowing the hyphen to act as a kind of place-holder earlier in the sentence:

'Both full- and part-time employees will receive bonuses this year.'

'We don't see many two-, three- and four-year-old children in nightclubs.'

Be careful not to overuse this feature of the hyphen; it's clever and literary but readers have to wait until that final instance to know what you're talking about, and that can be annoying. Of course, you could always rewrite the sentences:

'All employees will receive bonuses this year.'

'We don't see many under-fives in nightclubs.'

Parentheses ()

Parentheses (round brackets) should be used occasionally (and sparingly) for extra, non-essential material included in a sentence. For example, dates, sources or ideas that are subordinate or tangential to the rest of the sentence are set apart in parentheses.

'Just as it crossed the finish line, the convertible Mini (which was rebuilt in 1997 by an assistant of John Cooper) caught fire.'

You can also use them for separate complete sentences that are almost incidental to the main body of the text. (Remember that, like altar boys, parentheses always appear in pairs.) Use a full stop inside the parentheses only when they contain a complete sentence.

They are also helpful in text as a means of definition, explanation, reference or translation:

Parentheses (round brackets)
Machtpolitik (power politics)

The question mark (?)

This should follow every question where a separate answer is required. A question mark is not required after an indirect or rhetorical question:

'The lecturer asked how many of us used calculators exclusively.' (indirect)
'Why me, Lord...' (rhetorical)

A question mark in parentheses may also be placed after a word or date whose accuracy is doubted:

'*This Business of Writing* was first published in 2005 (?) by The Institute of Chartered Accountants in Ireland.'

Quotation marks (")

The use of quotation marks, also called inverted commas, is complicated somewhat by the fact that there are two types: single quotes (') and double quotes ("). As a general rule, British English prefers single quotes for ordinary use, whereas American English prefers double quotes. Given that we're publishing on this side of the pond, our editor has favoured the use of single quotes in this book.

The chief use of quotation marks is quite easy to understand: a pair of quotation marks encloses a direct quotation, which is the repetition of someone's exact words. Quotations within quotations are indicated by the use of double quotation marks within single (or vice versa if you're writing in American). Some examples:

'President Kennedy famously exclaimed: "Ich bin ein Berliner!" '

'According to Thomas Edison, "Genius is one percent inspiration and ninety-nine percent perspiration." '

When you're quoting in text, all extracts in the precise words of the original have quotation marks:

• at the beginning
• at the start (but not the end) of each paragraph if it's flowing over more than one
• at the end of the extract

Punctuation within the extract should be exactly as in the original, and the concluding full stop goes within the quotation marks when it's part of the original. When a whole sentence is a quotation, full stops, commas and other punctuation marks are placed inside the quotation marks; if the quoted matter forms only part of the sentence, and the punctuation mark is not part of the quote, it comes outside the quotation marks:

'The Secretary General praised the "tireless efforts of the Medecins Sans Frontieres volunteers to help the people of Bali after the Tsunami".'

You can use quotation marks to indicate words used ironically, with reservations, or in some unusual way.

Don't overuse them in this sense, or they will lose their impact:

'Isolating words with quotations more than once or twice in a page will leave your "considered" text open to "accusations" of "curranty-bun complex".'

If you're indenting a quotation and setting it down in smaller type, which you should do if it's longer than five lines, don't use inverted commas. Generally, no more than 10 percent of any document should be direct quotation. If you're writing an essay or report and do find yourself relying on other people's material, it's better to paraphrase, always with the proviso that you're attributing the material correctly. (See Plagiarism, Section 1.) Seek permission to use quotes of more than 200 words.

Single quotes and roman (regular) type are used when citing the titles of articles in newspapers, journals, chapters of books, essays and speeches. (See Citation of Authorities, Section 2.)

Square brackets [ ]

Square brackets should be used around a word or words you have inserted into a quote:

'He [Justin Timberlake] burst onto the dance scene with a Number 1 solo album after leaving the boyband, *NSYNC.'

They can also be used within parentheses:

'The man responsible for the arrest (James Hudson [1885-1940]) was never given credit.'

Underlining and italics

Italics are generally used for the titles of books, magazines, newspapers, motion pictures, plays, works of art, ships and aircraft. In addition, if you're a Trekkie, italicise the names of spacecraft, real or imaginary.

The titles of short stories, poems and songs are used in roman style with inverted commas. Long poems, published as a single volume, and music albums (not photographic ones) are styled in italics.

Underlining and italics aren't punctuation in strict terms, but they are significant textual effects used in a variety of situations. Before word processors, writers would underline certain terms in handwritten or manually typed pages, and the underlining would be replaced by italics or bold in the published version. Because word processing allows us many options for font and text effects, we generally recommend you choose either underlining or italics and use it consistently throughout a document if you need to add emphasis or highlight certain points. Use italics sparingly and principally for foreign words and phrases. (See Latin Terms and Foreign Words – A Glossary, Section 6.) It is okay to use them for emphasis but confine this to one or two instances per page.

A LIST OF USAGES

accept/except
Accept means to receive. Except means to exclude. 'I accept your points, except where you are wrong.'

access
We gain access to buildings. When using 'access' as a verb, confine it to the technological sense. 'We access our money at a cash-dispenser.'

Achilles' heel
Note the use of the possessive.

acre/hectare
An acre is 43,560 square feet, 4840 square yards. To convert to hectares, simply multiply by 0.4. Five acres equals two hectares. Note that the abbreviation for hectares, like metres and centimetres, does not take as 's' in the plural form: 15 ha.

Actors' Equity
Thespians offer their talents in troupes: note the use of the possessive.

AD
See BC below.

Adrenalin/adrenaline
Adrenalin is the trademark for synthetic or chemically extracted forms of epinephrine, the substance produced by adrenal glands. It's used in the treatment of asthma. Adrenaline is the natural hormone that is secreted in response to stress and increases in heart rate and blood pressure.

adverse/averse
'Adverse' means unfavourable and 'averse' means unwilling or reluctant. You may well be averse to flying to East Asia because you are expecting turbulence and adverse weather.

adviser/advisor
Modern use prefers adviser.

affect/effect
'Change in anything can *affect* our lives. With a strong will, we can sometimes *effect* change in an organisation. Failing that, 20 minutes after swallowing one, a Valium will take *effect* and make everything seem easier.'

AIDS
The acronym is acceptable in references to the disease acquired immune deficiency syndrome. Distinction should be made between AIDS, the disease, and HIV, the virus. People infected with HIV, known as HIV-positive, can remain healthy. Only after they develop serious symptoms should they be described as having AIDS. (See The Language of Illness, Section 1.)

alcoholic
Use 'recovering' not 'reformed' when referring to those who have suffered from the disease of alcoholism. (See The Language of Illness, Section 1.)

alien
Avoid using the word when referring to an immigrant or foreigner. For those who enter a country illegally, the term illegal immigrant should be used. (See The Language of Diversity, Section 1.)

allowable
Use 'permissible' instead.

all-round
Daly Thompson was an all-round athlete. Not an all-around one.

allude/refer
You allude to something when you speak of it without direct mention. You refer when you mention it directly.

alternate/alternative
'Alternate' can mean every second one. (The British prime minister meets the Queen on alternate Tuesdays.) The noun 'alternative' means a choice between only two. When there are several 'alternatives', use 'options' instead.

Americas Cup (for golf)/America's Cup (for yachting)
Notice how the apostrophe distinguishes the sports.

amount
The word 'amount' denotes quantity. If the objects referred to can be counted, use 'number' instead. There was a small amount of honey to go around the table. The number of bees in the hive was terrifying.

ampersand (&)
Ampersands should be avoided unless used as part of a brand, company name or title – for example, Proctor & Gamble or *Will & Grace.*

anxious/eager
In strict terms, 'anxious' means worried whereas 'eager' means enthusiastic.

anyone/any one
'Anyone can do it.' 'Any one of them can do it.' (Two words stress the individual elements.)

attorney general/attorneys general
Note the spelling of the plural.

auger/augur
An auger is a tool for boring holes whereas 'augur' is used as a verb meaning 'to foreshadow'.

authoress
Prefer the generic word 'author'.

baker's dozen
To the horror of accountants, this means 13.

bankrupt
Avoid calling a debtor bankrupt unless he or she has been legally declared so. It's pejorative and can lead to you being sued.

BBC
Spell out British Broadcasting Corporation on the first reference.

BC
The abbreviation for 'before Christ' follows the year: 'Mark's Gospel was written circa 60 BC according to biblical scholars.' The abbreviation AD precedes the year: 'The settlement where the tome was located is likely to have been founded in AD 43.' There is no need to use AD in text that does not have BC dates where its meaning is clear.

between
Use this word when you're treating two people, objects or ideas. For three or more items or people, use 'among'. Discuss or dispute this point between you and a colleague. Argue the finer details of this point among your team members.

biennial/biannual

Biennial events occur every two years; biannual events occur twice a year.

Bible

Use capitals when referring to the word 'Bible' and the Old or New Testaments; however, 'biblical' is lower case. (See 'religious terms' below.) The same rule applies to most other proper nouns and their adjectives, with the Continent (in reference to Europe) and Continental being the exception. In this instance Continental remains upper case to distinguish Continental breakfast from continental drift.

blond/blonde

Use blond to refer to men and blonde when describing women. American English favours blond in both instances.

bridal/bridle

Bridal refers to matrimony. Bridle refers to a horse's harness.

both… and

'Both her mother *and her* father were on the committee.' Not, 'Both her mother and father were on the committee.' This is one of text's great redundancies. As part of any edit, we recommend doing a 'both-hunt' to cull the word from your writing.

Burma

Now called Myanmar. (See List of Countries, Section 6.)

byte

A unit of measure of computer information, typically consisting of eight bits or binary digits, equivalent to the average word (not to be misspelt as bite). (See Cyberstyling, Section 3.)

can/may

The word 'can' means 'has the ability'. The word 'may' means 'being allowed'. For example, The answer to 'Can I take a day's leave?' depends on whether you have time available. 'May I take a day's leave?' could suggest you're planning a stag or hen night and have a sympathetic boss.

cash on delivery

COD is acceptable in all instances.

cater for/cater to

We cater *for* your need to write and our printers cater *to* your preference for hardback or soft cover.

catsup/ketchup
The great Irish cook and writer, Maura Laverty, included catsup in some recipes. If we were doing the cooking, we'd use ketchup.

Celsius
Use this term rather than centigrade for the metric temperature scale. In this scale, zero represents the freezing point of water and 100 degrees is the boiling point of water at sea level.

If you want to convert to Fahrenheit and revisit your primary school days, multiply a temperature by 9, divide by 5 and add 32.

centre
'Centred on', never 'around' or 'in'.

century/Century
Use in lower case when spelling out numbers fewer than 10. 'The town was founded in the second century.' Use in upper case when preceded by digits. That's the correct use in 21st-Century writing.

chairman/chairwoman/chairperson
Simplify life – and the minutes of your meeting – by using the word 'Chair'. (See Minute Writing, Section 2.)

character/reputation
Character refers to ethical standards and reputation is how a person is regarded by others.

Christmas Day
Never abbreviate to Xmas Day.

cite/site
To cite something is to mention it as proof of what is being said. It is generally used in a legal sense. To site it, on the other hand, is to physically place something somewhere.

cocaine
Use the slang term 'coke' only in quoted matter.

Common Market
Predecessor to the European Union.

compare
'Compare to' is used for similarities and 'compare with' for describing differences. It usually works but it's not strictly true. Think of it this way: 'compare to' equals 'liken to'.

compose/comprise

'Compose' means to create or put together. Ireland is composed of four provinces. 'Comprise' means 'to contain'. Use it in the active voice: 'Ireland comprises 32 counties.' Ireland is not comprised of anything. 'Comprise' should never be followed by 'of', even when it is used in the passive.

contact

A word better used as a noun, so don't contact someone. Call him, arrange to meet her, or write your uncle a letter.

continual/continuous

'Continual' means regular, but not constant. 'Continuous' means constant.

crescendo

This is where something is increasing or building up. It doesn't mean a loud point or a climax.

criterion/criteria

The former is singular, the latter plural.

cult

Because of its negative connotations, it's better not used.

curriculum

'Curricula' in plural form.

data

This is plural noun, which takes plural verbs and pronouns.

days of the week

Don't abbreviate unless in tabular form. Likewise, don't abbreviate months except in tables or spreadsheets.

decades

1800s, 1940s, 1990s, the Swinging Sixties, the Roaring Twenties. (Note there is no apostrophe. See Apostrophes in this section.)

deficit

Deficits widen or narrow but don't increase or decline.

déjà vu

This means coming into a situation and believing you have been there before. It's not to be confused with repetitive happenings (like work, for example).

de-fuse/diffuse
You de-fuse a bomb. To diffuse information is to scatter it.

desert/dessert
Desert as a noun is a dry, barren sandy region, home of the Foreign Legion. Desert can also mean something that is deserved. (Usually, punishment.) Desert as a verb means to turn your back on, leave or abandon. Dessert is a sweet food such as chocolate, ice cream or crème brulee.

dilemma
This is similar to alternative. It refers to a choice between only two. You may be in a dilemma whether to read this book or seek an answer to your query online.

disinterested/uninterested
Disinterested means that you're not influenced by any personal concern in something. Therefore, you can be a disinterested party in a lawsuit if you don't care about the outcome. You may well be uninterested in the whole dispute.

divorcée
Avoid using this term. Prefer 'His or her marriage ended in divorce.'

dyeing/dying
Dyeing refers to the change of colour. Dying refers to the end of life.

Easter, Easter Sunday, Easter egg, Easter parade
Note the use of the upper-case E.

enormity
This suggests wickedness, outrageousness or malice, as well as size. The enormity of the September 11th bombings will be judged by historians.

Eskimo
Prefer Inuit.

etc
Avoid this if possible. It's an ugly distraction in a sentence, and puts the onus on the reader to supply what the writer is too lazy to provide.

everyday/every day
'Everyday' is an adjective meaning ordinary or daily. Use it only as a modifier. Every day is not an adjective – it means each day.

Emmy/Emmys
The television equivalent of the Oscars, awarded by the Academy of Television Arts and Sciences (which, in recent years, were most often won by the casts of *Sex and the City*, *Boston Legal* and *The Sopranos*). Note the plural spelling without the apostrophe.

extract/extricate
She will find it difficult to extricate herself from a situation. Her dentist extracts teeth.

factor
Apart from its mathematical definition, do not confuse with the words 'component' or 'element'. A factor contributes to a result. It does not refer to a part of a plan or an arrangement.

farther/further
Farther refers to strict physical distance. The farther we travel, the more we see, assuming we have open minds and open eyes. Although modern usage has diminished the distinction, your authors are closed-minded and don't intend to discuss this further.

fewer/less
'Fewer' is best used for numbers and 'less' for aggregates or quantity. 'Fewer than 210 seats were lost by the British Labour party in the 2006 local elections.' 'Less than 70 Maltese lira per day will hire a family car in Valetta.'

fiancé/fiancée
One French word where we retain the gender distinction in common parlance.

fireman
Fire-fighter is a more inclusive (and accurate) description.

first, second, third
'First of all' makes sense when you want to emphasise the primacy of the first item in a series, but it should not be followed by 'second of all', where the expression serves no such function. And 'secondly' is an adverbial form that makes no sense in enumeration. (Neither does 'firstly'.) As you go through your list, simply say: second, third, fourth.

first come, first served
Note the lack of hyphens and use of the comma.

flammable/inflammable
'Flammable' and 'inflammable', although appearing contradictory, are interchangeable when describing the combustible properties of materials. However, to avoid confusion and even immolation, use 'flammable' in warning labels. 'Inflammable' is used more in figurative contexts:

'As history has shown, military action in the Middle East has proved inflammatory.'

forego/forgo
'Forego' means 'to go before' or 'to precede'. 'Forgo' means 'to abstain from' or 'to go without' – it goes without the e.)

founder
Should not be confused with 'flounder'. When we say that the project foundered, it means that it broke down or failed. The reason may be that the project manager floundered around in the minutiae.

fulsome
Don't give 'fulsome' praise unless you mean it to be insincere, offensive or disgusting. It's a word loaded with irony (and baggage), and is best thought of as 'excessive to the point of causing disgust'. If you like something, by all means be full of praise for it.

furnish
Best used in *Wallpaper* magazine and *Image Interiors*. 'Send', 'give' or 'inform' are to be preferred in business English.

future planning
The word 'future' is redundant. (See 'tautology' below.)

gentlemen's agreement
Not gentleman's.

Hobson's choice
This means no choice. Prefer 'dilemma' or 'quandary'.

Holy Father
Refers to the pope or the pontiff. Always use capitals.

Holy Spirit
The Holy Spirit replaced the Holy Ghost in Catholic terminology after the Second Vatican Council.

historic/historical
Historic refers to something famous or important in history. Historical is used in the more general sense of having existed.

hanged/hung
'Hanged' refers to capital punishment; 'hung' to clothes and pheasant.

housewife

Today, use the word 'homemaker'.

however

This is best not used at the start of a sentence unless it means 'in whatever way' or 'to what extent'. The word 'nevertheless' can usually be substituted for accuracy. However hard we try, we cannot always use the correct phrase. Nevertheless, we should aim for best practice.

human/human being

The latter may seem a tautology but, in common parlance, either has become acceptable.

I/ me

'Marsha and I went to the bookshop. She bought a dictionary for Terry and me.'

imply/infer

At its simplest, imply means what was intended by the speaker, whereas infer refers to what is understood by the listener. 'What did the manager imply in his remarks? What should we infer from his tone given the year-end statement?'

individual(s)

As a noun, prefer person, people, man, woman, child, children. It's a dehumanising word. And on no account use the phrase 'each individual' anything.

inside of, outside of

There's no need for 'of' in either instance.

intense/intensive

'Intense' means to a high degree or extreme. 'Intensive' means highly concentrated. 'The break-up prompted intense anger. Intensive debate showed it was because he left his socks in the living room.'

in terms of

This is padding. 'The 2006 national pay negotiations proved difficult in terms of pensions,' reads better as, 'Pensions made the 2006 pay agreement talks more difficult.'

irregardless
This is a made-up word that doesn't even feature in a spell-check. 'Regardless' is the correct form.

invaluable
Invaluable is an absolute adjective. Something cannot be absolutely invaluable.

its/it's
We have hammered this point throughout the book – it is the most common misuse of the apostrophe. So, here we go again. Never use an apostrophe to show possession for it. It's is always a contraction for 'it is' or 'it has'.

last/past
Last and past are often confused. 'The last year's activities' can almost always be rewritten (more accurately and elegantly) as 'the past year's activities' Likewise, 'the past week' is preferable to 'the last week' unless it is the last week of a set period.

least/less
Use 'less' when comparing two persons or things – for example, 'He was the less effective of the two salesmen.' Use 'least' when referring to more than two. 'She was the least nervous of the three singers on the night.'

legible/readable
When handwriting is easily read it is legible. Dan Brown's novels are considered readable. (Which still didn't entice his readers to see the movie after those lukewarm reviews.)

licence/license
We've all been grateful for the late-night off-licence. We've walked there so we wouldn't lose our driving licences. We're taking poetic licence devising this scenario. Ask us nicely and we'll license the rights to this book.

living death/living dead
The ultimate oxymoron. Anyone who uses this expression should be killed.

loan/lend
Loan is a noun. Lend is a verb. You will give a loan of this book to your friend. You will lend it for one night only and strongly encourage him to buy a copy.

mathematics

Always spell this word in full; do not use 'math' or 'maths'. It's ugly in text and reminiscent of homework.

measurements

A common style is to spell out numbers up to nine and use digits for 10 and above.

Use commas (not spaces) when a number has more than three digits: 10 and 100 and 1,000 but 10,000 and 100,000.

Combine figures and units (of millions or billions) when referring to very large numbers: 8.5 million, 13 billion, 25 trillion.

Avoid starting sentences with numbers. If you can't, spell them out: 'One hundred and ninety-seven people attended the reception.' (Or you can rewrite as: 'Almost 200 people came to wish Stephen McKenna well at the opening of his retrospective at the RHA Gallery.')

Use figures to express heights, decimals and percentages: 5 metres, 32.6, 62 percent (or 62% in tabular form).

When units of measurement are shown as abbreviations or symbols, only use figures: 359g, 1kg, 2ml.

Use figures in addresses: 234 Albert Road, Donnybrook, Dublin 4. (Which, in traditional English styling, would have been written with a comma after the digits. A throwback to the days when houses had names. It's up to you whether you want to write like a young fogey: 234, Albert Road, Donnybook, Dublin 4.)

The plurals of figures and decades are formed by adding an s: 'The temperature was in the 80s.' 'Elvis Presley changed the sound of music forever in the 1950s.'

media

This is a plural noun, which takes plural verbs and pronouns.

Mount

Spell it out in all uses. Mount Everest is sufficiently imposing to merit a full spelling.

nauseous/nauseated

Strunk and White deal with this succinctly. 'The first means 'sickening to contemplate'; the second means 'sick to the stomach'. Do not, therefore, say 'I feel nauseous' unless you are sure you have that effect on others.

New York Stock Exchange

Note the use of capitals, but 'the London stock exchange' because that's only its informal name.

newspaper titles

We're not going to argue with *The Economist* or *Guardian* style guides on this one. They're usually set in italics and with lower case 'the': the *Irish Independent* or the *Guardian*. The exceptions to this are *The Irish Times*, *The Times* and *The Economist*.

nice

This is no longer a nice word. It's overused and inaccurate. In strict terms, it refers to something delicate. 'It was a nice specimen orchid before the cat got at it.'

nicknames

Don't use them in your writing. Dubya Bush is downright disrespectful. But Bertie Ahern or Tony Blair are acceptable because they seem to prefer to be so known.

not-for-profit/non-profit

There's an important difference between these terms. A not-for-profit organisation can make a profit; a non-profit organisation cannot make a profit. When referring to an organisation, make sure to use the term that the organisation itself uses.

oceans

In order of size, the Pacific Ocean, Atlantic Ocean, Indian Ocean, Antarctic Ocean and Arctic Ocean.

on the part of

This is ghastly. Prefer the use of 'by', 'among' or 'for'. 'A little effort by writers will achieve more elegant prose.'

one

Avoid 'one' as a personal pronoun unless you're the Queen of England. Even Margaret Thatcher couldn't pull this off when commenting on the birth of her grandchild: 'One is a grandmother.' (Remember the joke: Why is Margaret Thatcher like a pound coin? Because she's thick, brassy and thinks she's a sovereign.) 'You' or 'I' will do instead. In addition, one is not followed by 'his' or 'her' in a sentence. One must take care with one's grammar.

only

Place the word 'only' close to the word it describes. 'She sold only five raffle tickets,' (which means she didn't mange to sell six) as opposed to, 'She only sold five raffle tickets' (which implies she didn't do anything that day other than sell raffle tickets. Did the woman not eat or breathe?).

Pacific

Please don't confuse with 'specific'. (Happens more often than you'd think.)

peculiar to

This phrase means characteristic of and has nothing to do with being strange. Did you know that deafness is peculiar to Dalmatian dogs?

people/persons

Prefer people to persons in all plural uses. Use persons only in quotes, official names or in the singular: 'People of all races participated in the conference at UCD. More than 80 people gathered for the first seminar. One person waited in vain at the door for his companion, who had visited Mulligan's the previous night.'

percent/per cent

Percent can be written as one word or two. Given the spelling of the word 'percentage', your authors believe it's cleaner to use it as one. Use the % sign only in tables.

personal

'Our personal favourite' – as opposed to 'our personal favourite of someone else's'? – or simply 'our favourite'? You decide. We think it's unnecessary.

personally

Another superfluous word. 'Personally, I need a dictionary on my desk,' adds nothing to 'I need a dictionary on my desk.'

phenomena

This is plural noun, which takes plural verbs and pronouns.

planets

In order of their distance from the sun, they are Mercury, Venus, Earth, Mars, Jupiter, Saturn, Uranus and Neptune. Pluto is not a planet.

please do not hesitate

This sounds patronising rather than indicative of a genuine willingness to serve.

politics

This noun can take a singular or plural verb.

pore/pour

As a verb, 'pore' means 'to examine closely'. We hope that you will pore over every page of this book. We want to pour oil on the troubled waters of business writing.

possess

This sounds pompous even in formal writing. Prefer 'have' or 'own'.

postman

Prefer postal worker.

practice/practise

If you practise as an accountant and build a wide client base, you may decide to set up a practice of your own. (Of course, you won't take your address book with you.)

practicable/practical

'Practicable' means something is feasible. 'Practical' refers to actual practice. It may be practicable to drive a vintage Rolls-Royce to work in rush-hour traffic but it is hardly practical.

preface/foreword

A preface to a book is written by its author. A foreword is written by someone else.

presently

This word means shortly. It does not mean currently.

principal/principle

Principal is an adjective meaning 'foremost' or 'most important'. Principle is a noun meaning 'fundamental law' or 'guiding idea'. Here's a way to distinguish. Princple = e for ethics or elementary rule. The principal is your pal once you've passed the Leaving Cert.

Reader's Digest

Note the use of the apostrophe.

recur/recurred
Events or problems don't 'reoccur'. They recur.

refer back
You don't refer back to something. The word 'back' is unnecessary.

relative
Fine when used as an adjective, but as a noun prefer 'relation'.

religious terms
Capitalise most religious terms – and forgive any omissions – including Advent, Baptist, Bible, Blessed Sacrament, Blessed Virgin, Catholic, Christian, Christian Science (properly known as the Church of Christ, Scientist), Commandments, Cross, Crucifixion, Eucharist, Gospels, Holy Communion, Islam, Jewish, Judaism, Kabbala, Kaddish, Koran, Mass, Morman, Muslim, Nativity (but a nativity play), Protestant, Resurrection, Sabbath and Sikh.

right of way
The plural is 'rights of way'.

rock'n'roll
Some of us are old enough to remember how to spell this phrase.

rosary
You can 'say' or 'recite' this prayer pattern. It is lower case.

run
The Economist Style Guide makes the following distinction. In countries with a presidential system you may run for office. In those with a parliamentary system, one stands.

same difference
This is a jokey, deliberately illogical slang expression that doesn't belong in formal writing.

Scot/Scots/Scotch/Scottish
The word 'scotch' refers only to whisky and eggs.

sculptor
This word can be safely used for men and woman who are blessed with the ability to carve wood and stone into beauty. 'Sculptress' is an ugly word.

seasons
Use as lowercase in run-on text: spring, summer, autumn and winter.
(See Capitalisation in this section.)

semi-annual
Means occurring every six months or twice a year.

setback
Do not confuse with drawback.

Siamese twins
Derived from twins Chang and Eng, who were born in 19th Century
Siam (Thailand) and died in the US. Banned in 21st Century English.
Use conjoined instead.

silicon/silicone
Silicon is a chemical element, the basic material of which microchips are
made. Silicones are plastics and other materials containing silicon, the
most commonly discussed example being silicone breast implants.

simplistic
Simplistic already has 'too' as part of its meaning. It's tautology to refer
to something being 'too simplistic' or 'overly simplistic'.

since
A word that should be used in the context of time when introducing a
clause. Otherwise, prefer 'because' or 'as'.

slang
Better to avoid words a dictionary defines as slang. (See Slang, Section 1.)

sleight of hand
Note the spelling of the word 'sleight'.

small capitals
Should be banned. Full stop.

SOS
Whoever signs this cry for help most definitely doesn't have time to use
points or periods between the letters.

slash
Don't use spaces on either side of a slash – for example, and/or.

spartan

The word is lower case when referring to prudent or frugal. But the Romans did slaughter the Spartans.

stadium/stadiums

We may eventually have a national sports stadium. We may find the funds for two stadiums. We will never have stadia.

stationary/stationery

'Stationary' means unmoving or stopped. 'Stationery' is material used for writing. Remember 'e' for envelope.

stewardess

Prefer flight attendant.

strata

This is plural noun, which takes plural verbs and pronouns.

teaspoon/teaspoonful

You may stir your morning cuppa with a teaspoon. But four teaspoonfuls of sugar probably isn't good for you.

tautology

Avoid it – as in 'reverse backwards', 'enter into', 'follow along' or, worse still, 'follow behind'.

Ten Commandments

The divine instructions passed to Moses are too important to use digits or take lower-case letters.

terrorists

Terrorists attack civilians. Guerrillas fight governments or armies. (Proceed with caution when using either noun.)

thanking you in advance

Dreadful, and implies that you won't bother to thank someone afterwards.

that/which

'That' should be used for defining clauses and 'which' for non-defining ones. Therefore, 'which' should always have a comma preceding it, and the non-defining clause it introduces must be followed by a comma or a full stop. Consider the difference between these examples (from Bill Bryson's *Troublesome Words*):

swear words

Though still likely to cause offence to older or more conservative people, many words have lost their shock value in modern English. For example, in 2000 the British Advertising Standards Authority rejected complaints about the use of the word 'shag' in advertising material for the Austin Powers movie, *The Spy Who Shagged Me*. However, do remember that the use of the word 'fuck' retains its negative connotations when used in writing – where it is particularly stark –- although everyday speech has lessened its impact as an expletive.

'The tree that had no leaves was a birch.'

'The tree, which had no leaves, was a birch.'

You don't need the word 'that' after believe, presume, suppose and think. In most instances, it can left out after the word 'said'.

that/who
For people or anything personalised (such as your beloved hamster, Charlie), use 'who' or 'whom'. For objects, things and less-important pets or animals, use 'that' or 'which'.

their/there/they're
'Their' is a possessive form of they. 'There' is generally an adverb. 'They're' is a contraction of 'they are'. (See Punctuation, The apostrophe, in this section.)

Third World
'Developing countries' is preferable.

through
In American English, the word 'through' can be used to mean 'until'. For example, 'September 19th through October 1st', would be in British English 'the 19th of September until 1st of October'.

time
When writing about time use the 12-hour clock, as in 5.15 pm. It's universally recognised. Note the use of the full stop and the space before pm.

total
Prefer 'add up to' or 'amount to'.

try and/try to
Prefer 'try to' in formal writing.

UFO
Ubiquity has made the acronym acceptable in all instances.

under way
This is always two words.

unique
If something is unique, it's one of a kind. This doesn't make it strange, odd or bizarre.

upcoming

Use 'coming' instead. (Except in direct quotation.)

upside down/upside-down

'Upside down' is adverbial. 'Her world turned upside down.' 'Upside-down' is adjectival. 'She is now living in an upside-down world.'

usher

Another word without a gender distinction.

utilise

The word 'use' can be used in most instances.

VHF

It stands for 'very high frequency' but the acronym is so common it can be used in all references.

vitamin

'She swallows a vitamin A capsule every day without noticing that it is used in lower case.'

was/were

These are invariably confused. When expressing a hypothetical condition or conditions contrary to fact, use 'were'. 'He behaves as though he were Brad Pitt. If I were him, I would not do so.' But, 'If she was at the dinner, I did not see her.

WASP

White Anglo-Saxon Protestants have never liked this acronym. (See Abbreviations, Acronyms and Initialisms in this section.)

weatherman

'Weather forecaster' is to be preferred.

where are we at

This is dreadful and should be banned from speech and writing.

whence

Use 'from where' but never 'from whence'.

who/whom

Who is the subject of a verb; whom is the object. Modern usage has diminished the distinction but it should be maintained in writing. Who will be the candidate for South Dublin? Whom will the cumann select?

while/whilst
Both 'while' and 'whilst' are used in British English. In American English, 'whilst' is considered a pretentious affectation. *The Economist Style Guide* makes the point that 'while' is not interchangeable with 'although' or 'whereas' (although common usage has eroded the distinction).

whereabouts
This is plural noun, which takes plural verbs and pronouns.

vital
In strict terms this refers to the maintenance of life – for example, the kidneys perform a vital function. Prefer the use of 'crucial' or 'important' in business English.

yin and yang
The pair of female and male terms in Chinese thought consists of 'yin and yang' not 'ying and yang'.

YMCA
This is an acceptable abbreviation in all instances.

your/you're
This is another important distinction. 'Your' is possessive. 'You're' is the contraction for 'you are'. (See Punctuation, The apostrophe, in this section.)

X-ray
Note the hyphen.

'You can't have your cake and eat it too.'

The original – and only sensible – version of this saying is, 'You can't eat your cake and have it too,' meaning that if you eat your cake you won't have it any more. People get confused because we use the expression 'have some cake' to mean 'eat some cake' and they misunderstand what 'have' means in this expression.

5. IRISH IN WRITING

USING IRISH IN CORRESPONDENCE
Pádhraic Ó Ciardha, Leascheannasaí TG4

Irish is a beautiful language. It has flourished and waned in cycles through the centuries but, like all living things, survives by adapting. Many times in history it has managed to co-exist alongside the dominant world language – Latin, French or, more recently, English. It will take Chinese in its stride too, no doubt.

Some linguists even claim that a new dialect of Irish – 'Dartais' – has developed and is spoken by those pupils of Gaelscoileanna who live in the more affluent suburbs of our capital city. This dialect has its own syntax and mores – and is the subject of much mirth among native speakers from the more traditional rural Gaeltachtaí.

Whatever our address, Irish literature and folklore, prose, poetry and song are rich sources of wisdom, wit and invective. Used properly, they can enhance most professional writing in correspondence or other formats.

The Official Languages Act 2003 obliges many public bodies to provide an Irish-language service to clients and customers. This means that most of these bodies, if they have not already done so, will have to put in place measures to satisfy this statutory duty. In theory at least, you will have, close by, someone with a facility and fluency in Irish – your own in-house style counsellor when using the language or are unsure about correct usage.

Whatever your level of competence, you can use Irish to give your text a more-personal or natural tone. Depending on your ability and confidence with Irish, it can be as simple as a greeting at the beginning or end of a letter – or the use of a phrase, proverb, saying or quotation.

Don't be afraid to have a go. Remember, it's your language too.

Personal Names

Starting a letter in Irish is easy – but don't forget the vocative case:

A Sheáin, a chara
A Éamoinn, a chara
A Mhichíl, a chara

Ending a letter is also easy:

Is mise le meas
Is mise
Le gach beannacht
Le dúththracht

As with surnames in all languages, check the spelling that the person uses – people do not always use the standard version. For example, one 'Ó Murchú' may be one person's choice but 'Ó Murchadha' may be another's.

Irish does not have an apostrophe in surnames:

O'Sullivan is English.
Ó Súilleabháin is Irish. There is no such name as O'Súilleabháin.

Don't forget that Irish has a vocative case. People's forenames change when being addressed, as at the start of a letter:

A Phádraig, a chara for Pádraig
A Chiaráin, a chara for Ciarán
A Mhichíl, a chara for Micheál (Note that Micheál does not have a síneadh fada on the first 'i' in either.)

Women's surnames can be tricky but are simple to decipher:

Máire Ní Mhurchú is the name of a female whose marital status is not clear from her name but whose surname as a single woman we do know.

Máire Uí Mhurchú is the name of a woman who is (or was) married to a man called Ó Murchú.

Máire Nic Giolla Íosa is a single woman's surname.

Máire Mhic Giolla Íosa is a married woman.

Some women now choose to style themselves using the 'Ó' (Máire Ó Murchú) but this can cause confusion because the literal meaning of the Irish letter 'Ó' is 'grandson'.

Placenames

The Irish version of a placename will often be more poetic than the English because most of our indigenous placenames are originally Irish that has been transmogrified into English of some kind, often badly.

The correct Irish language version of major counties, towns, cities and villages (anywhere with a post office) has been codified and officially sanctioned.

The standard reference work for these is *Gasaitéar na hÉireann, Gazetteer of Ireland*, published by Oifig an tSoláthair and available in many bookshops and all libraries.

There are thousands of placenames in Ireland and not all of them have been codified – but a little enquiry will probably reveal a lot more about the place and its history and will tend to be more mellifluous as well. Isn't Droichead na Dothra (telling you the bridge is on the Dodder) a lot more interesting than Ballsbridge)?

Titles/Forms of Address

Ireland is a much less formal place than before – but people still like to be addressed properly. The little reference book *Maidir le do Litir* (published by An Gúm) is a treasure trove and contains a chapter on how to address everyone from officials and dignitaries to bishops and judges of all grades. It also contains the correct forms of many titles in the public service.

The official name of departments and organisations will often appear on the home pages of their website – or in the Irish language version of the site. The IPA *Administration Yearbook and Diary* is also a good place to find the official Irish names for many bodies. If these sources fail you, telephone and ask.

Quotations

Notwithstanding all of the advice earlier in this book, there are some of us who still believe it is hard to beat a good proverb to start or finish a key paragraph. *Sin scéal eile* can cover a multitude of circumstances as can *Beidh lá eile ag an bPaorach*. Sayings like *Ní neart go cur le chéile* (Unity is strength) and *Ar scáth a chéile a mhairimid* (We're all in this together) may also come in useful.

Táim ag súil le freagra go luath (I expect an early reply) and *Cuir glaoch orm faoi sin* (Telephone me about that) can also strike a chord.

The best advice to all scriptwriters is *Bíonn blas ar an mbeagán* (Less is more)!

Where to look for help

When using Irish, take time to check that you are using it correctly. There are a myriad of good dictionaries and reference books that will give you the correct spellings:

The standard full-size dictionaries, *English-Irish Dictionary (De Bhaldraithe)* and *Foclóir Gaeilge-Béarla (Ó Dónaill)*, are both published by An Gúm and widely available. They are both still in daily use although slightly outdated by now.

The small but really useful *Foclóir Póca* (also from An Gúm) is, as the title suggests, pocket sized, more recent than either of the standard works, and very easy to use.

The website www.focal.ie is wonderful for more recent terms and phrases, particularly in the area of technology.

Provinces and counties

Connacht
Galway, Leitrim, Mayo, Roscommon and Sligo

Gaillimh, Liatroim, Maigh Eo, Ros Comáin agus Sligeach

Leinster
Carlow, Dublin, Kildare, Kilkenny, Laois, Longford, Louth, Meath, Offaly, Westmeath, Wexford and Wicklow

Ceatharlach, Baile Átha Cliath, Cill Dara, Cill Chainnigh, Laois, An Longfort, Lú, An Mhí, Uíbh Fhailí, An Iarmhí, Loch Garman agus Cill Mhantáin

Munster
Clare, Cork, Kerry, Limerick, Tipperary and Waterford

An Clár, Corcaigh, Ciarraí, Luimneach, Tiobraid Árann agus Port Láirge

Ulster
Antrim, Armagh, Cavan, Derry, Donegal, Down, Fermanagh, Monaghan and Tyrone

Aontroim, Ard Mhacha, An Cabhán, Doire, Dún na nGall, An Dún, Fear Manah, Muineachán agus Tír Eoghain

List of Irish counties by size

County	Population	Density (km²)	County Town
1. Dublin	1,122,821	1,219	Dublin
2. Antrim	616,384	217	Antrim
3. Cork	447,829	60	Cork
4. Down	410,487	168	Downpatrick
5. Derry	211,669	102	Derry
6. Galway	209,077	34	Galway
7. Limerick	175,304	65	Limerick
8. Kildare	163,944	97	Naas
9. Tyrone	158,460	50	Omagh
10. Tipperary	140,131	33	Tipperary
11. Donegal	137,575	28	Lifford
12. Meath	134,005	57	Navan
13. Kerry	132,527	28	Tralee
14. Armagh	126,803	101	Armagh
15. Mayo	117,446	21	Castlebar
16. Wexford	116596	50	Wexford
17. Wicklow	114,676	57	Wicklow
18. Clare	103,277	33	Ennis
19. Louth	101,821	124	Dundalk
20. Waterford	101,546	55	Waterford
21. Kilkenny	80,339	39	Kilkenny
22. Westmeath	71,858	39	Mullingar
23. Offaly	63,663	32	Tullamore
24. Laois	58,774	34	Portlaoise
25. Sligo	58,200	32	Sligo
26. Cavan	56,546	29	Cavan
27. Fermanagh	54,033	32	Enniskillen
28. Roscommon	53,744	21	Roscommon
29. Monaghan	52,593	41	Monaghan
30. Carlow	45,845	51	Carlow
31. Longford	31,068	28	Longford
32. Leitrim	25,799	16	Carrick-on-Shannon
Ireland	5,458,352		

Source: Census Data for Northern and Southern Ireland, 2002 and 2004.

HIBERNO-ENGLISH, ULSTER-SCOTS, IRISH-ENGLISH
Jo O'Donoghue, Editor of *Brewer's Dictionary of Irish Phrase and Fable*

More than most nationalities the Irish have contributed, as Dr Johnson said of his friend and former pupil, David Garrick, to the gaiety of nations. Among our foremost contributions have been music and song, literature (in both the native Irish and the adopted Anglo-Irish language) and art. Along with these have come a certain indefinable but undeniable talent for the *mot juste*, the memorable, often scurrilous phrase, witness to a sense of humour, certainly, but also to an ironic lack of respect, perhaps inherited from the mindset of an oppressed, colonised people.

Ireland, although a small country, has traditionally had an extensive Diaspora. Whether it be the besieged and outnumbered Irish fighting off the police at the Eureka Stockade in Australia in 1854; supplying America's first cardinal; grubbing a living in the Five Points in Manhattan, a slum that terrified even Charles Dickens; tattie-howking in Scotland; or the navvies building the Jubilee tube line in London after the Second World War – all these are part of the Irishness of the globe and the creators of the language or varieties of language we speak.

The first Irish hunter-gatherers are thought to have built their circular dwellings to Mount Sandel, near Coleraine in County Derry circa 7000 BC. In the intervening years, heading now for ten millennia, the languages of Ireland have been, naturally, Irish in its Old, Middle and Modern forms; Latin, the international language of scholars and churchmen, enabling us to read what was written 2000 years ago throughout western Europe; and English, now the vernacular of most of the country, brought by the not-always-welcome strangers, the *Gaill*, as the natives called them. All these means of communication are part of the complicated tapestry of Irish history and thought.

With the Irish language and a predominantly oral culture survived the belief of Irish people in the older myths. Cuchulainn and his battle at the Ford, Deirdre and the sons of Usna, Fionnuala and the other Children of Lir, the Red Branch Knights, the Fianna band of warriors (led by the paladin Fionn Mac Cumhail, his gifted son, Oisin, and *his* warrior son, Oscar) were part of the oral culture of the country. Folk memory had registered a series of invasions so they had to be incorporated into the history. Mythology provided an explanation for the mysteries of life as experienced by a literally unlettered but far from primitive

Kibosh. A colloquial noun (also, less commonly, a verb) used in Hiberno-English (and also in Britain) in phrases such as 'to put the kibosh on…' meaning to 'put an end to', 'finish off', 'do for' something. The derivation of the word is disputed, but it possibly comes from the Irish *caidhpín báis* (death cap), the black cap traditionally assumed by judges when pronouncing the death sentence, or perhaps referring to the black pitch cap used as a means of torture after the Rebellion of 1798.

Put manners on. A Hiberno-English phrase meaning to teach a lesson, correct or discipline, or bring down a peg or two: 'That'll put manners on him.' It is sometimes used to express *schadenfreude*, for instance of a TD who has lost his seat in the Dáil or an individual who has lost her job.

From Brewer's Dictionary of Irish Phrase & Fable

people. Meteorology, topography, the changing seasons, darkness and light, crop growth and failure, reproduction in humans and animals all needed to be accounted for. Immortal longings, wish-fulfilment, courage, magnanimity and a sense of greater predecessors demanded some kind of objective correlative. And mythology supplied it. This mythology is testimony of the deep imagination of the Irish people.

Much later, the merging of English and Irish – and in northern counties the lowlands Scots of the Ulster planters – produced two unique sub-linguistic forms, Hiberno-English and Ulster-Scots. Sentimental, now outdated terms such as 'asthore', 'mavourneen', 'macushla' are straight from the Irish, hiding in a kind of lexical halfway-house. When an Irish tenor sings of Kathleen Mavourneen or hears the voice of Macushla calling him ever again and again he is consciously or unconsciously rehearsing the terms of endearment of the older language. Just as frequent are not-so-endearing terms – *dulamú, lúdramán, táthaire, óinseach.* The Irish language has few rivals when it comes to terms of abuse (in case you wondered, all the preceding mean a stupid or useless person, the last being restricted to a female). Not too long ago, I heard a Kerryman (in English) deliver a veritable litany of abuse about a recalcitrant worker: in one sentence he called him a *mí-ádh* (misfortune); a *táthaire* (trifler); a *dulamú* (stupid) and – best of all – a *clúrachán* (type of gnomish sprite). Hiberno-English has also supplied a literary language, although some earlier playwrights and novelists, such as Sheridan, Farquhar and Boucicault, created stage-Oirish characters speaking with strong brogues.

Experts say Hiberno-English is in decline – specifically the type of English spoken in western and rural areas that was strongly influenced by the Irish language, abandoned only a few generations ago. Under the influence of British and especially American mass-culture, our children's vocabulary and idiom, if not their accents, will soon be indistinguishable from those of Anglophones the world over. (Hopefully, because of the popularity of Eddie Hobbs, regional accents at least will come back into vogue and help stem the tide of uniformity.)

Ulster-Scots (also called Ullans) is regional variation of the lowland Scots dialect, Lallans, which was brought to north-east Ireland by 17th-Century settlers and colonists. The greatest concentration of these was in Antrim, north Derry, east Donegal and north-west Tyrone; and residual elements of their dialect survive, mitigated somewhat by intrusion of Hiberno-English. Ulster-Scots has since the 1990s acquired a political and cultural element, its advocates suggesting, with more energy than conviction, that it deserves its place alongside Irish as a living language. Its detractors insist it is merely a dialect, used by an elderly and therefore diminishing population.

We may lament the linguistic upheaval of the 19th Century, the wholesale abandonment of the Irish language by a people, Irish in every other respect, who 'turned their back' as the philosopher John Moriarty recently said of the means of communication and creative expression that had served them for millennia in one form or another. But recent immigration into a very different Ireland helps us understand that if the millions who left this country were turning their back on one life, they were turning their faces to the great English-speaking world. When meeting Poles or Latvians who struggle to understand the language of the Irish building site or factory, it is possible to appreciate the resourcefulness and intelligence of those who determined that, poor and hungry as they were, they would at least be able to communicate.

The term 'Hiberno-English', which was until recently in general, non-specific use – and which anyone older than ten will have grown up with – has been officially replaced with an awkward and feeble umbrella term 'Irish-English' to cater for the sensibilities of those with a loyalty to Ulster-Scots (as described above). The Belfast Agreement of 1998 brought with it, along with very many positive developments, a statutory commitment to 'parity of esteem' so you will no longer find any official or government agencies using the term 'Hiberno-English'. Such have become the demands of political correctness.

A NOTE FROM THE (FOREIGN) EDITOR
Marsha Swan

A debate arose in the course of working on this book as to whether all distinctly Irish references – the smoking ban, Enterprise Ireland, An Taisce, CIÉ – should be stripped out to make it more accessible to a foreign market. It has, almost without exception, been the custom in Irish non-fiction to use a British style, and to avoid Irish references where the book is intended for foreign sale. When it is not the will of editors at a UK or US publishing house, it is my guess that this comes from the authors' desire to be taken 'seriously' and also to deflect any political associations that are sometimes attached to Hiberno English.

The British are quite happy to refer to chavs and the National Express; the Americans are allowed the South and sidewalks; why do the Irish shy away from local references, and should they? It is an anomaly that British references and phrasing are considered neutral in Ireland, and it is an anomaly that some Irish people consider their own vernacular politicised. To a foreign reader, there is nothing incorrect, or political, about saying 'press' for 'cupboard', or 'just after'. A British author would not worry that 'the north', referring to the north of England, would be misunderstood, but an Irish author in the equivalent situation would be more likely to write 'Northern Ireland', even though 'the North' is a legitimate and unambiguous term in general conversation.

Famous examples of changing language to appeal to a foreign market are the Harry Potter books in America and, going back a bit further, the UK edition of *The Great Gatsby*. We know why the British editors of *Gatsby* wanted to change 'color' to 'colour', but was it really necessary to change 'a crop of caterers' to 'a corps of caterers'? Many hope to learn about another culture by reading about it, and changing the language strips away much of this pleasure. It also introduces numerous editorial mistakes and oddities: *Gatsby*'s 'Biloxi, Mississippi' became 'Biloxi, Tennessee', and for some reason 'six' was translated into 'half a dozen' for British readers. But the greatest danger is that this tendency will dumb down language, diminishing our understanding of other cultures, and further remove the written word from the oral tradition it represents.

In business writing it may be preferable to use language that is as universal as possible, but consider the phrasing, the uniquely Irish use of certain prepositions and verb tenses. These can be seen as informal, or they can be seen as equally legitimate to every other type of English. This should not be confused with sprinkling your writing with *begorrah and begosh*s – there is an enormous difference between the phrases foreigners assign to a culture and true, contemporary language. The real decision should be whether a phrase is too informal for the context, or if a reference is so obscure that it would put readers off or confuse the meaning.

Reference

Neea Paatero, 'Differences Between British and American English in Two Versions of F. Scott Fitzgerald's *The Great Gatsby*' (December 2002) www.uta.fi/FAST/US1/LP/np-great.html

6. A–Z RESOURCES

ACCOUNTING ABBREVIATIONS

AAA
American Accounting Association

ABCUL
Association of British Credit Unions Limited

ACCORD
Australian Centre for Cooperative Research and Development

AGM
Annual General Meeting

AICPA
American Institute of Certified Public Accountants

AIDB
Accountancy Investigation and Discipline Board

AIU
Audit Inspection Unit

APB
Auditing Practices Board

ARC
Audit Registration Committee

ASB
Accounting Standards Board

ASC
Accounting Standards Committee, UK

BAS
Board for Actuarial Standards

C(AICE)
Companies (Audit, Investigations & Community Enterprise) Act 2004

CCAB
Consultative Committee of Accountancy Bodies

CESR
Committee of European Securities Regulators

CGU
Corporate Governance Unit

CICA
Canadian Institute of Chartered Accountants

CUDA
Credit Union Development Association

CUNA
Credit Union National Association

DETI (NI)
Department of Enterprise, Trade and Investment, Northern Ireland

DIRT
Deposit Interest Retention Tax

DTI
Department of Trade and Industry

EFRAG
European Financial Reporting Advisory Group

FASB
Financial Accounting Standards Board, US

FRC
Financial Reporting Council

FRRP
Financial Reporting Review Panel

Accounting Abbreviations

FRS
Financial Reporting Standard

FRSSE
Financial Reporting Standard for Smaller Entities

FSA
Financial Services Authority, UK

GAAP
Generally Accepted Accounting Principles

GASB
Government Accounting Standards Board, US

HMT
Her Majesty's Treasury

IAASB
International Auditing and Assurance Standards Board

IAS
International Accounting Standard

IASB
International Accounting Standards Board

ICA
International Cooperative Alliance

ICAEW
Institute of Chartered Accountants in England and Wales

ICAI
Institute of Chartered Accountants in Ireland

ICAS
Institute of Chartered Accountants in Scotland

IFRIC
International Financial Reporting Interpretations Committee

IFRS
International Financial Reporting Standard

IFSRA
Irish Financial Services Regulatory Authority

ILCU
Irish League of Credit Unions

IMSA
Irish Mortgage and Savings Association

ISA
International Standard on Auditing

NFCU
National Federation of Savings and Cooperative Credit Unions

OFR
Operating and Financial Review

PCAOB
Public Company Accounting Oversight Board

POBA
Professional Oversight Board for Accountancy

SEG
Select Employee Group

SIR
Standards for Investment Reporting

UITF
Urgent Issues Task Force

AIRCRAFT AND AIRLINES

Aircraft names
As a general rule, use a hyphen when changing from letters to figures and no hyphen when adding a letter after figures:

B-1
BAC-111
DC-10
F-15 Eagle
Lockheed P-3 Orion
MiG-21
727-100C

Airbus models are the exception: Airbus A300 and A320.

Do not use quotation marks for aircraft names: Air Force One, Air Force Two (used by the vice-president), Concorde, the Enola Gay, the Spirit of St Louis, the Stealth Bomber.

Airlines

Aer Lingus
Aeroflot
AeroMexico – the short form of Aerovias de Mexico
Air Canada
Air France
Air India
Alaska Airlines
Alitalia
American Airlines
Avianca
British Airways (BA)
Cathy Pacific Airways
Continental Airlines
Delta Air Lines
easyJet
El Al Israeli Airlines (El Al)
Iberia
Japan Airlines (which uses the abbreviation JAL)
KLM
Lufthansa
Qantas Airways
Ryanair
Saudi Arabian Airlines
Scandanavian Airlines System (SAS)
Swissair
Transworld Airlines (TWA)
United Airlines
US Airways (US Air)
Virgin Atlantic Airways

CAR AND MOTORCYCLE MANUFACTURERS

Take care with caps and hyphens when spelling the following:

Acura	Lexus
Alfa Romeo	Lincoln
Aston Martin	Lotus
Audi	Maserati
Austin	Maybach
Bentley	Mazda
BMW	Mercedes-Benz
Bristol	MG
Buick	Mini
Cadillac	Mitsubishi
Chevrolet	Morgan
Chrysler	Nissan
Citroën	Oldsmobile
Daewoo	Opel
Daihatsu	Peugeot
Daimler	Pontiac
Dodge	Porsche
Ducati	Renault
Ferrari	Rolls-Royce
Fiat	Rover
Ford	Saab
Harley-Davidson	SEAT
Honda	Skoda
Hummer	Smart
Hyundai	Subaru
Isuzu	Suzuki
Jaguar	Toyota
Jeep	Triumph
Jensen	Vauxhall
Kawasaki	Volkswagen
Kia	Volvo
Lamborghini	Winnebago
Lancia	Yamaha
Land Rover	

COUNTRIES AND WORLD CURRENCIES

Country/Territory	Population	Capital/Principal City	Currency
Afghanistan	31,056,997	Kabul	afghani (AFA)
Albania	3,581,655	Tirana	lek (ALL)
Algeria	32,930,091	Algiers	Algerian dinar (DZD)
American Samoa	57,794	Pago Pago	US dollar (USD)
Andorra	71,201	Andorra la Vella	euro (EUR)
Angola	12,127,071	Luanda	kwanza (AOA)
Anguilla (Overseas Territory of the UK)	13,477	The Valley	East Caribbean dollar (XCD)
Antigua and Barbuda	69,108	Saint John's	East Caribbean dollar (XCD)
Argentina	39,921,833	Buenos Aires	Argentine peso (ARS)
Armenia	2,976,372	Yerevan	dram (AMD)
Aruba	71,891	Oranjestad	Aruban guilder/florin (AWG)
Australia	20,264,082	Canberra	Australian dollar (AUD)
Austria	8,192,880	Vienna	euro (EUR)
Azerbaijan	7,961,619	Baku	Azerbaijani manat (AZM)
The Bahamas	303,770	Nassau	Bahamian dollar (BSD)
Bahrain	698,585	Manama	Bahraini dinar (BHD)
Bangladesh	147,365,352	Dhaka	taka (BDT)
Barbados	279,912	Bridgetown	Barbadian dollar (BBD)
Belarus	10,293,011	Minsk	Belarusian ruble (BYB/BYR)
Belgium	10,379,067	Brussels	euro (EUR)
Belize	287,730	Belmopan	Belizean dollar (BZD)
Benin	7,862,944	Porto-Novo	CFA franc (XOF)
Bermuda	65,773	Hamilton	Bermudian dollar (BMD)
Bhutan	2,279,723	Thimphu	ngultrum (BTN); Indian rupee (INR)
Bolivia	8,989,046	La Paz (administrative) Sucre (judicial)	boliviano (BOB)
Bosnia and Herzegovina	4,498,976	Sarajevo	marka (BAM)
Botswana	1,639,833	Gaborone	pula (BWP)
Brazil	188,078,227	Brasília	real (BRL)
British Virgin Islands (Overseas Territory of the UK)	23,098	Road Town	US dollar (USD)
Brunei	379,444	Bandar Seri Begawan	Bruneian dollar (BND)
Bulgaria	7,385,367	Sofia	lev (BGL)
Burkina Faso	13,902,972	Ouagadougou	CFA franc (XOF)

Country/Territory	Population	Capital/Principal City	Currency
Burma	47,382,633	Rangoon	kyat (MMK)
Burundi	8,090,068	Bujumbura	Burundi franc (BIF)
Cambodia	13,881,427	Phnom Penh	riel (KHR)
Cameroon	17,340,702	Yaoundé	CFA franc (XAF)
Canada	33,098,932	Ottawa	Canadian dollar (CAD)
Cape Verde	420,979	Praia	Cape Verdean escudo (CVE)
Cayman Islands (Overseas Territory of the UK)	45,436	George Town	Caymanian dollar (KYD)
Central African Republic	4,303,356	Bangui	CFA franc (XAF)
Chad	9,944,201	N'Djamena	CFA franc (XAF)
Chile	16,134,219	Santiago	Chilean peso (CLP)
China	1,313,973,713	Beijing	yuan (CNY), also referred to as the Renminbi (RMB)
Christmas Island (Territory of Australia)	1,493	The Settlement	Australian dollar (AUD)
Cocos (Keeling) Islands	574	West Island	Australian dollar (AUD)
Colombia	43,593,035	Bogotá	Colombian peso (COP)
Comoros	690,948	Moroni	Comoran franc (KMF)
Congo, Democratic Republic of the	62,660,551	Kinshasa	Congolese franc (CDF)
Congo, Republic of the	3,702,314	Brazzaville	CFA franc (XAF)
Cook Islands (Self-governing in association with New Zealand)	21,388	Avarua	New Zealand dollar (NZD)
Costa Rica	4,075,261	San José	Costa Rican colon (CRC)
Côte d'Ivoire	17,654,843	Yamoussoukro (official) Abidjan (de facto)	CFA franc (XAF)
Croatia	4,494,749	Zagreb	kuna (HRK)
Cuba	11,382,820	Havana	Cuban peso (CUP) and Convertible peso (CUC), and the US dollar (USD)
Cyprus	784,301	Nicosia	Republic of Cyprus: Cypriot pound (CYP); Turkish Cypriot area: Turkish New lira (YTL)
Czech Republic	10,235,455	Prague	Czech koruna (CZK)
Denmark	5,450,661	Copenhagen	Danish krone (DKK)
Djibouti	486,530	Djibouti	Djiboutian franc (DJF)
Dominica	68,910	Roseau	East Caribbean dollar (XCD)
Dominican Republic	9,183,984	Santo Domingo	Dominican peso (DOP)

Country/Territory	Population	Capital/Principal City	Currency
East Timor	1,062,777	Dili	US dollar (USD)
Ecuador	13,547,510	Quito	US dollar (USD)
Egypt	78,887,007	Cairo	Egyptian pound (EGP)
El Salvador	6,822,378	San Salvador	US dollar (USD)
Equatorial Guinea	540,109	Malabo	CFA franc (XAF)
Eritrea	4,786,994	Asmara	nafka (ERN)
Estonia	1,324,333	Tallinn	Estonian kroon (EEK)
Ethiopia	74,777,981	Addis Ababa	birr (ETB)
Falkland Islands (Islas Malvinas) (Overseas Territory of the UK)	2,967	Stanley	Falkland pound (FKP)
Faroe Islands (Part of the Kingdom of Denmark)	47,246	Tórshavn	Danish krone (DKK)
Fiji	905,949	Suva	Fijian dollar (FJD)
Finland	5,231,372	Helsinki	euro (EUR)
France	60,876,136	Paris	euro (EUR)
French Guiana (Overseas Department of France)	199,509	Cayenne	euro (EUR)
French Polynesia (Overseas Department of France)	274,578	Papeete	Comptoirs Francais du Pacifique franc (XPF)
Gabon	1,424,906	Libreville	CFA franc (XAF)
The Gambia	1,641,564	Banjul	dalasi (GMD)
Gaza Strip	1,428,757	Gaza	new Israeli shekel (ILS)
Georgia	4,661,473	Tbilisi	lari (GEL)
Germany	82,422,299	Berlin	euro (EUR)
Ghana	22,409,572	Accra	cedi (GHC)
Gibraltar	27,928	Gibraltar	Gilbraltar Pound (GIP)
Greece	10,688,058	Athens	euro (EUR)
Greenland	56,361	Nuuk (Godtháb)	Danish krone (DKK)
Grenada	89,703	Saint George's	East Caribbean dollar (XCD)
Guadeloupe (Overseas Department of France)	452,776	Basse-Terre	euro (EUR)
Guam	171,019	Hagátña (Agana)	US dollar (USD)
Guatemala	12,293,545	Guatemala City	quetzal (GTQ) and US dollar (USD)
Guernsey (British Crown Dependency)	65,409	St. Peter Port	British pound (GBP); also Guernsey pound
Guinea	9,690,222	Conakry	Guinean franc (GNF) and syli (GNS)

Country/Territory	Population	Capital/Principal City	Currency
Guinea-Bissau	1,442,029	Bissau	CFA franc (XOF)
Guyana	767,245	Georgetown	Guyanese dollar (GYD)
Haiti	8,308,504	Port-au-Prince	gourde (HTG) and US dollar (USD)
Honduras	7,326,496	Tegucigalpa	lempira (HNL)
Hong Kong (Special Administrative Region of China)	6,940,432		Hong Kong dollar (HKD)
Hungary	9,981,334	Budapest	forint (HUF)
Iceland	299,388	Reykjavík	Icelandic krona (ISK)
India	1,095,351,995	New Delhi	Indian rupee (INR)
Indonesia	245,452,739	Jakarta	Indonesian rupiah (IDR)
Iran	68,688,433	Tehran	Iranian rial (IRR)
Iraq	26,783,383	Baghdad	New Iraqi dinar (NID)
Ireland	4,062,235	Dublin	euro (EUR)
Isle of Man (British Crown Dependency)	75,441	Douglas	British pound (GBP); also Manx pound
Israel	6,352,117	Jerusalem	new Israeli shekel (ILS); NIS is the currency abbreviation; ILS is the International Organization for Standardization (ISO) code for the NIS
Italy	58,133,509	Rome	euro (EUR)
Jamaica	2,758,124	Kingston	Jamaican dollar (JMD)
Japan	127,463,611	Tokyo	yen (JPY)
Jersey (British Crown Dependency)	91,084	Saint Helier	British pound (GBP), also Jersey pound
Jordan	5,906,760	Amman	Jordanian dinar (JOD)
Kazakhstan	15,233,244	Astana	tenge (KZT)
Kenya	34,707,817	Nairobi	Kenyan shilling (KES)
Kiribati	105,432	Tarawa	Australian dollar (AUD)
Korea, North	23,113,019	Pyongyang	North Korean won (KPW)
Korea, South	48,846,823	Seoul	South Korean won (KRW)
Kuwait	2,418,393	Kuwait City	Kuwaiti dinar (KD)
Kyrgyzstan	5,213,898	Bishkek	som (KGS)
Laos	6,368,481	Vientiane	kip (LAK)
Latvia	2,274,735	Riga	Latvian lat (LVL)
Lebanon	3,874,050	Beirut	Lebanese pound (LBP)
Lesotho	2,022,331	Maseru	loti (LSL); South African rand (ZAR)
Liberia	3,042,004	Monrovia	Liberian dollar (LRD)

Country/Territory	Population	Capital/Principal City	Currency
Libya	5,900,754	Tripoli	Libyan dinar (LYD)
Liechtenstein	33,987	Vaduz	Swiss franc (CHF)
Lithuania	3,585,906	Vilnius	litas (LTL)
Luxembourg	474,413	Luxembourg	euro (EUR)
Macau (Region of China)	453,125	Macau	Pataca (MOP)
Macedonia	2,050,554	Skopje	Macedonian denar (MKD)
Madagascar	18,595,469	Antananarivo	Madagascar ariary (MGA)
Malawi	13,013,926	Lilongwe	Malawian kwacha (MWK)
Malaysia	24,385,858	Kuala Lumpur	ringgit (MYR)
Maldives	359,008	Male	rufiyaa (MVR)
Mali	11,716,829	Bamako	CFA franc (XOF)
Malta	400,214	Valletta	Maltese lira (MTL)
Marshall Islands	60,422	Majuro	US dollar (USD)
Martinique (Overseas Department of France)	436,131	Fort-De-France	euro (EUR)
Mauritania	3,177,388	Nouakchott	ouguiya (MRO)
Mauritius	1,240,827	Port Louis	Mauritian rupee (MUR)
Mayotte (French Territory)	201,234	Mamoudzou	euro (EUR)
Mexico	107,449,525	Mexico City	Mexican peso (MXN)
Micronesia Federated States of	108,004	Palikir	US dollar (USD)
Moldova	4,466,706	Chisinau	Moldovan leu (MDL)
Monaco	32,543	Monaco	euro (EUR)
Mongolia	2,832,224	Ulaanbaatar	togrog/tugrik (MNT)
Montenegro	630,548	Podgorica	euro (EUR)
Montserrat	9,439	Plymouth	East Caribbean dollar (XCD)
Morocco	33,241,259	Rabat	Moroccan dirham (MAD)
Mozambique	19,686,505	Maputo	metical (MZM)
Namibia	2,044,147	Windhoek	Namibian dollar (NAD) or South African rand (ZAR)
Nauru	13,287	No official capital; government offices in Yaren District	Australian dollar (AUD)
Nepal	28,287,147	Kathmandu	Nepalese rupee (NPR)
Netherlands	16,491,461	Amsterdam	euro (EUR)

Country/Territory	Population	Capital/Principal City	Currency
Netherlands Antilles	221,736	Willemstad	Netherlands Antillean guilder (ANG)
New Caladonia (Territory of France)	219,246	Nouméa	Comptoirs Francais du Pacifique franc (XPF)
New Zealand	4,076,140	Wellington	New Zealand dollar (NZD)
Nicaragua	5,570,129	Managua	gold cordoba (NIO)
Niger	12,525,094	Niamey	CFA franc (XOF)
Nigeria	131,859,731	Abuja	naira (NGN)
Niue (Self-governing in association with New Zealand)	2,166	Alofi	New Zealand dollar (NZD)
Norfolk Island (Territory of Australia)	1,828	Kingston	Australian dollar (AUD)
Northern Mariana Islands	82,459	Saipan	US dollar (USD)
Norway	4,610,820	Oslo	Norwegian krone (NOK)
Oman	3,102,229	Muscat	Omani rial (OMR)
Pakistan	165,803,560	Islamabad	Pakistani rupee (PKR)
Palau	20,579	Koror	US dollar (USD)
Panama	3,191,319	Panama City	balboa (PAB) and US dollar (USD)
Papua New Guinea	5,670,544	Port Moresby	kina (PGK)
Paraguay	6,506,464	Asunción	guarani (PYG)
Peru	28,302,603	Lima	nuevo sol (PEN)
Philippines	89,468,677	Manila	Philippine peso (PHP)
Pitcairn Islands (Territory of the UK)	45	Adamstown	New Zealand dollar (NZD)
Poland	38,536,869	Warsaw	zloty (PLN)
Portugal	10,605,870	Lisbon	euro (EUR)
Puerto Rico	3,927,188	San Juan	US dollar (USD)
Qatar	885,359	Doha	Qatari rial (QAR)
Reunion (Overseas Department of France)	787,584	Saint-Denis	euro (EUR)
Romania	22,303,552	Bucharest	leu (ROL) New leu (RON) in 2006
Russia	142,893,540	Moscow	Russian ruble (RUR)
Rwanda	8,648,248	Kigali	Rwandan franc (RWF)
Saint Helena (Territory of the UK)	7,502	Jamestown	Saint Helenian pound (SHP)
Saint Kitts and Nevis	39,129	Basseterre	East Caribbean dollar (XCD)
Saint Lucia	168,458	Castries	East Caribbean dollar (XCD)

Country/Territory	Population	Capital/Principal City	Currency
Saint Pierre & Miquelon (Territorial collectivity of France)	7,026	Saint-Pierre	euro (EUR)
Saint Vincent and the Grenadines	117,848	Kingstown	East Caribbean dollar (XCD)
Samoa	176,908	Apia	tala (SAT)
San Marino	29,251	San Marino	euro (EUR)
Sao Tome and Principe	193,413	Sao Tomé	dobra (STD)
Saudi Arabia	27,019,731	Riyadh	Saudi riyal (SAR)
Senegal	11,987,121	Dakar	CFA franc (XOF)
Serbia	9,396,411	Belgrade	new Yugoslav dinar (YUM); in Montenegro the euro is legal tender; in Kosovo both the euro and the Yugoslav dinar are legal
Seychelles	81,541	Victoria	Seychelles rupee (SCR)
Sierra Leone	6,005,250	Freetown	leone (SLL)
Singapore	4,492,150	Singapore	Singapore dollar (SGD)
Slovakia	5,439,448	Bratislava	Slovak koruna (SKK)
Slovenia	2,010,347	Ljubljana	tolar (SIT)
Solomon Islands	552,438	Honiara	Solomon Islands dollar (SBD)
Somalia	8,863,338	Mogadishu	Somali shilling (SOS)
South Africa	44,187,637	Cape Town (legislative) Pretoria (administrative) Bloemfontein (judiciary)	rand (ZAR)
Spain	40,397,842	Madrid	euro (EUR)
Sri Lanka	20,222,240	Colombo	Sri Lankan rupee (LKR)
Sudan	41,236,378	Khartoum	Sudanese dinar (SDD)
Suriname	439,117	Paramaribo	Surinam dollar (SRD)
Svalbard (Territory of Norway)	2,701	Longyearbyen	Norwegian krone (NOK)
Swaziland	1,136,334	Mbabane	lilangeni (SZL)
Sweden	9,016,596	Stockholm	Swedish krona (SEK)
Switzerland	7,523,934	Bern	Swiss franc (CHF)
Syria	18,881,361	Damascus	Syrian pound (SYP)
Taiwan	23,036,087	Taipei	New Taiwan dollar (TWD)
Tajikistan	7,320,815	Dushanbe	ruble (TJR)
Tanzania	37,445,392	Dar es Salaam	Tanzanian shilling (TZS)
Thailand	64,631,595	Bangkok	baht (THB)

Country/Territory	Population	Capital/Principal City	Currency
Togo	5,548,702	Lomé	CFA franc (XOF)
Tokelau (Territory of New Zealand)	1,392	No Capital	New Zealand dollar (NZD)
Tonga	114,689	Nuku'alofa	pa'anga (TOP)
Trinidad and Tobago	1,065,842	Port-of-Spain	Trinidad and Tobago dollar (TTD)
Tunisia	10,175,014	Tunis	Tunisian dinar (TND)
Turkey	70,413,958	Ankara	Turkish lira (YTL)
Turkmenistan	5,042,920	Ashgabat	Turkmen manat (TMM)
Turks & Caicos Islands (Overseas Territory of the UK)	21,152	Grand Turk	US dollar (USD)
Tuvalu	11,810	Funafuti	Australian dollar (AUD); also Tuvaluan dollar
Uganda	28,195,754	Kampala	Ugandan shilling (UGX)
Ukraine	46,710,816	Kiev	hryvnia (UAH)
United Arab Emirates	2,602,713	Abu Dhabi	Emirati dirham (AED)
United Kingdom	60,609,153	London	British pound (GBP)
United States	298,444,215	Washington D.C.	US dollar (USD)
Uruguay	3,431,932	Montevideo	Uruguayan peso (UYU)
Uzbekistan	27,307,134	Tashkent	Uzbekistani soum (UZS)
Vanuatu	208,869	Port-Vila	vatu (VUV)
Vatican City (Holy See)	932		euro (EUR)
Venezuela	25,730,435	Caracas	bolivar (VEB)
Vietnam	84,402,966	Hanoi	dong (VND)
Virgin Islands	108,605	Charlotte Amalie	US dollar (USD)
Wallis & Futuna	16,025	Mata-Utu	Comptoirs Francais du Pacifique franc (XPF)
West Bank	2,460,492	None	new Israeli shekel (ILS); Jordanian dinar (JOD)
Western Sahara	273,008	None	Moroccan dirham (MAD)
Yemen	21,456,188	Sanaa	Yemeni rial (YER)
Zambia	11,502,010	Lusaka	Zambian kwacha (ZMK)
Zimbabwe	12,236,805	Harare	Zimbabwean dollar (ZWD)

Economic and Political Groupings

Asia-Pacific Economic Cooperation (APEC)

Its 21 members are Australia, Brunei, Canada, Chile, China, Chinese Taipei, Hong Kong, Indonesia, Japan, Korea, Malaysia, Mexico, New Zealand, Papua New Guinea, Peru, the Philippines, Russia, Singapore, Thailand, the United States and Vietnam. Leaders of this Pacific Rim trade forum meet annually. www.apec.org

Association of Southeast Nations (ASEAN)

The Association was founded in 1967 with five members: Thailand, Indonesia, Malaysia, Singapore and the Philippines. The organisation aims to accelerate economic growth, social progress and cultural development among its members and the promotion of regional peace. As of 2006, there are 10 member states: Brunei Darussalam, Cambodia, Indonesia, Laos, Malaysia, Myanmar, the Philippines, Singapore, Thailand and Vietnam.

Common Economic Space (CES)

Belarus, Kazakhstan, Russia and Ukraine signed an agreement in 2003 to create the CES.

Commonwealth of Independent States (CIS)

This is the proper name for the organisation founded by former members of the republics of the Soviet Union in 1991. Membership has changed in recent years but in 2006 consisted of Azerbaijan, Armenia, Belarus, Georgia, Kazakhstan, Kyrgyzstan, Moldova, Russia, Tajikistan, Turkmenistan, Uzbekistan and Ukraine. www.cisstat.com

Commonwealth of Nations

Formerly known as the British Commonwealth, membership now comprises 53 independent states: Antigua and Barbuda, Australia, Bahamas, Bangladesh, Barbados, Belize, Botswana, Brunei Darussalam, Cameroon, Canada, Cyprus, Dominica, Fiji Islands, the Gambia, Ghana, Grenada, Guyana, India, Jamaica, Kenya, Kiribati, Lesotho, Malawi, Malaysia, Maldives, Malta, Mauritius, Mozambique, Namibia, Nauru (as a special member), New Zealand, Nigeria, Pakistan, Papua New Guinea, St Kitts and Nevis, St Lucia, St Vincent and the Grenadine, Samoa, Seychelles, Sierra Leone, Singapore, Solomon Islands, South Africa, Sri Lanka, Swaziland, Tonga, Trinidad and Tobago, Tuvalu, Uganda, United Kingdom, United Republic of Tanzania, Vanuatu and Zambia. www.thecommonwealth.org

Countries and their people
Bangaladesh (Bangladeshi)
Bhutan (Bhutanese)
Argentina (prefer Argentine to Argentinian)
China (Chinese)
Bosnia and Herzegovina (Bosnian, Bosnian Croat, Bosnian Serb)
Botswana (Batswana)
Britain (British or Briton[s])
El Salvador (San Salvador)
Israel (Israelis, not the Biblical Israelites)
Sri Lanka (Ceylonese)

The Economic Community of West African States (ECOWAS)

ECOWAS is a regional group founded in 1975 when 16 West African countries signed the Treaty of Lagos. Its mission is to promote economic integration. The members are: Benin, Burkina Faso, Cape Verde, Côte d'Ivoire, The Gambia, Ghana, Guinea, Guinea Bissau, Liberia, Mali, Niger, Nigeria, Senegal, Sierra Leone and Togo. Mauritania withdrew its membership in 2000.

Eurasian Economic Community (EurAsEc)

Founded in 2000, its members were Belarus, Kazakhstan, Kyrgyzstan, Russia and Tajikistan. Uzbekistan joined in 2006.

European Free Trade Association (EFTA)

Established in 1960 and based in Geneva, its members are Iceland, Liechtenstein, Norway and Switzerland. www.efta.int

European Union (EU)

In 2006, the 25 Member States of the EU were Austria, Belgium, Cyprus, Czech Republic, Denmark, Estonia, Finland, France, Germany, Greece, Hungary, Ireland, Italy, Latvia, Lithuania, Luxemburg, Malta, Netherlands, Poland, Portugal, Spain, Slovakia, Slovenia, Sweden and the United Kingdom. www.europa.eu.int

G-3

The three leading industrial nations: Germany, Japan and the United States.

G-7

The Group of Seven leading industrial nations is composed of Canada, France, Germany, Italy, Japan, the United Kingdom and the United States.

G-8

The Group of Seven and Russia.

G-15

This is a group of developing nations who form an advisory trade body. Its 17 members are Algeria, Argentina, Brazil, Chile, Egypt, India, Indonesia, Jamaica, Kenya, Malaysia, Mexico, Nigeria, Peru, Senegal, Sri Lanka, Venezuela and Zimbabwe.

North American Free Trade Agreement (NAFTA)

NAFTA is a free trade agreement among Canada, the United States and Mexico.

Organisation for Economic Co-operation and Development (OECD)

The OECD groups 30 member countries sharing a commitment to democratic government and the market economy. It has active relationships in some 70 other countries, organisations and NGOs. In 2006 its members were: Australia, Austria, Belgium, Canada, Czech Republic, Denmark, Finland, France, Germany, Greece, Hungary, Iceland, Ireland, Italy, Japan, Korea, Luxembourg, Mexico, Netherlands, New Zealand, Norway, Poland, Portugal, Slovak Republic, Spain, Sweden, Switzerland, Turkey, United Kingdom and the United States. www.oecd.org

Organization of Petroleum Exporting Countries (OPEC)

Founded in 1960 by Iran, Iraq, Kuwait, Saudi Arabia and Venezuela, its membership has grown to 11. Later additions to the original members were Algeria, Indonesia, Libya, Nigeria, Qatar and the United Arab Emirates. Ecuador was a member until 1992. (The acronym OPEC is acceptable in second reference and in headlines.) www.opec.org

Pacific Islands Forum (PIF)

Founded in 1971 as the South Pacific Forum, the name was changed in 2000 to reflect the geographic locations of its member states both in the north and the south Pacific. Member states are: Australia, the Cook Islands, the Federated States of Micronesia, Fiji, Kiribati, the Marshall Islands, Nauru, New Zealand, Niue, Palau, Papua New Guinea, Samoa, the Solomon Islands, Tonga, Tuvalu and Vanuatu.

The South Asian Association for Regional Cooperation (SAARC)

Established in 1985, it comprises seven countries: Bangladesh, Bhutan, India, Maldives, Nepal, Pakistan and Sri Lanka.

United Arab League (UAL)

Seven states formed the Arab League in 1945. Membership has expanded to include Algeria, Bahrain, Comoros, Djibouti, Iraq, Jordan, Kuwait, Lebanon, Syria, Libya, Mauritania, Morocco, Oman, Qatar, Saudi Arabia, Somalia, State of Palestine, Sudan, Tunisia, United Arab Emirates and Yemen. www.arableagueonline.org

Country and State Groupings
Asian subcontinent

This encompasses Bangladesh, Bhutan, India, Nepal, Sikkim and Sri Lanka.

The 50 United States

Although it is a single country, because so many people ask, here's a list:

Alabama, Alaska, Arizona, Arkansas, California, Colorado, Connecticut, Delaware, Florida, Georgia, Hawaii, Idaho, Illinois, Indiana, Iowa, Kansas, Kentucky, Louisiana, Maine, Maryland, Massachusetts, Michigan, Minnesota, Mississippi, Missouri, Montana, Nebraska, Nevada, New Hampshire, New Jersey, New Mexico, New York, North Carolina, North Dakota, Ohio, Oklahoma, Oregon, Pennsylvania, Rhode Island, South Carolina, South Dakota, Tennessee, Texas, Utah, Vermont, Virginia, Washington, West Virginia, Wisconsin and Wyoming.

Australasia

Australasia comprises Australia, New Zealand and Papua New Guinea.

Far East

Politically incorrect and geographically outdated, it was taken to refer to the eastern portions of the Asian continent and included China, Japan, North and South Korea, Taiwan, Hong Kong and the eastern part of Russia.

Middle East

The Middle East comprises Cyprus, Egypt, Iran, Iraq, Israel, Jordan, Kuwait, Lebanon, Libya, Oman, Qatar, Saudi Arabia, South Yemen, Sudan, Syria, Turkey, United Arab Emirates and Yemen.

Scandinavia

In strict terms Scandinavia comprises Denmark, Norway and Sweden. Sometimes, however, Finland is included, even in official communiqués.

Southeast Asia

Southeast Asia refers to Brunei, Cambodia, Indonesia, Laos, Malaysia, Myanmar, the Philippines, Singapore, Thailand and Vietnam.

LATIN TERMS, FOREIGN WORDS AND PHRASES – A GLOSSARY

Depending on convention and context, foreign words and phrases are treated differently in text. In general, American English favours the use of roman format, whereas European academics and Latin scholars prefer a strict style, borne out of scholastic and traditional usage. Increasingly, as these phrases have become homogenised and more familiar, they are styled in roman. However, in the interest of best practice, we have compiled this list from the *Collins*, *Oxford* and *Webster's* dictionaries:

Roman or italic	Definition
actus reus	elements of a criminal offence, including those that concern the mind of an accused
ad hoc	for a particular purpose

ad valorem	according to the value
à la carte	priced separately on a menu
à la mode	in the latest fashion
alma mater	school, college or university formerly attended
apartheid	political system in South Africa
apropos	in regard to
au courant	abreast of
au fait	conversant
avant-garde	artistically innovative
bona fide(s)	in good faith
bourgeois	middle class and conventional
café	coffee house
caveat	warning
caveat emptor	buyer beware
coup de grace	final blow
coup d'état	overthrow, seizure of power
coup de foudre	something overwhelming, usually love
de facto	in fact
de jure	by right
de novo	anew
de rigueur	strictly required by current fashion or etiquette
elite	privileged minority
en masse	as a body or in a group
en route	on the way
ex gratia	as a favour
ex parte	on behalf of one side only

in camera	hearing of a court case in private
in loco parentis	in the place of a parent
in re	in the matter of
in situ	in its original position
inter alia	among others
intra vires	within the power or scope of
ipso facto	by the fact of
locus standi	the right to be heard in court
machismo	exaggerated display of masculinity
mens rea	guilty purpose
nouveau riche	a former member of a lower class
obiter dicta	utterances by the way
per annum	a year
per capita	a head
percent	as expressed in hundredths
per se	taken alone or by itself
pogrom	campaign of persecution or extermination
post mortem	autopsy or retrospective analysis
prima facie	on first appearance
pro forma	as a matter of form, a standard document
pro rata	in proportion
quasi	as if it were
raison d'être	justification or purpose
sine qua non	an essential requirement
status quo	the state in which things are or were
sub judice	in the course of a trial

subpoena	a document or order requiring a person to be in a specific place at a specific time
supra	above
ultra vires	beyond the power of, in excess of the authority of
verbatim	using identical words
versus	against
via	by way of or through
vice versa	the other way around
vis-à-vis	regarding or opposite to
viz	an abbreviation for videlicet, which means namely, that is to say

References

Catherine Soanes, *Oxford Dictionary of English* (Oxford University Press, 2005).
Collins English Dictionary (Collins, 2006).
Merriam-Webster, *Webster's New World Dictionary of the American Language* (World Publishing, 1976).

PREPOSITIONAL USAGE

In *Prepositions and Adverbial Particles*, the writer J.B. Heaton stated that 'prepositions cause more difficulty than any other aspect of the English language'. Prepositions are not to be trifled with. The collision of two 747s in 1977 at Tenerife Airport, killing 583 people, resulted from a misunderstanding of the preposition 'at'. 'At take-off' was understood by an air traffic controller to mean that a plane was waiting at the take-off point – in fact, it was actually taking off.

Using a wrong preposition will not often have such tragic consequences, but using the correct one will always be a source of satisfaction and speak well of your writing competence.

This list contains nouns, verbs, adjectives and adverbs that are sometimes used with the wrong preposition. The correct use is given here:

abhorrence of
abhorrent to
abide by
abreast of
absence of fear
abstain from
(in) accordance with
act on
agree on
allow for
aspire to
associate with
averse to
aware of

baffled by
basis for discussion
basis in fact
bask in
balk at
bearing on

capacity for
centre on
commensurate with
compliment on
comply with
concur with
conform to
consist of
consistent with
contend with
converge on
conversant with

correspond to
  (resemble)
correspond with
  (communicate)
culminate in

default on
delve into
differ from or to, and
  never than
disagree with
discourage from
dispense with
divest of

elaborate on
embark on
enamoured of

focus on
forbid to
free from or of

grasp of

immune from
impinge on
incapable of
indifferent to
insight into
integrate into
intercede for, on behalf
  of or with
invest in

levy on
liable to

link to or with

oblivious to
originate in or with but
  not from

persist in
preference for
preoccupied with
preside over
prevent from
prohibit from
pursuant to
put in or into place

register with
remand in
research in or into

satisfied with
speculate about
substitute for
sympathise with

take account of
take into account
take exception to
tamper with
tend towards

unconscious of

(at) variance with
versed in

wary of
withhold from

Further reading

J.B. Heaton, *Prepositions and Adverbial Particles* (Longman Group UK, 1965).

Funk & Wagnalls, *Standard Handbook of Prepositions, Conjunctions, Relative Pronouns & Adverbs* (Funk & Wagnalls Company, 1953).

James Champlin Fernald, *Funk and Wagnalls Standard Handbook of Synonyms, Antonyms, and Prepositions* (Funk & Wagnalls Company, 1947).

ROMAN NUMERALS

In general, Roman numerals can be converted mathematically by simply assigning a numerical value to each letter, according to the chart below, and calculating a total:

M = 1000 | D = 500 | C = 100 | L = 50 | X = 10 | V = 5 | I = 1

Although the historical practice has varied, the modern convention is to arrange the letters from left to right in order of decreasing value for higher numbers; the total is then calculated by adding the numerical values of all the letters in the sequence. For example:

MDCLXVI = 1000 + 500 + 100 + 50 + 10 + 5 + 1 = 1666

Roman numerals

1	I	27	XXVII	53	LIII	79	LXXIX
2	II	28	XXVIII	54	LIV	80	LXXX
3	III	29	XXIX	55	LV	81	LXXXI
4	IV	30	XXX	56	LVI	82	LXXXII
5	V	31	XXXI	57	LVII	83	LXXXIII
6	VI	32	XXXII	58	LVIII	84	LXXXIV
7	VII	33	XXXIII	59	LIX	85	LXXXV
8	VIII	34	XXXIV	60	LX	86	LXXXVI
9	IX	35	XXXV	61	LXI	87	LXXXVII
10	X	36	XXXVI	62	LXII	88	LXXXVIII
11	XI	37	XXXVII	63	LXIII	89	LXXXIX
12	XII	38	XXXVIII	64	LXIV	90	XC
13	XIII	39	XXXIX	65	LXV	91	XCI
14	XIV	40	XL	66	LXVI	92	XCII
15	XV	41	XLI	67	LXVII	93	XCIII
16	XVI	42	XLII	68	LXVIII	94	XCIV
17	XVII	43	XLIII	69	LXIX	95	XCV
18	XVIII	44	XLIV	70	LXX	96	XCVI
19	XIX	45	XLV	71	LXXI	97	XCVII
20	XX	46	XLVI	72	LXXII	98	XCVIII
21	XXI	47	XLVII	73	LXXIII	99	XCIX
22	XXII	48	XLVIII	74	LXXIV	100	C
23	XXIII	49	XLIX	75	LXXV	101	CI
24	XXIV	50	L	76	LXXVI	500	D
25	XXV	51	LI	77	LXXVII	1000	M
26	XXVI	52	LII	78	LXXVIII		

THE SUFFIX: -ABLE, -EABLE AND -IBLE

The following are the most commonly used (and misspelt) words ending with the suffix able, eable or ible:

-able
adoptable
advisable
allowable
billable
cashable
collectable
correctable
culpable
debatable
defendable
deliverable
dispensable
disputable
erectable
forgivable
imaginable
implacable
imputable
inalienable
indescribable
indictable
indispensable
indistinguishable
knowable
losable
lovable
mistakable
movable

penetrable
provable
prunable
receivable
removable
salable (but prefer
   sellable)
seizable
storable
tradable
unmistakable
unshakable
unusable
usable
writable

-eable
blameable
bridgeable
knowledgeable
likeable
liveable
impermeable
manageable
nameable
peaceable
rateable
serviceable
sliceable

sizeable
stateable
traceable
tradeable
unenforceable
unpronounceable
unshakeable

-ible
accessible
convertible
comprehensible
credible
digestible
edible
flexible
forcible
inadmissible
indestructible
investible
irresistible
perceptible
permissible
reversible
submersible
visible

References
www.morewords.com
Jeanette Kuether, *The Collins English Dictionary Complete and Unabridged* (Collins, 2004).

TEMPERATURE CONVERSION

The equation for converting Fahrenheit to Celsius is:

([Deg. F] − 32) x (5/9) = Deg. C

Celsius	Fahrenheit
0 C	32.0 F
1 C	33.8 F
2 C	35.6 F
3 C	37.4 F
4 C	39.2 F
5 C	41.0 F
6 C	42.8 F
7 C	44.6 F
8 C	46.4 F
9 C	48.2 F
10 C	50.0 F
11 C	51.8 F
12 C	53.6 F
13 C	55.4 F
14 C	57.2 F
15 C	59.0 F
16 C	60.8 F
17 C	62.6 F
18 C	64.4 F
19 C	66.2 F
20 C	68.0 F
21 C	69.8 F
22 C	71.6 F
23 C	73.4 F
24 C	75.2 F
25 C	77.0 F
26 C	78.8 F
27 C	80.6 F
28 C	82.4 F
29 C	84.2 F
30 C	86.0 F

Oven Temperature Conversion

As a rule of thumb, Celsius is roughly half the Fahrenheit temperature. The chart below offers greater precision:

Fahrenheit	Celsius	Gas Mark	Description
225	110	1/4	very slow
250	120-130	1/2	very slow
275	140	1	slow
300	150	2	slow
325	160-170	3	moderate
350	180	4	moderate
375	190	5	moderately hot
400	200	6	moderately hot
425	220	7	hot
450	230	8	hot
475	240	9	very hot

AN A–Z OF THE 1,000 MOST COMMONLY MISSPELT WORDS

Top 10 Most Commonly Misspelled Words

1. minuscule
2. millennium
3. embarrassment
4. occurrence
5. accommodate
6. perseverance
7. supersede
8. noticeable
9. harass
10. inoculate

Source: Cornell Kimball of The Simplified Spelling Society. Formed in 1908 with the aim of updating English spelling, the society publishes leaflets, newsletters, journals, books and bulletins to promote spelling reform of the English language.
www.spellingsociety.org

Take the test

An excellent online spelling test can be found at www.sentex. net/~mmcadams/spelling.html. Compiled by Mindy McAdams after a decade of work as a senior copy-editor, you can whiz through it in 60 seconds and determine your level of competence. We found it humbling…

The average retentive vocabulary is 630 words. According to studies by the University of Washington undertaken in 2000, spelling difficulties (not only among children) are inhibiting an expanded range of expression.

This was confirmed by 2003 research commissioned by Bloomsbury, publisher of the Encarta Dictionary, which concluded that the reading and writing skills of second and third-level students in the UK were better before the first world war. The study defined 15 percent of people aged 15 to 21 as 'functionally illiterate'. Contrast that with 1912 statistics when school inspectors reported that only 2 percent of young people were unable to read or write.

The research team also found a high level of overestimation of ability to spell among the 15- to 21-year-olds surveyed. Seven out of ten believed they were 'pretty good' at spelling words correctly. But when asked to spot 14 mistakes in a piece of text none was able to identify them all. (Girls did better than boys but they were still unable to pinpoint more than two-thirds of the errors.)

Spelling dictionaries – yes, such publications do exist – are a quick and easy way of rectifying such difficulties. To save you having to buy a spelling dictionary, the following have been identified by Internet studies, an ICAI questionnaire of 50 Irish academics and businesspeople, and the Encarta lexicon as the most commonly misspelt words and phrases:

abattoir
absence
acceptable
accidentally
accommodate
accomplish
accordion
accumulate
acetic
acknowledge, acknowledgment
acquaintance
acquiesce
acquire, acquired, acquiring

acquit, acquittal, acquitted, acquitting
across
addendum
adolescence
adrenalin
adviser, advisory
aeon
aeroplane, aircraft
aesthetic
affront
aficionado
Afghanistan

Afrikaans, (language), Afrikaner
   (person)
ageing (but caging, paging,
   raging, waging)
agnostic
agri-business
allegiance
amiable
amid (not amidst)
amok
annals
annex (verb), annexe (noun)
anniversary
apocryphal
apogee
appal, appals, appalling, appalled
apropos
aqueduct
aquifer
arbitrage
archetype
arctic
argument
armadillo
arraign
artefact
askance
asinine
assiduous
assignments
atheist
auxiliary
avalanche
awesome
ayatollah

balk (not baulk)
balloted, balloting
bandanna

bandwagon
bankruptcy
bannisters
barbecue
battalion
beatific
beginning
believe
benefiting, benefited
berserk
betrothal
biased
bicentenary (noun, not
   bicentennial)
biennial
blanketing, blanketed
block (never bloc)
bogey (bogie is on a locomotive)
boloney
brethren
breviary
bridging
brusque
bulwark
business
by-election, bypass, by-product,
   bylaw, byword

Cabal
cactus
calendar
calorie
Cameroon
camouflage
cannon (gun), canon (criterion,
   clergyman)
capital (money), capitol (main
   city)
cappuccino

carcass

Caribbean

caviar

cemetery

census

chancy

channelling, channelled

check (US), cheque

chintzy

choosy

Church of Jesus Christ of
Latter-day Saints (note the
lower case d)

cipher

clavicle

clientele

coagulate

cockatiel

codology

combating, combated

commemorate

commensurate

commission

commitment

committed

committee

competence

composite

conceive

connection

connote

conscience

conscientious

conscious

consensus

controversy

cooled, cooler, cooly

coral (found in the sea), corral
(cattle pen)

correlate

coruscate

cosseted, cosseting

crick

cryptic

cubicle

cyberspace

cypress

daub

debilitate

defendant

demagogue

de mode

dependant (person), dependent
(adjective)

de rigueur

description

desiccate, desiccation

détente

development

dexterous

diarrhoea

dignitary

dilapidate

dilemma

diligence

disabilities

discuss, discussing

disingenuous

disk (in a computer context),
otherwise disc (including
compact disc)

dispatch (not despatch)

dispel, dispelling

dispossess

distil, distiller

divergences

doppel-ganger(s)

drudgery
drunkenness
dryer, dryly
duplicity
dwelt
dyeing (colour)
dyke
dynamics
dyspepsia

echo
eclectic
ecstasy
eighth
elevate
elliptical
elucidate
embarrass, embarrassment
encyclopedia
enroll, enrolment
ensure (make certain), insure
    (against risks)
enterprise
enthral
espresso
evangelism
eviscerate
exaggerate
exemplary
exhilarate
expanse
extrovert
exuberance

facsimile
fajitas
farther (distance), further
    (additional)
favour, favourable
February

felicitous
fenestration
ferreted
fjord
fiery
Filipino, Filipina (person),
    Philippine (referring to the
    Philippines)
filleting, filleted
flagellate
flotation
flourescent
flyer, frequent flyer, high-flyer
focused, focusing (not focussed or
    focussing)
forbear (abstain), forebear
    (ancestor)
forbid, forbade
forcibly
foreboding
foreclose
forefather
foreign
forestall
forewarn
forgather
forgo (do without), forego
    (precede)
forty
forsake
forswear, forsworn
forth (to go out), fourth (number
    four)
fractious
fraught
frieze
fuelled
-ful, not -full (thus armful,
    bathful, handful, etc)

fulfil, fulfilling
fullness
fulsome
functionary
funnelling, funnelled
furore

gaiety
gauge
gauntlet
Gibraltar
gigabyte
Gingham
gingivitis
ginkgo
glamour, glamorous
glimpse
gnaw
government
governor
graffiti
gram (not gramme)
grammar
granule
gregarious
grievous
grisly (horrifying), grizzly (bear)
grey
Guadeloupe
guarantee
guardian
guerrilla
gypsy

halibut
hallucination
hallowed
Halloween
handkerchief

hangar (building), hanger (for clothes)
happiness
harass
height
heinous
heuristic
Hezbollah
hiccup (not hiccough)
hierarchy
high-tech
hindrance
hippopotamus
hoist
honour, honourable
hopscotch
hotch-potch
household
humidor
humour, humorous
hurrah
hygiene
hysterectomy

identification
idiosyncrasy
ignominy
illusory
immediately
implement
impostor
impresario
inadvertent
incidentally
incorporated
inculpate
incumbency
incur, incurring
indicted, indictment

indispensable
information
innocuous
inoculate
inquest
inquire, inquiry (not enquire,
    enquiry)
install, instalment, installation
instil, instilling
interpretive
interrupt
intransigent
iridescent
iterative

jail (not gaol)
Jamaica
jealousy
jewellery (not jewelry [US])
joinery
judgment (court decision),
    judgement (appraisal)
judicial
jujitsu
junction
juvenescence

kaolin
keloid
ketone
khaki
kilogram or kilo (not
    kilogramme)
kingdom
knickknack
knotty
knowledge
kudos

labelling, labelled
laboratory
lacrosse
lactic
laisser-faire
lama (priest), llama (beast)
lambaste
largess (or largesse)
length
leukaemia
levelled
liaise
libel, libelling, libelled
libretto
licence (noun), license (verb)
Liechtenstein
lieutenant
lightning
likelihood
likely
limited
limousine
linchpin
linguine
liquefy
literal
literary
literature
lollipop
loneliness
loose (untied), lose (mislay),
    losing
loth (reluctant), loathe (hate),
    loathsome
low-tech
luxury
lymphoma
lyre
lyricist

macaroon
mahogany
maintain, maintenance
malleable
maniacal
manilla envelope, but Manila,
    capital of the Philippines
manoeuvre, manoeuvring
mantel (shelf), mantle (cloak)
manufacture
marriage
marshal (noun and verb),
    marshalled
mayonnaise
Médecins Sans Frontières (MSF)
medieval
mêlée
memento
metronome
mentally
mileage
millennium
millionaire
miniature
minuscule
miscellaneous
mischievous
mischief
Mississippi
moccasin
modelling, modelled
monotonous
moot
mosquito, mosquitoes
Mossad
mould
Moult
moustache
mujahideen

mummify
mundane
murmur, murmured
muscle
Muslim (not Moslem)
mutilate
mythical
mythology

naivety
narrative
naught
Neanderthal
necessary, necessity
nectarine
nighttime
nihilism
ninetieth
ninety
ninth
nonplussed
notary
noticeable
nought (for numerals), otherwise
    naught
nowadays
nucleus
nuisance
nutrition

objet(s) d'art
occasion, occasionally
occur, occurred, occurrence,
    occurring
oligopoly
omission
omit, omitted
omniscient
omnivore
ooze

opinion

opponent

optics (optician, etc) ophthalmic
    (ophthalmology, etc)

oratory

orchestra

ordinarily

oregano

origin

Ouija

outrageous

overrun

paediatric, paediatrician

pamphlets

panache

pandemonium

panel, panelled

paraffin

parallel, paralleled

Parliament

Parliamentary

particular

partisan

pastime

pavilion

peculiar

peptic

perceive

periphery

persevere, perseverance

personal (relating to self),
    personnel (staff-members)

petrify

phoney (not phony)

piety

pigeon

pigeonhole

piggyback

pitch

platinum

plebeian

plebiscite

plummeted, plummeting

pockmarked

Politburo

politicking

polyurethane

populous

possess, possessed, possession

practice (noun), practise (verb)

prairie

precede

precedent

predilection

preferred (preferring, but
    proffered)

preventive (not preventative)

pricey

principal (head, loan or adjectival
    use), principle (abstract noun)

privilege

proffered (proffering, but
    preferred)

profited

Profumo

program (only in a computer
    context), otherwise
    programme

propaganda

propagate

propeller

protester

proviso, provisos

provocation

psychiatrist

psychic

psychologist

psychosis
publicly
pursue
putsch
pygmy
pzazz

quaint
qualitative
quantity
quarantine
quarter
quartermaster
quartet
question
questionable
questionnaire
queue, queuing
quiz, quizzes
quixotic
quotient
Quran

raccoon
rack, racked, racking (as in
    racked with pain,
    nerve-racking)
racket
rankle
rarefy
razzle-dazzle
razzmatazz
recede
receipt
receive
recommend
recur, recurrent, recurring
refer, referral, referred
reference
regretted, regretting

registry
reminisce, reminiscence
remittance
Requiem
resemblance
reservoir
resilience
restaurant
restaurateur
resuscitate
rhapsody
rheumatism
rhythm
ridiculous
rococo
roommate
ropy
Rottweiler
rubella
rubric
ruinous
Rwanda

saboteur
sacrifice
sacrilegious
salvo, salvos
sanatorium
sandal
satellite
schedule
scissors
sculpture
scurrilous
secede
seesaw
seize
selectivity
sensible

separate

sepulchre

sequence

sergeant

shaky

sheik

shenanigans

siege

sieve

simultaneous

skiing

smelt

smidgen

smoky

smooth (both noun and verb)

soothe

souped up

soya bean

specialty (only in context of
    medicine, steel and chemicals),
    otherwise speciality

species

spelled (verb), spelt (how words
    are)

sphinx

spoilt

storey (floor)

straitjacket and strait-laced but
    straight-faced

stratagem, strategy

stubbornness

supersede

susceptible

suspicious

swap

swathe

syllable

symmetrical

synonym, synonymous

tangible

tariff

teammate

techie

temperamental

temperature

tenterhooks

theatre

threshold

tincture

tinnitus

tipster

titillate

tournament

trade union, trade unions (but
    Trades Union Congress)

transatlantic

transferred, transferring

travelled

trestle

tricolour

triptych

triweekly

trouper (as in old trouper)

trousseau

truncate

tungsten

turboprop

tureen

twelfth

tyranny

tyres

unanimous

undoubtedly

unforgettable

uniformity

unilateral

unnecessary

unparalleled
uptick
ureter
usage
usually
usury
utensil
Utopia

vaccinate
vacillate
vacuum
valuable
vendor
vengeance
vermilion
vertebrate
vesicle
vexatious
vigorous
villain
voodoo

wacky
wagon
wallop
warrant, warranty
watchful
waylay

weasel, weaselly
wedge
Wednesday
Weight
werewolf
wheeler-dealer
whimsical
whimsy
whodunnit
wholly
width
wigwam
wilful
withhold
wrest, wrestle
writhe

yacht
yearn
yield
yogurt
yo-yo
yule, yuletide

zenith
zigzag
Zirconia
zucchini
zoology

References

A.C.E. Spelling Dictionary (LDA Publications, 1998).
Christine Maxwell, Dictionary of Perfect Spelling (Barrington Stoke, 2005).
Encarta Essential English Dictionary (Bloomsbury Publishing, 2002).
Improve Your Spelling: The Key to Mistake-Free Writing (Bloomsbury, 2002).
New Oxford Spelling Dictionary (Oxford University Press, 2005).

BIBLIOGRAPHY

A.C.E. Spelling Dictionary (LDA Publications, 1998).

Administration Yearbook and Diary (Institute of Public Administration, annually).

Aristotle, *Politics*, translated by Peter Simpson (Dover Publications, 2000).

Balshem, Martha, *Cancer in the Community: Class and Medical Authority* (Smithsonian Books, 1993).

Bennett, W. Lance, *News: The Politics of Illusion* (Addison Wesley Longman, 2005).

Bernstein, Theodore, *Dos, Don'ts & Maybes of English Usage* (Gramercy Books, New York, 1999).

Bierce, Ambrose, *The Devil's Dictionary* (Aegypan, 2006).

Brown, Dan, *The Da Vinci Code* (DoubleDay 2003).

Bryson, Bill, *Troublesome Words* (Penguin, 1997).

Burchfield, R.W., *The New Fowler's Modern English Usage* (Oxford University Press, 2004).

The Chicago Manual of Style, 15th Edition (University of Chicago Press, 2003).

Coolidge, Susan, *What Katy Did Next* (Puffin Classics, 1994).

Conan Doyle, Sir Arthur, *The Complete Sherlock Holmes* (Gramercy, 2002).

Cooper, Sheila; Patton, Rosemary, *Writing Logically, Thinking Critically* (Pearson Books, 2006).

Daltún, Seamus, *Maidir le do Litir* (An Gúm, 1998).

De Bhaldraithe, Tomás, *English-Irish Dictionary with Terminological Additions and Corrections* (An Gúm).

Dickens, Charles, *A Tale of Two Cities* (Everyman's Library, 1993).

Diversity at Work: The Business Case for Equity (John Wiley and Sons, 1996).

The Economist Style Guide, 9th Edition (Profile Books, 2005).

Elliot, Mark, *The Dynamics of Human Life* (Paternoster Press, 2001).

Encarta Essential English Dictionary (Bloomsbury Publishing, 2002).

Euripides, *Medea* (Prestwick House, 2005).

Fernald, James Champlin, *Funk and Wagnalls Standard Handbook of Synonyms, Antonyms, and Prepositions* (Funk & Wagnalls Company, 1947).

Gasaitéar na hÉireann, Gazetteer of Ireland (Oifig an tSoláthair).

Gelardi, Julia, *Born to Rule: Five Reigning Consorts, Granddaughters of Queen Victoria* (Saint Martin's Press, 2005).

Gordon, J. Randy, *BusiBUZZ: Business Buzzwords for Survivin' and Thrivin' in the Big City* (Booksurge Publishing, 2006).

Heaton, J.B., *Prepositions and Adverbial Particles* (Longman Group UK, 1965).

The Holy Bible King James Version, 1611 Edition (Hendrickson Publishers, 2003).

Improve Your Spelling: The Key to Mistake-Free Writing (Bloomsbury, 2002).

Johnson, Greg, *Invisible: A Biography of Joyce Carol Oates* (Plume Books, 1999).

Bibliography

Kuether, Jeanette, *The Collins English Dictionary Complete and Unabridged* (Collins, 2004).

McKenna, Neil, *The Secret Life of Oscar Wilde* (Basic Books, 2005).

McMahon, Sean; O'Donoghue, Jo, *Brewer's Dictionary of Irish Phrase & Fable* (Weidenfeld & Nicolson, 2004).

Maxwell, Christine, *Dictionary of Perfect Spelling* (Barrington Stoke, 2005).

Merriam-Webster's Collegiate Dictionary (Merriam-Webster Inc, 2003).

Meyers, Jeffrey, *Somerset Maugham: A Life* (Vintage, 2005).

Mind Your Language, Diversity Matters Briefing Paper (Disability Action, Belfast, March 2004). www.disabilityaction.org/publications

New Oxford Spelling Dictionary (Oxford University Press, 2005).

Nuland, Sherwin, *The Doctors' Plague: Germs, Childbed Fever, and the Strange Story of Ignac Semmelweis* (W.W. Norton & Company, 2004).

O'Casey, Sean, *Three Plays: Juno and the Paycock; The Shadow of a Gunman; The Plough and the Stars* (Macmillan, 1966).

O'Connor, Patricia T., *Words Fail Me* (Harcourt Brace, 1999).

Ó Dónaill, Niall, *Foclóir Poca English-Irish Irish-English Dictionary* (An Gúm).

Paatero, Neea, 'Differences Between British and American English in Two Versions of F. Scott Fitzgerald's *The Great Gatsby*' (December 2002). www.uta.fi/FAST/US1/LP/np-great.html

Persaud, Raj, *Staying Sane* (Bantam, 2001).

Powers, Ron, *Mark Twain: A Life* (Free Press, 2005).

Quindlen, Anna, *Thinking Out Loud: On the Personal, the Political, the Public and the Private* (Ballentine Books, 1994).

Quirk, Randolph; Greenbaum, Sidney, *A University Grammar of English* (Longman Group, 1993).

Ritter, Robert, *The Oxford Style Manual* (Oxford University Press, 2003).

Rushdie, Salman, *Midnight's Children* (Penguin, 1991).

Sabin, William A., *The Gregg Reference Manual* (McGraw-Hill, New York, 2001).

Schick, Theodore; Vaughn, Lewis, *How to Think about Weird Things* (McGraw-Hill, 2005).

Schulberg, Budd, *What Makes Sammy Run?* (Vintage, 1993).

Soanes, Catherine, *Oxford Dictionary of English* (Oxford University Press, 2005).

Solotaroff, Ted, *Alfred Kazin's America: Critical and Personal Writings* (Harper Perennial, 2004).

Sontag, Susan, *AIDS and Its Metaphors* (Farrar, Straus and Giroux, 1988).

Sontag, Susan, *Illness as Metaphor* (Farrar, Straus and Giroux, 1978).

Standard Handbook of Prepositions, Conjunctions, Relative Pronouns & Adverbs (Funk & Wagnalls Company, 1953).

Stephens, Leigh Aldrich, *Covering the Community – A Diversity Handbook for Media* (Sage Publications, 1999).

Sypri, Johanna, *Heidi* (Children's Classics, 1998).

Tarver, John Charles, *Gustave Flaubert as Seen in His Works and Correspondence* (Kessinger Publishing, 2005).

Troyka, Lynn Quitman; Hess, Doug, *Quick Access: Reference for Writers* (Simon & Schuster, 2006).

Tufte, Edward, *Beautiful Evidence* (Graphic Press, 2006).

Tufte, Edward, *Envisioning Information* (Graphic Press, 1990).

Tufte, Edward, *The Visual Display of Quantitative Information* (Graphic Press, 2001).

Walsh, Bill, *Lapsing into a Comma* (Contemporary Books, New York, 2000).

INDEX

READER NOTES

READER NOTES